צא ולמד
A Passover Haggadah
Go Forth and Learn

Rabbi Silber has given us two books in one: the Haggadah itself, in English and Hebrew, with a line-by-line commentary, and a collection of essays that provide close readings of the biblical and Rabbinic texts that inform seder-night ritual. Together, the two sections illuminate the central themes of the Passover Haggadah, pointing to different voices within the tradition and exploring new interpretive possibilities. Just as midrash attempts to bridge the gap between ancient text and contemporary meaning, *A Passover Haggadah* provides new sources of insight that deepen the Passover experience for today's readers.

"Silber's genius is close reading of texts, bringing together a keen literary sensibility and a deep familiarity with biblical and Rabbinic sources."—Ellen Frankel, Editor Emerita, The Jewish Publication Society

"Clear, engaging and accessible, yet sophisticated and insightful . . . Rabbi Silber offers us a rich and meaningful plate of ideas and concepts for our seder table."—Rabbi Nathaniel Helfgot, Chair, Departments of Bible and Jewish Thought, Yeshivat Chovevei Torah

"Silber's scholarship is solid and accessible and will appeal to a range of Jewishly literate readers seeking to better understand and appreciate the richness of the Haggadah text."—Rabbi Sue Levi Elwell, PhD, Union Rabbi and Worship Specialist, Union for Reform Judaism.

Rabbi David Silber is the founder and dean of Drisha Institute for Jewish Education in New York City. A popular, nationally acclaimed lecturer, Silber is a recipient of the prestigious Covenant Award for excellence in innovative Jewish education.

Rachel Furst teaches Talmud and Rabbinic literature in Jerusalem, where she is a PhD candidate in medieval Jewish history. She has studied and taught at Drisha Institute for over a decade.

Drisha Institute for Jewish Education is the foremost center for the advanced study of classical Jewish texts by women in an open and thoughtful environment. It has grown significantly in scope and impact since its founding in 1979, and its graduates serve as educators, scholars, and leaders in the Jewish community and the world at large. Drisha's continuing education programs for women and men are a key community resource, and its Beit Midrash is open to all.

צא ולמד

A Passover Haggadah

Go Forth and Learn

צא ולמד
A Passover Haggadah
Go Forth and Learn

Rabbi David Silber
with
Rachel Furst

2011 • 5771
The Jewish Publication Society
Philadelphia

JPS is a nonprofit educational association and the oldest and foremost publisher of Judaica in English in North America. The mission of JPS is to enhance Jewish culture by promoting the dissemination of religious and secular works, in the United States and abroad, to all individuals and institutions interested in past and contemporary Jewish life.

The Jewish Publication Society
2100 Arch Street, 2nd floor
Philadelphia, PA 19103
www.jewishpub.org

Design by Masters Group Design
Composition by El Ot Ltd., Israel

Manufactured in the United States of America

11 12 13   10 9 8 7 6 5 4 3 2

Library of Congress Cataloging-in-Publication Data

Haggadah. English & Hebrew
    A Passover Haggadah : go forth and learn / David Silber with Rachel Furst.
      p. cm.
    Text of Haggadah in Hebrew with English translation; commentary in English.
    Includes bibliographical references.
    ISBN 978-0-8276-0925-9 (alk. paper)
    1. Haggadot–Texts.   2. Seder–Liturgy–Texts.   3. Judaism–Liturgy–Texts.
4. Haggadah. I. Silber, David. II. Furst, Rachel, 1978. III. Haggadah. English & Hebrew. IV. Title.
    BM674.643.S585 2011
    296.4'5371–dc22

                                        2010044149

JPS books are available at discounts for bulk purchases for reading groups, special sales, and fundraising purchases. Custom editions, including personalized covers, can be created in larger quantities for special needs. For more information, please contact us at marketing@jewishpub.org or at this address: 2100 Arch Street, Philadelphia, PA 19103.

In honor of my parents

Harry J. Silber ז"ל **and Martha C. Silber**

my first teachers

וַיְנַטְּלֵם וַיְנַשְּׂאֵם כָּל יְמֵי עוֹלָם

You have borne and sustained me all of my years

—Isaiah 63:9

Contents

Note to the Reader

This book is comprised of two parts: one section that includes eight essays on the Haggadah and related biblical texts and another section that includes the traditional Haggadah text in Hebrew and English translation, together with a line-by-line commentary.

The essays read from left to right, in standard English fashion, beginning on page 1. The Haggadah, along with its translation and commentary, reads from right to left, in standard Hebrew fashion, beginning in the back of the book.

Acknowledgments

The idea to publish a Haggadah commentary based on my classes at Drisha Institute was first suggested by the late Judith Tenzer, of blessed memory. She proposed the concept several years ago in conversation with Tova and Norman Bulow. The Bulows provided support and encouragement for this project from the beginning, and it has been a pleasure to work with them.

The English translation of the Haggadah has been emended from the *JPS Commentary on the Haggadah: Historical Introduction, Translation, and Commentary* (Philadelphia: The Jewish Publication Society, 2008) by Dr. Joseph Tabory. I thank Dr. Tabory for generously permitting me to use his translation as a basis for my own. In emending the JPS translation, I have consulted and considered various other works, including Dr. Joshua Kulp's translation in *The Schechter Haggadah: Art, History, and Commentary* (Jerusalem: Schechter Institute of Jewish Studies, 2009). All verses from the Torah and Psalms are translated according to *The Five Books of Moses: A Translation with Commentary* (New York: W.W. Norton, 2004) and *The Book of Psalms: A Translation With Commentary* (New York: W.W. Norton, 2007) by Professor Robert Alter, with a few minor changes. My thanks to Professor Alter and his publisher for granting us permission to use those editions. All other biblical texts are translated according to the *NJPS Hebrew-English Tanakh* (Philadelphia: The Jewish Publication Society, 1993).

The bibliography and suggested readings were compiled with the assistance of Rabbi Dr. Avraham Walfish. The essays were read at various stages by Dr. Rachel Adelman, Wendy Amsellem, Nechama Barash, Chana Lockshin Bob, Dr. Jerome Chanes, Daniel Feldman, Ilana Kurshan, Sara Labaton, Ayelet Libson, and Gavy Posner. Dan Baras read and commented extensively throughout the writing process. I thank them all for their time and energies. Thanks also to my children Akiva Steinmetz-Silber and Shifra Steinmetz-Silber for their assistance typing and proofing.

Over the years, I have benefited from discussions with my friends and colleagues Rabbi Shimon Deutsch and David Goshen, whose thinking and insights have helped me clarify my own work. I have learned much from my colleagues and students at Drisha Institute, whose comments and questions in the classroom and outside it have challenged and encouraged me.

The arduous task of collecting and selecting the material and all of the writing is the work of Rachel Furst. She has performed this task with integrity, grace, and great professionalism, and her work is infused with a love of Torah. In addition, her own observations have contributed to the commentary and essays, and this Haggadah should be viewed as a collaborative work. I do take full responsibility for misunderstandings or errors of interpretation.

I have been blessed throughout my life with the privilege of studying with great teachers who have modeled approaches to learning and life. At a formative stage, Rabbi Joseph B. Soloveitchik and Rabbi Aharon Lichtenstein taught me a rigorous mode of analysis and modeled a commitment to search for truth. Later in life, I became involved with the Carlebach synagogue in New York and the Hasidic teachings of Rabbi Shlomo Carlebach, which represented a different way of seeing the world and have had a profound impact on my thinking. My approach to life and to Torah has been greatly shaped and informed by the thought and the teaching of my wife, Devora Steinmetz. Although I have included only a few specific references to her published work in this Haggadah, her voice is present in much of my interpretation.

Yet another "rebbe" was instrumental in sparking my interest in the Bible and its study. Many years ago, when I was 13 years old and growing up in Jackson Heights, Queens, a young member of our synagogue asked me to attend a class he was teaching that *Shabbat* afternoon on the weekly Torah reading, Parashat Toledot. When I got home, I mentioned the invitation to my mother but added that it was cold, I was tired, and I did not plan to go. My mother insisted that I attend. Such a class would not draw many students, and the young teacher might feel slighted. So I attended, along with one other participant. The teacher had brought a passage from the work of Dr. Umberto Cassuto, an extended interpretation of Genesis 27, which argued that the Torah, read unmediated, offered a critique of Jacob's behavior. I never forgot that class, and many years later, when I first began teaching Bible, I went back to Cassuto, who became a point of departure in developing my own approach to biblical narrative.

I dedicate this book to my first rebbes, my mother and my father, who modeled honesty, compassion, commitment, self-sacrifice, and a love of Torah that continues to inform my life.

David Silber
New York
Kislev 5751/December 2010

Introduction

The Torah presents the Exodus from Egypt as the foundational experience of the Jewish nation and the Passover sacrifice as the necessary precondition to the Exodus. That experience is represented in the Torah as an attempt to build inclusive community. As ritually impure members of the desert generation said to Moses upon realizing that they could not participate in the Passover offering, *Lama nigara*? ("Why should we be barred from bringing God's sacrifice at its appointed time together with the rest of the People of Israel?") (Num. 9:7). The implication is that exclusion from the Passover ritual effectively means exclusion from the community.

Traditional Jewish texts and practices recall the Exodus frequently, and the Passover seder is chief among the rituals designed to commemorate the collective redemption from Egypt. But the seder does not only recount the community building that accompanied freedom and the birth of the Nation of Israel: it reenacts that experience. The seder itself is a collective ritual whose liturgy focuses on a biblical text that is essentially about concern for and identification with the outsider. It is a ritual that emphasizes shared history and a shared vision of the future and promotes, above all, shared study of Torah. The invitation to join the seder that we extend formally at the beginning of the *Maggid* section is an invitation to serve God by joining such a community.

The term "seder" means order, and the Passover seder is a strictly ordered rite. In the Torah, Passover ritual centers on the *korban Pesah*, the Passover offering, and in Rabbinic parlance, the term "seder" is often associated with a sacrificial service—for example, *seder avodah* (the order of the sacrificial service) and *seder ha-yom* (the order of the day's sacrifices). Today too the term "seder" refers to a ritual that stands in for the Passover offering and its attendant rites. But beyond the sacrificial connection, the ordered events of the seder are emblematic of the central idea of *Maggid*: that the Exodus was the fulfillment of an earlier covenant whose dynamic repeats throughout

A PASSOVER HAGGADAH: GO FORTH AND LEARN

history. The claim of Passover night is that there is a divine plan in history and that the Exodus is testimony to that plan.

In Mishnah *Pesahim*, the evening's ritual is organized around the four cups of wine, which are poured and drunk at specific intervals. The Haggadah divides the seder into fifteen distinct stages, or sections, each of which represents a ritual act or liturgical theme. But on a most basic level, the seder orders and intertwines eating and speech. The eating originally entailed the sacrificial meal, which today is commemorated with symbolic foods, and the speech consists of both study (*Maggid*) and songs of thanksgiving (*Hallel*). The idea that Jewish experience and Jewish community is fundamentally founded on both practice and intellectual inquiry is a core message of the seder.

Maggid, the telling of the Exodus story, is prescribed by the Mishnah, which instructs us to read a set of verses from Deuteronomy and to expound upon the entire passage (*ve-doresh et kol ha-parashah kulah*). In Rabbinic literature, this is a singular instruction to engage in the activity of midrash. Rabbinic midrash presupposes a text with limitless possibilities and invites the student to find difficulties or questions within the text and to search for their solutions. It also presupposes connections between different biblical passages and often interprets one text in light of another. In every biblical narrative, the Midrash hears resonances and echoes of different stories. The use of midrash at the Passover seder is not arbitrary. At its core, midrash connects the present student to the ancient text, rendering that text alive and pregnant with interpretive possibility. Its fundamental claim is that deep analysis of the historical text can provide answers and insights into questions of the moment. What mode of study could be more appropriate for an evening whose stated goal is that "in every generation one . . . see oneself as if one had [personally] gone out of Egypt"!

Several scholarly works published in recent years attempt to trace the historical development of the Passover seder and the genesis of the Haggadah text. That is not the goal of this book, although we will occasionally reference historical scholarship. This commentary focuses primarily on the biblical texts that form the core of the Haggadah and on the Torah passages that serve as a backdrop to the seder ritual and the Exodus narrative. In accordance with the Mishnah's directive, it is an attempt to engage in midrash, delving into the texts themselves and drawing meaning from their depths. This volume includes a series of essays that may be read individually or collectively, as well as a line-by-line commentary on the traditional Haggadah. It is intended both for advance preparation and for use at the seder itself.

The commentary presented herein is largely drawn from lectures that I have given at Drisha Institute in New York over the past thirty years. This presented my colleague Rachel Furst with two challenges. First, it was necessary to select from a great amount of material—to do otherwise would have resulted in a Haggadah of thousands of pages. The second challenge was to take lectures and classroom discussions that involve give and take, a constant questioning and reformulating, and transfer that experience to the written page. If midrash is about uncovering the dynamic possibilities of the written text, our challenge was to write a text that does not only present one interpretation but also encourages additional and alternative readings. It is my hope that this Haggadah will inspire the reader to continue studying and searching for new meaning and insight. I trust that this study will foster the understanding, connection, and common language that are at the heart of a truly inclusive community.

Go forth and study!

1

Arami Oved Avi:
The Core Text of the Haggadah

The main features of the Rabbinic Passover seder, including the essential components of the *Maggid* (storytelling) section, are outlined in the last chapter of tractate *Pesahim*. Listed among these is the requirement to engage in exegesis on a specific set of verses from Deuteronomy that function as the core text of the Haggadah (M. Pes. 10:4). The complete passage, which the Mishnah refers to by its opening words, *Arami oved avi*, reads:

> ... אֲרַמִּי אֹבֵד אָבִי וַיֵּרֶד מִצְרַיְמָה וַיָּגָר שָׁם בִּמְתֵי מְעָט וַיְהִי שָׁם לְגוֹי גָּדוֹל עָצוּם
> וָרָב: וַיָּרֵעוּ אֹתָנוּ הַמִּצְרִים וַיְעַנּוּנוּ וַיִּתְּנוּ עָלֵינוּ עֲבֹדָה קָשָׁה: וַנִּצְעַק אֶל יהוה אֱלֹהֵי
> אֲבֹתֵינוּ וַיִּשְׁמַע יהוה אֶת קֹלֵנוּ וַיַּרְא אֶת עָנְיֵנוּ וְאֶת עֲמָלֵנוּ וְאֶת לַחֲצֵנוּ: וַיּוֹצִאֵנוּ יהוה
> מִמִּצְרַיִם בְּיָד חֲזָקָה וּבִזְרֹעַ נְטוּיָה וּבְמֹרָא גָּדֹל וּבְאֹתוֹת וּבְמֹפְתִים:

> ... *my father was an Aramean about to perish,*[1] *and he went down to Egypt, and he sojourned there with a few people, and he became there a great and mighty and multitudinous nation. And the Egyptians did evil to us and abused us and set upon us hard labor. And we cried out to the* LORD *God of our fathers, and the* LORD *heard our voice and saw our abuse and our trouble and our oppression. And the* LORD *brought us out from Egypt with a strong hand and with an outstretched arm and with great terror and with signs and with portents.* (Deut. 26:5–8)

Arami oved avi is the only biblical text explicitly prescribed by the Mishnah for inclusion in the *Maggid* section. But this passage, known in Rabbinic parlance as *mikrah bikkurim*, is actually the pilgrim's recitation upon bringing first fruits to the Temple, making it an odd choice for the Passover seder: Yom

---

[1]The Haggadah assumes a different translation of this phrase: rather than "My father was an Aramean about to perish," the Haggadah renders it "An Aramean [namely, Laban] attempted to destroy my father [i.e., Jacob]." The significance of this interpretation will be discussed in essay 2.

ha-Bikkurim, the Day of the First Fruits, is observed not on Pesach but on Shavuot! Selections from the book of Exodus would seemingly have been a more sensible choice for the Haggadah. Why, then, did the Rabbis choose this passage to serve as the focal point of the seder?

Many scholars have dealt with this question.

In his classic study on the historical development of the Haggadah, Daniel Goldschmidt posited that the choice of this particular passage was based on the familiarity of the masses with the text in question.[2] Although the Mishnah was written down many years after the Temple was destroyed and the *bikkurim* offering had ceased, this passage was presumably seared into the nation's collective memory or was chosen to commemorate the reality of an earlier era.[3] Israel Yuval suggests that the authors of the Haggadah chose to focus the seder-night liturgy on the passage from Deuteronomy to distance themselves from the practice of the early church fathers who based their Easter homilies on the Exodus version of the Passover story.[4] And in the recently published *Schechter Haggadah*, Joshua Kulp argues that the passage from Deuteronomy 26 was chosen primarily because of its brevity, which rendered it better material for the midrashic exegesis that was the Rabbis' principal interest.[5] Along similar lines, R. Joseph B. Soloveitchik suggested that the Haggadah's choice of these verses, which indeed provide a markedly concise description of the Exodus experience, was intended to emphasize that the evening's goal is to draw meaning out of the text;[6] thus, the main activity

---

[2] E. D. Goldschmidt, *The Passover Haggadah: Its Sources and History* (in Hebrew) (Jerusalem: Bialik Institute, 1960), 30.

[3] Goldschmidt's explanation is difficult if only because it does not accord with the claim made by the Mishnah itself, that many pilgrims either did not know how to read or did not know how to recite the verses of *mikrah bikkurim* by heart and, therefore, needed to have the passage recited aloud for them; see M. Bik. 3:7.

[4] Israel Jacob Yuval, *Two Nations in Your Womb: Perceptions of Jews and Christians in Late Antiquity and the Middle Ages* (Berkeley: University of California Press, 2006), 109.

[5] Joshua Kulp and David Golinkin, *The Schechter Haggadah: Art, History, and Commentary* (Jerusalem: Schechter Institute of Jewish Studies, 2009), 213–15.

[6] The seder is the one time we are instructed to engage in midrash, the act of explication, as a core mitzvah. See J. B. Soloveitchik, *Shiurim le-zekher abba mari*, vol. 2 (Jerusalem: Mosad Ha-Rav Kook, 2002), 156–57.

of the seder is not a recitation or reading of biblical texts but rather explication of Torah. According to R. Soloveitchik, the selection of this outstandingly brief passage was designed to encourage participants to focus on questioning, on learning, and on intellectual engagement rather than on the text itself.[7]

Each of these explanations has its merits and its shortcomings, many of which have been discussed in both scholarly and popular literature. The question that I wish to focus on is a different one, and it is independent of the historical reasons for the text's selection. What does the *Arami oved avi* passage contribute to the Haggadah, and what is its significance for the seder participant? To answer this question, this essay offers four readings of the text in its original biblical context, each of which highlights messages and motifs central to the seder experience.[8]

Narrative and Sacrifice

The Rabbinic seder is constructed on a distinct two-part model composed of eating and speech.[9] In fact, it entails an intricate interweaving of these two elements: we begin the seder by drinking wine and eating the

---

[7] The difficulty with this explanation is that it does not presume any particular significance for the passage from Deuteronomy 26 other than its brevity. Moreover, were brevity the sole consideration, *Arami oved avi* would not have been the best choice: the message that Moses sends to the king of Edom to request passage through his land includes an even more concise account of the Exodus where the same basic events are narrated in two verses rather than four (Num. 20:15–16).

[8] A fifth reading will be the subject of essay 2.

[9] This is in contrast to the Torah's account of the Passover ritual, both in Exodus 12 and Deuteronomy 16, which focuses almost exclusively on the communal eating of the Passover sacrifice. The Bible does require teaching one's children the Exodus story on no less than four occasions (Exod. 12:26–27, 13:8, 13:14–15, and Deut. 6:20–25), but in only one of these instances is it clear that the exchange between parent and child is meant to take place on the holiday itself (Exod. 13:8). (In Exod. 12:26–27 the telling is explicitly linked to the sacrificial rite, but it is less clear that it needs to be conducted on the night of the holiday). R. Moses Maimonides (Rambam), in particular, seems to have been sensitive to the Rabbis' innovation in linking the Exodus storytelling directly with the eating of the sacrifice on the night of Passover (see *Mishneh Torah, Hilkhot Hametz u-Matzah* 7:1). Rather than citing one of the obvious verses (Exod. 12:26–27, 13:8, 13:14, or Deut. 6:20–25) as a prooftext for the commandment "to tell of the Exodus from Egypt," he cited the verse "Remember [*zakhor*] this day on which you went out of Egypt, from the house of slaves" (Exod. 13:3)

A PASSOVER HAGGADAH: GO FORTH AND LEARN

karpas, and then we pause to tell the Passover story;[10] we conclude the story-telling with a partial recitation of *Hallel* (psalms of thanksgiving), and then we go back to eating (matzah and *maror*, the *korekh* sandwich, and the main meal); and finally, we conclude the evening's ritual by completing the *Hallel* recitation. Deuteronomy 26, which describes the bringing of first fruits—a temple offering that is accompanied by the recitation of a historical narrative—provides a paradigm for this type of ritual.

In the verses that immediately precede the *Arami oved avi* passage, the Torah describes the interaction between the fruit-bearing pilgrim and the *Kohen* who receives his offering:

וְלָקַחְתָּ מֵרֵאשִׁית כָּל פְּרִי הָאֲדָמָה אֲשֶׁר תָּבִיא מֵאַרְצְךָ אֲשֶׁר יהוה אֱלֹהֶיךָ נֹתֵן לָךְ
וְשַׂמְתָּ בַטֶּנֶא וְהָלַכְתָּ אֶל הַמָּקוֹם אֲשֶׁר יִבְחַר יהוה אֱלֹהֶיךָ לְשַׁכֵּן שְׁמוֹ שָׁם: וּבָאתָ אֶל
הַכֹּהֵן אֲשֶׁר יִהְיֶה בַּיָּמִים הָהֵם וְאָמַרְתָּ אֵלָיו הִגַּדְתִּי הַיּוֹם לַיהוה אֱלֹהֶיךָ כִּי בָאתִי אֶל
הָאָרֶץ אֲשֶׁר נִשְׁבַּע יהוה לַאֲבֹתֵינוּ לָתֶת לָנוּ: וְלָקַח הַכֹּהֵן הַטֶּנֶא מִיָּדֶךָ וְהִנִּיחוֹ לִפְנֵי
מִזְבַּח יהוה אֱלֹהֶיךָ:

You shall take from the first yield of all the fruit of the soil that you will bring from your land which the **Lord** *your God is about to give you, and you shall put it in a basket and go to the place that the* **Lord** *your God chooses to make His name dwell there. And you shall come to the priest who will be in those days, and you shall say to him, "I have told today to the* **Lord** *your God that I have come into the land which the* **Lord** *swore to our fathers to give us." And the priest shall take the basket from your hand and lay it down before the altar of the* **Lord** *your God. (Deut. 26:2–4)*

---

and added, "As it is written: Remember [*zakhor*] the Sabbath day to hallow it" (Exod. 20:7). The Rabbis understood the latter verse as a reference to *Kiddush*, the formal act of remembering or pronouncing the Sabbath that is performed on the Sabbath day itself. In appending this verse to the prooftext regarding the Exodus story, Rambam meant to suggest that there too "remember" does not only mean intellectually but also declaratively, on the very day God took us out of Egypt—that is, on the night of Passover.

[10] In *Maggid*, much of the storytelling is presented in a question-answer format that is reminiscent of the questions concerning the Exodus posed by children in the Torah. Unlike the Torah's questions, however, the Haggadah's questions are particular to the seder night: the four *Mah Nishtanah* questions, the midrash concerning the Four Children, etc.

Arami Oved Avi: The Core Text of the Haggadah

The *Kohen* takes the basket from the pilgrim and places it before the altar, emphasizing that the first fruits are not a standard priestly offering but rather a form of sacrifice.[11] Next, the pilgrim is to declaim the *Arami oved avi* passage. Curiously, after providing the text of the pilgrim's recitation, the Torah repeats an instruction from the beginning of the section:

וְהִנַּחְתּוֹ לִפְנֵי יהוה אֱלֹהֶיךָ וְהִשְׁתַּחֲוִיתָ לִפְנֵי יהוה אֱלֹהֶיךָ׃...

> *...And you shall lay it down before the* LORD *your God, and you shall bow before the* LORD *your God.* (Deut. 26:10)

On a literary level, the repetition of this instruction serves to bookend the oral performance with the "laying down" of (*le-haniah*) verse 4 and the "laying down" of verse 10, underscoring that the recitation is bound up with bringing the sacrifice. Thus, the *Arami oved avi* passage provides the Haggadah with a biblical model for its ritual program: narrating the Exodus story in conjunction with eating the Passover offering (or its symbolic successors).

Telling versus Remembering

The *Arami oved avi* passage further highlights the significance of the storytelling act in contrast to simple remembering. This emerges from consideration of the text in its broader literary context. The biblical passage that immediately precedes *Arami oved avi* in Deuteronomy 26 mandates remembering Amalek's despicable actions toward the People of Israel shortly after their departure from Egypt:

זָכוֹר אֵת אֲשֶׁר עָשָׂה לְךָ עֲמָלֵק בַּדֶּרֶךְ בְּצֵאתְכֶם מִמִּצְרָיִם׃ אֲשֶׁר קָרְךָ בַּדֶּרֶךְ וַיְזַנֵּב בְּךָ
כָּל הַנֶּחֱשָׁלִים אַחֲרֶיךָ וְאַתָּה עָיֵף וְיָגֵעַ וְלֹא יָרֵא אֱלֹהִים׃ וְהָיָה בְּהָנִיחַ יהוה אֱלֹהֶיךָ
לְךָ מִכָּל אֹיְבֶיךָ מִסָּבִיב בָּאָרֶץ אֲשֶׁר יהוה אֱלֹהֶיךָ נֹתֵן לְךָ נַחֲלָה לְרִשְׁתָּהּ תִּמְחֶה אֶת
זֵכֶר עֲמָלֵק מִתַּחַת הַשָּׁמָיִם לֹא תִּשְׁכָּח׃

> *Remember what Amalek did to you on the way when you came out of Egypt, how he fell upon you on the way and cut down all the*

---

[11] See *Mishneh Torah*, *Hilkhot Bikkurim* 2:18, where Rambam refers to the first fruits as *kodshei mikdash*, a temple offering.

stragglers, with you famished and exhausted, and you[12] *did not fear God. And it shall be, when the LORD your God grants you respite from all your enemies around in the land that the LORD your God is about to give you in estate to take hold of it, you shall wipe out the remembrance of Amalek from under the heavens, you shall not forget.* (Deut. 25:17–19)

This requirement to remember Amalek is seemingly unrelated to the bringing of first fruits in the verses that follow. But in addition to the textual juxtaposition, the wording of the Amalek passage should alert the reader to its deep connection with the *Arami oved avi* verses. Strikingly, the phrase *nahalah le-rishtah* ("in estate to take hold of it") that appears in the concluding verse of the Amalek passage is echoed in the opening verse of the first-fruits section:

וְהָיָה כִּי תָבוֹא אֶל הָאָרֶץ אֲשֶׁר יהוה אֱלֹהֶיךָ נֹתֵן לְךָ נַחֲלָה וִירִשְׁתָּהּ וְיָשַׁבְתָּ בָּהּ׃

And it shall be, when you come into the land that the LORD your God is about to give you in estate, and you shall take hold of it and dwell in it. (Deut. 26:1)

And the verb *le-haniah*, which is used in the final verse of the Amalek passage, appears twice in the first-fruits passage (26:4,10), as we have noted.

However, these literary links serve primarily to highlight the distinction between the two commandments: whereas the requirement regarding Amalek is to remember, the requirement regarding first fruits is to recite a narrative. Remembering is an activity that can be done privately, whereas narrating—or in the Haggadah's language, "telling" (*le-sapper*)—is an activity that requires the presence of another. Indeed, the first-fruits recitation must be performed in the presence of two entities: the *Kohen* before whom the basket is placed and God, to whom the pilgrim's statement is directed. The juxtaposition of the Amalek passage to the first-fruits verses underscores this unique feature

---

[12] Translation has been emended: the original reads "he"; however, on the most basic level this phrase refers to the People of Israel and not to Amalek.

of the pilgrim's requirement, which lies at the heart of the seder-night experience as well.[13]

The Torah emphasizes that the pilgrim's story entails not only recitation but also performance. It involves actual physical activity: not just "and you shall lay it down before the LORD your God," but also "and you shall bow before the LORD your God" (Deut. 26:10). The storytelling at the seder similarly requires physical performance: one is obligated to recline at the seder, to physically demonstrate the freedom of the Exodus (M. Pes. 10:1 and B.T. Pes. 108a).[14] The Haggadah also enlists visual aids: the *Pesah*, the matzah, and the *maror*, which according to Rabban Gamliel are requisite props for the Exodus narration (M. Pes. 10:5). As a paradigm of what it means to tell a story, the *bikkurim* passage teaches that it is necessary to acknowledge God not only in speech but also in action. Transposing this passage to the seder serves to emphasize this basic tenet of Passover ritual.

The Deuteronomy passage highlights another facet of seder-night storytelling as well. When the pilgrim first approaches the *Kohen*, he says, in the first person:

...הִגַּדְתִּי הַיּוֹם לַיהוה אֱלֹהֶיךָ כִּי בָאתִי אֶל הָאָרֶץ אֲשֶׁר נִשְׁבַּע יהוה לַאֲבֹתֵינוּ לָתֶת לָנוּ:

. . . I have told today to the LORD your God that I have come into the land which the LORD swore to our fathers to give to us. (Deut. 26:3)

The individual who brings first fruits describes his personal arrival in the Land of Israel, although it is likely that his family has been rooted there for

---

[13] The distinction between remembering and telling is posited at the very beginning of the *Maggid* section, which records a talmudic dispute between Rabbi Eleazar (in the name of Ben Zoma) and the Sages concerning the number of times a day a person is required to actively remember the Exodus from Egypt. The Haggadah's point in citing this passage (which originates in M. Ber. 1:5) is that one is obligated "to remember" every day of the year; but the obligation "to tell" is relevant to the night of Passover alone.

[14] Rambam thinks that the four cups of wine are also a physical demonstration of the Exodus; see *Mishneh Torah, Hilkhot Hametz u-Matzah* 7:7. Some communities have a custom of walking around the table to convey the sense of personally escaping Egypt.

A PASSOVER HAGGADAH: GO FORTH AND LEARN

many generations. He relates similarly to the Exodus experience, as though it were his own: he does not say "they suffered in Egypt," "they cried out to God," or "God responded to them," but rather "we suffered," "we cried," and "we were redeemed." This sense of relating intimately to an ancient event is precisely what the Haggadah means to achieve by requiring participants of every generation to view themselves as though they personally escaped bondage in Egypt.[15]

But the Haggadah takes the performative recitation of the first-fruits formula one step further: on the seder night the requirement is not to declaim, but rather *le-sapper*, to tell, suggesting that each recitation should be distinct. Storytelling requires an audience, and since no two audiences are the same, narrative dynamics virtually ensure that each telling will be different. The Haggadah records this truism in the *Midrash* of the Four Children: what the parent says to one child is not what he says to another. It's always a different story.

God versus Amalek

The juxtaposition of the commandment to remember Amalek and the first-fruits recitation is even more significant for its theological implications than for its lessons regarding storytelling. The Torah's placement of the Amalek passage just before the *Arami oved avi* passage highlights God's role as protector of the weak and downtrodden, the very qualities of God that the Haggadah wishes to emphasize in the Exodus narrative.

In commanding us to remember Amalek, the Torah instructs us to consider that they attacked the People of Israel at a moment of vulnerability: *ba-derekh,* on the way, when they were tired and weak and did not fear God. A careful reader cannot help but recall the first description of the Israelites' encounter with Amalek, in Exodus 17. After crossing the sea, the people were

---

[15] The author of the Haggadah cites a different verse from Deuteronomy as a prooftext for this idea: "But us [*ve-otanu*] did He take out from there" (Deut. 6:23); but in truth, the theme is already embedded in the *Arami oved avi* passage.

wandering in the desert, complaining about the lack of water and questioning God's concern for them. They came to a place named Rephidim, and the Torah tells us that it was thereafter known as Masah u-Merivah (Testing and Dispute) because of their challenge to God (Exod. 17:7). Yet in the very next verse the Torah reports that Amalek came and fought with the Israelites at Rephidim (17:8). After having renamed the place Masah u-Merivah, why does the Torah revert to calling it by its former name? The *Mekhilta* suggests that the name Rephidim was a reference to the people's current condition: their hands had become too weak (*rafu yedeihem*) to bear the Torah. In fact, this explanation seems to accord with a plain reading of the text. The battle story that follows describes Moses' hands becoming heavy and weak, symbolic of the people's weakness that was exploited by Amalek, which was not a physical ailment but a spiritual one.

In addition to these descriptions of spiritual weariness, the two Amalek passages also share words and phrases. Indeed, many of the words that appear in Deuteronomy 25 seem to be drawn from the story in Exodus 17. The verse in Deuteronomy that provides the setting for God's command,

$$\text{וְהָיָה בְּהָנִיחַ יהוה אֱלֹהֶיךָ לְךָ מִכָּל אֹיְבֶיךָ מִסָּבִיב} \ldots$$

> And it shall be, when the LORD your God grants you respite from all your enemies around . . . (Deut. 25:19)

recalls the phrase from Exodus describing Moses' role during the battle with Amalek,

$$\text{וְהָיָה כַּאֲשֶׁר יָרִים מֹשֶׁה יָדוֹ וְגָבַר יִשְׂרָאֵל וְכַאֲשֶׁר יָנִיחַ יָדוֹ וְגָבַר עֲמָלֵק:}$$

> And so, when Moses would raise his hand, Israel prevailed, and when he put down his hand, Amalek prevailed. (Exod. 17:11)

The expression in Deuteronomy that describes Amalek's unheroic conduct,

$$\ldots \text{וַיְזַנֵּב בְּךָ כָּל הַנֶּחֱשָׁלִים אַחֲרֶיךָ} \ldots$$

> . . . and cut down all the straggler . . . (Deut. 25:18)

evokes the verse in Exodus depicting Joshua's success in battle,

A PASSOVER HAGGADAH: GO FORTH AND LEARN

וַיַּחֲלֹשׁ יְהוֹשֻׁעַ אֶת עֲמָלֵק וְאֶת עַמּוֹ לְפִי חָרֶב:

And Joshua disabled Amalek and its people by the edge of the sword.
(Exod. 17:13)

The opening phrase of the Deuteronomy passage,

זָכוֹר אֵת אֲשֶׁר עָשָׂה לְךָ עֲמָלֵק בַּדֶּרֶךְ בְּצֵאתְכֶם מִמִּצְרָיִם:

*Remember what Amalek did to you on the way when you came out of
Egypt.* (Deut. 25:17)

calls to mind the concluding segment of the Exodus narrative,

וַיֹּאמֶר יהוה אֶל מֹשֶׁה כְּתֹב זֹאת זִכָּרוֹן בַּסֵּפֶר ... כִּי מָחֹה אֶמְחֶה אֶת זֵכֶר עֲמָלֵק
מִתַּחַת הַשָּׁמָיִם:

And the LORD *said to Moses, "Write this down as a remembrance in a
record . . . that I will surely wipe out the name of Amalek under the
heavens."* (Exod. 17:14)

And the command in Deuteronomy to blot out Amalek's memory from under
the heavens,

... תִּמְחֶה אֶת זֵכֶר עֲמָלֵק מִתַּחַת הַשָּׁמָיִם לֹא תִּשְׁכָּח:

*. . . you shall wipe out the remembrance of Amalek from under the
heavens, you shall not forget.* (Deut. 25:19)

clearly echoes God's proclamation concerning Amalek in Exodus,

... כִּי מָחֹה אֶמְחֶה אֶת זֵכֶר עֲמָלֵק מִתַּחַת הַשָּׁמָיִם:

*. . . that I will surely wipe out the name of Amalek from under the
heavens.* (Exod. 17:14)

But strangely, a key word in Deuteronomy 25, *ba-derekh* (on the way), at first
blush does not seem to feature in the Exodus version. More careful analysis
reveals that the word is connected with the Exodus story, although it does
not appear in chapter 17. Instead, it appears in chapter 18, in the context of
Jethro's arrival at the Israelites' camp in the desert shortly after the battle with

Amalek. According to that narrative, Jethro comes after hearing reports of the Exodus and of all that God had done for Moses and the People of Israel (Exod. 18:1). When his father-in-law arrives, Moses takes him into his tent and updates him on the various hardships that they had encountered "on the way":

וַיְסַפֵּר מֹשֶׁה לְחֹתְנוֹ אֵת כָּל אֲשֶׁר עָשָׂה יהוה לְפַרְעֹה וּלְמִצְרַיִם עַל אוֹדֹת יִשְׂרָאֵל אֵת כָּל הַתְּלָאָה אֲשֶׁר מְצָאָתַם בַּדֶּרֶךְ וַיַּצִּלֵם יהוה:

And Moses recounted to his father-in-law all that the LORD had done to Pharaoh and to Egypt for the sake of Israel, all the hardship that had come upon them on the way, and the LORD had rescued them. (Exod. 18:8)

Jethro's response is to rejoice, praise God for having saved Israel, and declare that he now knows God to be the greatest of the deities, whereupon he offers a sacrifice (Exod. 18:9–12).

What did Moses tell his father-in-law that got him so excited? After all, according to the first verse of the chapter, Jethro has already heard about the Exodus before he comes to meet the people in the desert! Repeating the word "all" (*kol*) twice, the Torah emphasizes that Moses tells Jethro the complete story, including not only the triumphs but also the travails. The one hardship that Moses describes in detail is the only thing Jethro would not have already known: Amalek's attack *ba-derekh* (on the way). And unlike God's acts of redemption, with which Jethro is familiar, the story of Amalek, who assaulted the weak and the vulnerable, entailed an act of rescue (*hatzalah*) by God. What Moses reveals to Jethro is that the God of Israel is the God who takes care of the broken and the defenseless. And Jethro's response is: I knew that *you* had those qualities, Moses, but I didn't realize that your God was like that too; that is what makes your God the greatest.[16]

---

[16] In fact, an act of *hatzalah* is what drew Jethro to Moses in the first place. After meeting Moses at the well, the daughters of Jethro (there called Reu'el) return home and report that an Egyptian man "rescued" them from the other shepherds (Exod. 2:19). Jethro's response to Moses' kindness is precisely his response to hearing about God's act of *hatzalah* in Exod. 18: he invites Moses to break bread with him (2:20).

Returning to Deuteronomy 26, we can now posit an additional meaning for its selection as the central Haggadah text: the first-fruits recitation brings into sharp relief the distinction between the God of Israel and Amalek. Amalek is the only people that the Torah presents as God's enemy. They are God's enemy because they are the antithesis of God: they take advantage of people who are weak, of people who are "on the way," of people who are tired and weary.[17] In contrast, the God we praise on the night of Passover is the God of the lost and wandering Aramean who went down to the land of Egypt, where he was an exiled stranger, enslaved and tortured. That God heard the slave's cry and took him out with great miracles and wonders, ultimately bringing him to a safe haven, to the land of milk and honey. In other words, the pilgrim's statement is a theological one.

We have two statements about God in our tradition. The first is the twice-daily recitation of the *Shema* (Deut. 6:4–9, 11:13–21, and Num. 15:37–41), which references the one all-powerful, eternal God of history. The second is the statement about God that we make on the night of Passover, when God's role as rescuer and redeemer is the main theme. The *Arami oved avi* passage underscores, in concise form, the qualities of God that were on display in the Exodus: God who addresses the lost, the alienated, the afflicted, the slave.

The Message of Deuteronomy

Thus far, we have considered the *Arami oved avi* passage both as a text unto itself and in terms of its relationship to the Amalek passage that precedes it; now we need to consider chapter 26 in its larger context in Deuteronomy as a whole. From a religious standpoint it is no coincidence that the core text of the seder is taken from Deuteronomy, which reviews events from the forty years of desert wanderings, rather than from Exodus, where the original redemption story is told. Deuteronomy is not only the source of the *Arami oved avi* passage but also of the other key biblical passages that form the Haggadah liturgy, namely Deut. 6:21 (*Avadim hayinu*, the verse

---

[17] Amalek's significance as the symbolic "enemy of God" is discussed further in essay 7.

Arami Oved Avi: The Core Text of the Haggadah

with which the *Maggid* begins) and Deut. 6:20 (the response to the wise child's question).

Deuteronomy's uniqueness is based on its representation as Moses' final speeches to the People of Israel before they enter the Land. Oddly, Moses' addresses seem to be based on an inaccurate premise: that he is speaking to the same people who left Egypt and received the Torah forty years earlier. Indeed, Moses goes so far as to declare:

יהוה אֱלֹהֵינוּ כָּרַת עִמָּנוּ בְּרִית בְּחֹרֵב: לֹא אֶת אֲבֹתֵינוּ כָּרַת יהוה אֶת הַבְּרִית
הַזֹּאת כִּי אִתָּנוּ אֲנַחְנוּ אֵלֶּה פֹה הַיּוֹם כֻּלָּנוּ חַיִּים: פָּנִים בְּפָנִים דִּבֶּר יהוה עִמָּכֶם בָּהָר
מִתּוֹךְ הָאֵשׁ: אָנֹכִי עֹמֵד בֵּין יהוה וּבֵינֵיכֶם בָּעֵת הַהוּא לְהַגִּיד לָכֶם אֶת דְּבַר יהוה:
כִּי יְרֵאתֶם מִפְּנֵי הָאֵשׁ וְלֹא עֲלִיתֶם בָּהָר ...

The LORD our God sealed a covenant with us at Horeb. Not with our fathers did the LORD seal this covenant but with us—we who are here today, all of us alive. Face to face did the LORD speak with you on the mountain from the midst of the fire. I was standing between the LORD and you at that time to tell you the word of the LORD—for you were afraid in the face of the fire and did not go up the mountain . . .
(Deut. 5:2–5)

What did Moses mean in claiming that the covenant of Horeb (i.e., Sinai) was being made with the people about to enter the Land of Israel rather than with their ancestors? If we presume Deuteronomy to be in consonance with the rest of the Torah, that is simply not true. God did not speak with the people who entered the Land of Israel at all; God spoke only with their ancestors who died in the desert. Many of the people whom Moses addressed in Deuteronomy forty years after the Exodus from Egypt were not yet alive when God gave the Torah at Sinai!

A similar problem arises in Deuteronomy 29, where Moses refers to the people entering the Land as those who witnessed the plagues God wrought in Egypt. But here Moses clarifies the meaning of his cryptic claims. What he means is that only now are the people able to understanding the meaning of the signs and wonders that God displayed in Egypt:

A PASSOVER HAGGADAH: GO FORTH AND LEARN

...אַתֶּם רְאִיתֶם אֵת כָּל אֲשֶׁר עָשָׂה יהוה לְעֵינֵיכֶם בְּאֶרֶץ מִצְרַיִם לְפַרְעֹה וּלְכָל
עֲבָדָיו וּלְכָל אַרְצוֹ: הַמַּסּוֹת הַגְּדֹלֹת אֲשֶׁר רָאוּ עֵינֶיךָ הָאֹתֹת וְהַמֹּפְתִים הַגְּדֹלִים
הָהֵם: וְלֹא נָתַן יהוה לָכֶם לֵב לָדַעַת וְעֵינַיִם לִרְאוֹת וְאָזְנַיִם לִשְׁמֹעַ עַד הַיּוֹם הַזֶּה:

...You have seen all that the LORD *did before your own eyes in the
land of Egypt to Pharaoh and to all his servants and to all his land, the
great trials that your own eyes have seen, those great signs and portents. But the* LORD *has not given you a heart to know and eyes to see
and ears to hear until this day.* (Deut. 29:1–3)

The Torah seems to be suggesting that the people who actually witnessed the
Exodus and stood at Sinai were not fully there, in the sense that they never
understood or internalized the experience: the people who left Egypt and
stood at Sinai were the ones who made the Golden Calf and wanted to return
to their place of bondage! Deuteronomy, on the other hand, addresses the
people who were not physically present at those events: the generation that
was never in Egypt and was therefore able to attain critical distance from the
experience of slavery. To these people the Torah says: it is because you were
not in Egypt that you can understand Egypt. It is because you were not there
that you were "as if" there.[18]

---

[18]To clarify this point, it is worth noting one of the most interesting contrasts between Lev. 26 and
Deut. 28, the two *tokhehah* (admonition) passages in the Torah: the curse in Leviticus concludes
with an assurance that God has not forsaken the people or forgotten the covenant and that God will
bring them back, whereas the conclusion to the curse in Deuteronomy states simply that God
will send the people in boats to Egypt, where they will be sold to their enemies as slaves—it says
nothing about return. R. Moses Nachmanides (Ramban) was very troubled by this abrupt ending,
and he suggested that the actual conclusion to the admonition is the so-called *Parashat ha-Teshuvah*
(Repentance Passage), which appears two chapters later and promises that no matter where the
people are, if they return to God, God will return to them (Deut. 30:1–3). But what the Ramban
never explained is why the Torah did not build *Parashat ha-Teshuvah* directly into the *tokhehah*. The
answer is simple. The audience being addressed in Leviticus was the slaves who left Egypt; and the
Torah did not expect slaves to return to God on their own. Thus, the Torah promised them that if
they recognized their wrongs, confessed their sins, paid their debts, and maintained the covenant,
God would bring them back. But the people in the book of Deuteronomy were never slaves, and as
such they understood both freedom and slavery. They were able, and expected, to take themselves
out of "Egypt," or at least to take the first step of "turning back" to God. They were a different audience, with different possibilities.

The Rabbis who constructed the seder were concerned primarily with the Jew who was not a slave in Egypt, and as such they did not want to draw upon the book of Exodus and the original Exodus story. Deuteronomy is the book that addresses the Jew who, despite the historical divide, is able to say: "And the Egyptians did evil to us and abused us" (Deut. 26:6); but "I have come into the land" (26:3). In explicating the *Arami oved avi* passage we demonstrate that through our seder-night learning we are able to see ourselves in relation to Egypt and allow the Exodus to speak to us in the deepest way.

2
Gerut, Avdut, Innuy:
The Covenantal Formula

In one of its central passages, the Haggadah praises God for planning out the redemption of the Israelites even prior to their captivity, striking a covenant with Abraham that serves as a blueprint for the Exodus:

בָּרוּךְ שׁוֹמֵר הַבְטָחָתוֹ לְיִשְׂרָאֵל, בָּרוּךְ הוּא. שֶׁהַקָּדוֹשׁ בָּרוּךְ הוּא חִשַּׁב אֶת
הַקֵּץ, לַעֲשׂוֹת כְּמָה שֶׁאָמַר לְאַבְרָהָם אָבִינוּ בִּבְרִית בֵּין הַבְּתָרִים, שֶׁנֶּאֱמַר:
וַיֹּאמֶר לְאַבְרָם, יָדֹעַ תֵּדַע כִּי גֵר יִהְיֶה זַרְעֲךָ בְּאֶרֶץ לֹא לָהֶם, וַעֲבָדוּם וְעִנּוּ אֹתָם
אַרְבַּע מֵאוֹת שָׁנָה. וְגַם אֶת הַגּוֹי אֲשֶׁר יַעֲבֹדוּ דָּן אָנֹכִי וְאַחֲרֵי כֵן יֵצְאוּ בִּרְכֻשׁ גָּדוֹל.

Blessed is He who keeps His promise to Israel, Blessed is He. For the Blessed Holy One calculated the end, to do as He promised Abraham in the Covenant between the Pieces. As it says: *And He said to Abram, "Know well that your seed shall be strangers in a land not theirs and they shall be enslaved and afflicted four hundred years. But upon the nation for whom they slave I will bring judgment, and afterward they shall come forth with great substance."* (Gen. 15:13–14)

In the covenant, three forms of suffering are invoked—*gerut* (alienation), *avdut* (servitude), and *innuy* (affliction)—and God promises that once these have been endured, redemption will occur. But the enslavement in Egypt is not the first instantiation of this covenant: the Haggadah draws an additional link between God's promise to Abraham and Jacob's experiences in Laban's household:

וְהִיא שֶׁעָמְדָה לַאֲבוֹתֵינוּ וְלָנוּ שֶׁלֹּא אֶחָד בִּלְבָד עָמַד עָלֵינוּ לְכַלּוֹתֵנוּ, אֶלָּא
שֶׁבְּכָל דּוֹר וָדוֹר עוֹמְדִים עָלֵינוּ לְכַלּוֹתֵנוּ, וְהַקָּדוֹשׁ בָּרוּךְ הוּא מַצִּילֵנוּ מִיָּדָם.
צֵא וּלְמַד מַה בִּקֵּשׁ לָבָן הָאֲרַמִּי לַעֲשׂוֹת לְיַעֲקֹב אָבִינוּ . . .

And it is this promise that has sustained us, for not just once did somebody try to destroy us, rather in every generation they have tried to destroy us, but the Blessed Holy One saves us from them. Go forth and see what Laban the Aramean tried to do to our ancestor Jacob . . .

The verses from Deuteronomy that follow and serve as the core text of *Maggid* present a telescoped version of Israel's foundational narrative that, as we will see, echoes the language of all these stories, reinforcing the connection:

...אֲרַמִּי אֹבֵד אָבִי וַיֵּרֶד מִצְרַיְמָה וַיָּגָר שָׁם בִּמְתֵי מְעָט וַיְהִי שָׁם לְגוֹי גָּדוֹל עָצוּם
וָרָב: וַיָּרֵעוּ אֹתָנוּ הַמִּצְרִים וַיְעַנּוּנוּ וַיִּתְּנוּ עָלֵינוּ עֲבֹדָה קָשָׁה...

. . . *"My father was an Aramean about to perish,*[19] *and he went down to Egypt, and he sojourned there with a few people," and he became there a great and mighty and multitudinous nation. And the Egyptians did evil to us and abused us and set upon us hard labor . . .* (Deut. 26:5–6)

What is the significance of this recurring motif? Tracing its appearance in the books of Genesis and Exodus will allow us in order to examine the role of God's covenant in Israel's history.[20]

Berit bein ha-Betarim: The Covenant with Abraham

The covenant that God forged with Abraham at the *Berit bein ha-Betarim* (the Covenant between the Pieces) established the formula for God's relationship with his descendants for all generations. In Genesis 15, God promises the still-barren Abraham that he will be blessed with offspring who will inherit the Land; but Abraham questions how he is to know that he will indeed possess it. God instructs him to conduct an elaborate sacrificial ritual,

---

[19] As noted in the previous essay, the Haggadah assumes a different translation of this phrase: rather than "My father was an Aramean about to perish," the Haggadah renders it "An Aramean [namely, Laban] attempted to destroy my father [that is, Jacob]."
[20] Many of the insights presented in this essay are also discussed by Devora Steinmetz in her book *From Father to Son: Kinship, Conflict, and Continuity in Genesis* (Louisville, KY: Westminster/John Knox Press, 1991).

after which Abraham falls into a deep slumber and God speaks to him from the darkness:

יָדֹעַ תֵּדַע כִּי גֵר יִהְיֶה זַרְעֲךָ בְּאֶרֶץ לֹא לָהֶם וַעֲבָדוּם וְעִנּוּ אֹתָם אַרְבַּע מֵאוֹת שָׁנָה: וְגַם אֶת הַגּוֹי אֲשֶׁר יַעֲבֹדוּ דָּן אָנֹכִי וְאַחֲרֵי כֵן יֵצְאוּ בִּרְכֻשׁ גָּדוֹל: וְאַתָּה תָּבוֹא אֶל אֲבֹתֶיךָ בְּשָׁלוֹם תִּקָּבֵר בְּשֵׂיבָה טוֹבָה: וְדוֹר רְבִיעִי יָשׁוּבוּ הֵנָּה כִּי לֹא שָׁלֵם עֲוֹן הָאֱמֹרִי עַד הֵנָּה:

Know well that your seed shall be strangers in a land not theirs and they shall be enslaved and afflicted four hundred years. But upon the nation for whom they slave I will bring judgment, and afterward they shall come forth with great substance. As for you, you shall go to your fathers in peace you shall be buried in ripe old age. And in the fourth generation they shall return here, for the iniquity of the Amorites is not yet full. (Gen. 15:13–16)

God's promise to Abraham portends exile, suffering, and oppression but also pledges material wealth, redemption, and return to the Land. The Torah does not specify to whom the prediction in the text refers, but it does imply that three generations will suffer before the fourth will be redeemed. As noted, the basic terms of this covenant are threefold: *gerut*, *avdut*, and *innuy*.

As a backdrop to establishing this covenant, God tells Abraham to take a series of three animals and cut them in halves and to take a set of birds but leave them whole. The symbolism of this strange ritual is significant: the three animals that are cut in half represent the three generations of suffering (as well as the three covenantal terms: *gerut*, *avdut*, and *innuy*), while the birds, which are not cut, correspond to the fourth generation of redemption and repossession.[21] Both God's words to Abraham and the sacrificial ritual suggest a basic premise of the covenant: the generations that suffer will not themselves merit full redemption. Repossession of the ancestral homeland will be attained only by a generation that has not itself witnessed oppression.

---

[21] See the commentary of R. Samson Raphael Hirsch on Gen. 15:9–21, where he asserts: "The ידע תדע is nothing but the explanation of what had already been said symbolically, is nothing but the verbal translation of the symbolic performance which preceded it."

The dramatic staging of *Berit bein ha-Betarim* and the imposing tones of God's pledge to Abraham mark it as an event of magnitude. The consequence of the message is underscored by the reference to its covenantal nature in the concluding verses of the chapter:

בַּיּוֹם הַהוּא כָּרַת יהוה אֶת אַבְרָם בְּרִית לֵאמֹר לְזַרְעֲךָ נָתַתִּי אֶת הָאָרֶץ הַזֹּאת מִנְּהַר מִצְרַיִם עַד הַנָּהָר הַגָּדֹל נְהַר פְּרָת...

On that day the LORD *made a covenant with Abram, saying, "To your seed I have given this land from the river of Egypt to the great river, the river Euphrates . . ." (Gen. 15:18)*

But the designation of God's message as a covenant also indicates that it is not a unilateral pledge: inheritance of the Promised Land is contingent on accepting God's terms, namely *gerut, avdut,* and *innuy.* The fulfillment of these terms occurs both in Abraham's life and in the lives of Abraham's descendants.

Abraham Defines the Covenantal Life

In his 13th-century commentary on the Torah, R. Moses Nachmanides noted that the central narrative of Genesis 12—Abraham and Sarah's sojourn in Egypt—bears a remarkable similarity to the Exodus story.[22] In both cases, the protagonists journey to Egypt to escape famine in the land of Canaan; in both cases, they are exploited by the Egyptians; in both cases, the women play a central role; and in both cases, God responds by afflicting the Egyptians, who bestow great wealth upon those they have oppressed and send them from their land. But the stongest point of correspondence between the two narratives (which Nachmanides does not mention) is that both replicate the major elements of God's pledge to Abraham at *Berit bein ha-Betarim.* In fact, a careful reading of Genesis 12 demonstrates that events in Abraham's

---

[22] See Ramban on Gen. 12:10, *Va-yehi ra'av ba-aretz.* This observation is the basis for his oft-quoted thesis regarding the prophetic function of Genesis: *ma'aseh avot siman le-banim,* the acts of the fathers signal those of the sons.

own life prefigure the central themes of God's covenant, namely the motif of *gerut*, *avdut*, and *innuy* followed by redemption and acquisition of riches.

Shortly after arriving in the land of Canaan, Abraham encounters a famine and takes his family to seek food in Egypt. The Torah describes Abraham's purpose in traveling to Egypt as *la-gur* (to sojourn), implying that Abraham does not intend to settle there permanently:[23]

וַיְהִי רָעָב בָּאָרֶץ וַיֵּרֶד אַבְרָם מִצְרַיְמָה לָגוּר שָׁם כִּי כָבֵד הָרָעָב בָּאָרֶץ:

And there was a famine in the land and Abram went down to Egypt to sojourn there, for the famine was grave in the land. (Gen. 12:10)

Fearing that the Egyptians will kill him and abduct his wife, Abraham presents Sarah as his sister, but she is nonetheless apprehended by Pharaoh. After God intervenes, Sarah is released along with many gifts. Although the terms *avdut* and *innuy* do not appear in the text, the basic elements of Abraham and Sarah's saga clearly fit these categories. Abraham himself, who is complicit in Sarah's captivity, does not directly experience bondage or suffering. However, Sarah's experience is one of servitude in the sense that she is held forcibly and denied freedom of movement; and it is affliction insofar as she is threatened sexually.[24] The covenant of chapter 15, in which all three terms feature in God's promise to Abraham, is the Torah's reformulation of what has taken place.

The many linguistic associations between *Berit bein ha-Betarim* and Genesis 14, which tell of Abraham's participation in the battle of the Canaanite

---

[23] The sense of impermanence associated with the word *la-gur* emerges most clearly from Gen. 47:4, where Joseph's brothers use that term to explain to Pharaoh that they have come to Egypt on a temporary basis because of the famine in the land of Canaan. The word *la-gur* (to sojourn) is based on the same root as the word *gerut* (alienation).

[24] The Torah's use of the term *innuy* often indicates a sexual offense or a complicated sexual interaction. *Innuy* appears in the Sarah and Hagar story in the context of a complicated, three-way marriage (Gen. 16:6,9,11); it appears in the Dinah story to describe her molestation and rape by Shechem (34:2); it appears in the Joseph story, presumably to describe his experience in the home of Potiphar, which entailed a type of sexual harassment and abuse (41:52); and it appears at the beginning of Exodus, where it is proposed by Pharaoh as a solution to the problem of overpopulation (Exod. 1:11,12).

kings, imply that these two narratives are also deeply connected. The Hebrew root ש-ו-ב (to bring back, to return) features prominently in both passages (14:16, 15:16) as does the word *rekhush* (possessions), which refers both to the property that Abraham redeems and to the wealth God promises his descendants (14:16,21; 15:14). Similarly, the blessing that Melchizedek, king of Salem, bestows upon Abraham after he defeats the Canaanite kings (14:19–20) invokes the same seldom-used word *migen* (to surround, to defend) that appears in God's promise to Abraham preceding *Berit bein ha-Betarim* (15:1). Melchizedek's reference to God as "possessor of heaven and earth" (14:19) also resonates at the beginning of chapter 15 when God instructs Abraham to step outside and count the stars. And even Melchizedek's name reverberates in chapter 15, where Abraham's faith in God is deemed *tzedakah* (a merit).[25]

The number ten also features prominently in both chapters. In chapter 14, ten kings are mentioned (the four kings, the five kings, and Melchizedek); and Abraham gives Melchizedek a tenth of the spoils (Gen. 14:20).[26] At the end of chapter 15, the covenant is summarized as God's promise to Abraham that his descendants will inherit the Land by defeating ten nations, in contrast to the usual seven that are listed (15:19–21).

All these links between Genesis chapters 14 and 15 suggest that the struggle between the rulers of Canaan is merely the backdrop to a story that is really about Abraham and his symbolic conquest of the Land.[27] Abraham is driven by a sense of responsibility for his nephew Lot, who has been taken captive, to engage with the nations of Canaan in a manner that anticipates the

---

[25] The language of God's covenant in chap. 15 also echoes the places and people who feature in chap. 14. In chap. 14, Salem is the name of the city that Melchizedek rules, and the Amorites are both a nation that the four kings defeat (Gen. 14:7) and the nation of Mamre, on whose land Abraham resides (14:13). In chap. 15, God promises Abraham that his descendants will return to the Land only after the iniquities of the Amorites are *shalem*, "full" (15:16). In chap. 14, Abraham pursues Lot's captors first to a place called Dan (14:14) and subsequently to Hobah, north of Damascus (14:15), which is mentioned in chap. 15 as the hometown of Abraham's servant, Damessek Eliezer (15:2). In chap. 15, God promises to avenge Israel's 400-year enslavement: "But upon the nation for whom they slave I will bring judgment [*dan anokhi*]" (15:14).

[26] A play on the word *ma'aser* (a tenth) also appears in Abraham's refusal to take gifts from the king of Sodom: "You shall not say, 'It is I who made Abram rich [*he'esharti*]'" (Gen. 14:23).

[27] Of course, he does so by proxy: Abraham defeats the four kings who, in turn, have defeated all the powerful nations of Canaan.

eventual possession of that Land by his descendants. The significance of Abraham's "conquest" is reflected in the cosmic language of the blessing that Melchizedek bestows upon him, "Blessed be Abram to El Elyon, possessor of heaven and earth" (Gen. 14:19), marking Abraham as one who has participated in the fulfillment of God's plan for Creation.

Thus, the Covenant between the Pieces is essentially an articulation of Abraham's life experiences. By reformulating the events of chapters 12 and 14 in the language of *berit* (covenant), God indicates to Abraham that the divine covenant is modeled—indeed, predicated—on his life: God will enter into an eternal relationship specifically with those among Abraham's descendants who mirror his deeds and values.

Jacob Inherits the Covenantal Promise

As the author of the Haggadah indicates, Jacob is the first of Abraham's descendants to live out the terms of God's covenant: his self-imposed exile to Paddan-aram, his servitude and oppression in Laban's household, and his ultimate return to the land of Canaan fulfill all the major elements of God's promise. In addition to the thematic correlation, the Jacob narratives echo the language of *Berit bein ha-Betarim*—in particular, the *gerut, avdut, innuy* formula—alerting the reader to this instantiation of the divine covenant.

Jacob arrives in Paddan-aram penniless and alone, running from his brother Esau, who desires to kill him.[28] Over the course of twenty years in Laban's home, Jacob experiences personal and material growth, acquiring four wives, twelve children, and many flocks; but he is also beset with endless labor, repeated deception, and ongoing strife. Finally, following a souring of his

---

[28] The Torah offers two explanations for Jacob's departure from his parents' home and his journey to Paddan-aram: (1) to escape his brother Esau's wrath at having been deprived of their father's blessing; and (2) to find a wife. Each explanation reflects a different interpretation of the narrative: the first casts Jacob as a fugitive and his exile as a punishment; the second highlights his role as heir to the covenant.

relations with Laban and a direct command from God, Jacob gathers his family and possessions and sets off hastily for his father's home in Canaan. When Laban gets word of the unannounced departure, he chases after Jacob and overtakes his camp, accusing his son-in-law both of sneaking away with his daughters and grandchildren and of stealing his gods. After Laban searches the entire camp and finds nothing (Rachel, who did indeed take the idols, has hidden them well), Jacob verbally castigates his father-in-law, referring to his experience in Paddan-aram as both *avdut* and *innuy*:

מַה פִּשְׁעִי מַה חַטָּאתִי כִּי דָלַקְתָּ אַחֲרָי: כִּי מִשַּׁשְׁתָּ אֶת כָּל כֵּלַי מַה מָּצָאתָ מִכֹּל כְּלֵי בֵיתֶךָ שִׂים כֹּה נֶגֶד אַחַי וְאַחֶיךָ וְיוֹכִיחוּ בֵּין שְׁנֵינוּ: זֶה עֶשְׂרִים שָׁנָה אָנֹכִי עִמָּךְ רְחֵלֶיךָ וְעִזֶּיךָ לֹא שִׁכֵּלוּ וְאֵילֵי צֹאנְךָ לֹא אָכָלְתִּי: טְרֵפָה לֹא הֵבֵאתִי אֵלֶיךָ אָנֹכִי אֲחַטֶּנָּה מִיָּדִי תְּבַקְשֶׁנָּה גְּנֻבְתִי יוֹם וּגְנֻבְתִי לָיְלָה: הָיִיתִי בַיּוֹם אֲכָלַנִי חֹרֶב וְקֶרַח בַּלָּיְלָה וַתִּדַּד שְׁנָתִי מֵעֵינָי: זֶה לִּי עֶשְׂרִים שָׁנָה בְּבֵיתֶךָ עֲבַדְתִּיךָ אַרְבַּע עֶשְׂרֵה שָׁנָה בִּשְׁתֵּי בְנֹתֶיךָ וְשֵׁשׁ שָׁנִים בְּצֹאנֶךָ וַתַּחֲלֵף אֶת מַשְׂכֻּרְתִּי עֲשֶׂרֶת מֹנִים: לוּלֵי אֱלֹהֵי אָבִי אֱלֹהֵי אַבְרָהָם וּפַחַד יִצְחָק הָיָה לִי כִּי עַתָּה רֵיקָם שִׁלַּחְתָּנִי אֶת עָנְיִי וְאֶת יְגִיעַ כַּפַּי רָאָה אֱלֹהִים וַיּוֹכַח אָמֶשׁ:

What is my crime, what is my guilt, that you should race after me? Though you rummaged through all my things, what have you found of all your household things? Set it here before my kin and yours, and they shall determine between us two. These twenty years I have been with you, your ewes and your she-goats did not lose their young, the rams of your flock I have not eaten. What was torn up by beasts I brought not to you; I bore the loss; from my hand you could seek it—what was stolen by day and stolen by night. Often—by day parching heat ate me up and frost in the night, and sleep was a stranger to my eyes. These twenty years in your household I served you, fourteen years for your two daughters and six years for your flocks, and you switched my wages ten times over. Were it not that the God of my father, the God of Abraham and the Terror of Isaac, was with me, you would have sent me off empty handed. My suffering and the toil of my hands God has seen, and last night He determined in my favor. (Gen. 31:36–42)

Jacob means to suggest that he was a slave, in the most basic sense of the term.[29] A slave has no freedom of movement, and Laban has chased after him to detain him. A slave has no privacy, and Laban has searched all his possessions. A slave does not get paid properly, and Laban has changed his wages ten times. And in citing God as witness to his suffering at Laban's hands, Jacob definitively interprets the experience as *innuy*. However, it is only after parting ways with his father-in-law that Jacob identifies his experience in Paddan-aram as *gerut*. Approaching the land of Canaan, Jacob sends messengers to his brother Esau, saying:

כֹּה אָמַר עַבְדְּךָ יַעֲקֹב עִם לָבָן גַּרְתִּי וָאֵחַר עַד עָתָּה:

Thus says your servant Jacob: With Laban I have sojourned and I tarried until now. (Gen. 32:5)

The order in which the three covenantal terms appear in the Jacob narrative is different than the order in which God presented them at *Berit bein ha-Betarim*, where, *gerut* preceded *avdut* and *innuy*. In reordering the terms, the Torah seems to suggest that Jacob actually experienced *gerut* later. Indeed, it is possible that for most of Jacob's sojourn in Paddan-aram he felt included and engaged; but as he ran away from Laban, he felt deeply alienated and came to understand the whole experience as one of *gerut*. Recognition of himself as a stranger was only possible once Jacob had left, because self-reflection required critical distance from the experience itself; so long as he was in Laban's house, Jacob did not perceive himself as a *ger*.[30]

---

[29] Forms of the root ע-ב-ד appear in the Jacob/Laban narrative 14 times, the final instance being the statement "I served you [*avadetikha*] fourteen years for your two daughters..." (Gen. 31:41).

[30] To demonstrate this point, it is worth considering the Joseph narrative, a story about exile that follows the "covenantal pattern" except that the *gerut* element is missing. Joseph is explicitly referred to as a slave, both by Potiphar's wife (Gen. 39:17) and by the chief cupbearer (41:12). And Joseph refers to his own experience in Egypt as *innuy* when naming his second child Ephraim (41:52). Yet although the Egyptians call Joseph "*ivri*" (a Hebrew), reflecting their own perception of his otherness (39:17, 41:12, 43:32), we never hear Joseph, or anyone else, referring to his experience in Egypt as *gerut*. The feeling of alienation that marks *gerut* is contingent on a sense of belonging in some other location, and it is not clear that Joseph ever fully perceived any place to be his own. More significantly, Joseph did not identify his experience as *gerut* because he never left Egypt and so never attained the psychological distance that would have allowed him to do so.

GERUT, AVDUT, INNUY: THE COVENANTAL FORMULA

But Jacob is different than Abraham, who did not necessarily understand the deeper significance of his experiences in Egypt until God made those terms explicit at *Berit bein ha-Betarim*. The Torah suggests that by the end of his life, Jacob does recognize his own experiences as covenantal. This can be demonstrated by contrasting Jacob's interaction with God upon his first departure from Canaan with his second departure from Canaan decades later. The two departures—first to Paddan-aram (Gen. 28:10–16), then to meet Joseph in Egypt (46:1–4)—are similar in many ways. In both instances, the point of exit is Beersheba; in both instances, God appears to Jacob in a nighttime vision assuring him that there is no need to fear (suggesting that on both occasions Jacob was fearful); and in both instances, God cautions Jacob that the journey is likely to be much longer than expected.[31] The language of God's second address echoes and amplifies the language of the first, perhaps to indicate to Jacob that he is going to Egypt to reexperience, this time with his family, the events he had lived through in the house of Laban. In Genesis 28, God invokes the emphatic word *anokhi*—I Myself—in promising to guard Jacob:

וְהִנֵּה אָנֹכִי עִמָּךְ וּשְׁמַרְתִּיךָ בְּכֹל אֲשֶׁר תֵּלֵךְ וַהֲשִׁבֹתִיךָ אֶל הָאֲדָמָה הַזֹּאת כִּי לֹא
אֶעֱזָבְךָ עַד אֲשֶׁר אִם עָשִׂיתִי אֵת אֲשֶׁר דִּבַּרְתִּי לָךְ:

And, look, I Myself am with you and I will guard you wherever you go, and I will bring you back to this land, for I will not leave you until I have done that which I have spoken to you. (Gen. 28:15)

And in Genesis 46, God repeats the word *anokhi* three times:

אָנֹכִי הָאֵל אֱלֹהֵי אָבִיךָ אַל תִּירָא מֵרְדָה מִצְרַיְמָה כִּי לְגוֹי גָּדוֹל אֲשִׂימְךָ שָׁם: אָנֹכִי
אֵרֵד עִמְּךָ מִצְרַיְמָה וְאָנֹכִי אַעַלְךָ גַם עָלֹה וְיוֹסֵף יָשִׁית יָדוֹ עַל עֵינֶיךָ:

I Myself am the god, God of your father. Fear not to go down to Egypt, for a great nation I will make you there. I Myself will go down with you to Egypt and I Myself will surely bring you back up as well, and Joseph shall lay his hand on your eyes. (Gen. 46:3–4)

---

[31] Additionally, both passages employ images of ascent and descent: in Gen. 28:12, the angels of God ascend and descend the ladder in Jacob's dream; and in Gen. 46:4, God promises to accompany Jacob down to Egypt and back up (presumably to Canaan).

A PASSOVER HAGGADAH: GO FORTH AND LEARN

Yet Jacob responds differently on the second occasion. Whereas on the way to Paddan-aram Jacob did not answer God directly (and upon awakening expressed his surprise at God's presence), on the way to Egypt, Jacob answers God's call with a particularly pregnant expression: *hineni*—"Here I am" (Gen. 46:2). *Hineni* is the language with which Abraham accepts God's command to sacrifice his son (22:1, 7),[32] with which Isaac, Esau, and Jacob grapple with the conferring of ancestral blessing (27:1, 18), and with which Joseph agrees to meet his brothers, who will sell him into slavery (37:13). With the word *hineni*, Jacob, like the others before him, finally embraces his role as bearer of God's covenant.[33]

Assuming that Jacob understands the significance of his descent to Egypt at this stage, why does he agree to the journey? Having already experienced *avdut, innuy,* and *gerut* in Laban's household, why is Jacob willing to reenact his own exile and impose those conditions on his descendants? The Haggadah itself seems to be grappling with this question when it asserts that Jacob and his family went down to Egypt, forced to do so by the word of God (*anus al pi ha-dibur*). But this is not a fanciful midrashic interpretation. In fact, a plain reading of the biblical text indicates that Jacob feels compelled by divine decree.[34] By uttering *hineni* in response to God's thrice-repeated *anokhi* (this is My will), Jacob acknowledges that he is going to Egypt not because Joseph or Pharaoh has asked him to do so, but because God has ordained it and he is accepting his covenantal destiny. The significance of Jacob's recognition of and acquiescence to the terms of God's covenant is underscored through comparison with another individual who rejects this fate, a point to which we will return.

---

[32] It is also the language with which Abraham later agrees to sacrifice the ram in place of his son (Gen. 22:11). In fact, God's opening call in 46:1—"Jacob! Jacob!"—evokes the angel's command to substitute the ram for Isaac: "Abraham! Abraham!" (22:11).

[33] Jacob did use the word *hineni* once previously, but in a seemingly incongruous fashion that highlights his lifelong struggle with acceptance of his own covenantal role. According to what Jacob told his wives on the eve of their departure from Paddan-aram, when acquisition of material wealth was foremost in his mind, *hineni* was the manner in which he responded to the messenger of God in a dream about Laban's flocks (Gen. 31:11). For further analysis of the term *hineni* in the Genesis narratives, see Steinmetz, *From Father to Son*, 50–60.

[34] Indeed, the obviousness of this reading may explain why the Haggadah does not bring a prooftext for its claim that Jacob and his family went to Egypt "forced to do so by the word [of God]," as it does for most of its other interpretations of the verses in Deut. 26.

GERUT, AVDUT, INNUY: THE COVENANTAL FORMULA

Exodus: God Remembers the Covenant

The Torah's parallel construction of the youthful Jacob's solo journey to the house of Laban and the elderly Jacob's descent to Egypt with his extended household has already set the stage for the ultimate realization of God's covenantal formula: the story of slavery and national redemption that forms the book of Exodus. To emphasize that the Exodus narrative is the direct continuation of Jacob's life story—indeed, the fulfillment of God's promise to him—the book of Exodus begins by recalling the 70 members of Jacob's family who arrived with him in Egypt, as listed in detail in Genesis 46. The Torah highlights the underlying connection between these two narratives in another manner as well: the first time God speaks in Exodus—indeed, the first time God addresses humankind following Jacob's departure from Canaan—is at the Burning Bush, where God calls and Moses responds in language that clearly echoes Genesis 46:

וַיִּקְרָא אֵלָיו אֱלֹהִים מִתּוֹךְ הַסְּנֶה וַיֹּאמֶר מֹשֶׁה מֹשֶׁה וַיֹּאמֶר הִנֵּנִי ...

...and God called to him from the midst of the bush and said, "Moses, Moses!" And he said, "Here I am." (Exod. 3:4)[35]

But the definitive evidence that the Exodus story is the realization of God's covenant is the appearance of the terms *gerut, avdut,* and *innuy* in the Torah's depiction of Egyptian oppression.

The enslavement of Jacob's descendants and their suffering at the hands of the Egyptians is explicitly described as both *innuy* and *avdut* in the opening chapter of Exodus. The term *innuy* appears twice:

---

[35] The literary links between Exod. 3 and Gen. 46 are even more extensive. For example, God's pledge to redeem the Israelites (Exod. 3:8) echoes the language of God's promise to accompany Jacob to Egypt and watch over him (Gen. 46:4), with both employing the verbs ר-ד (to go down) and ע-ל-ה (to bring up) to depict God's actions. The various connections between the two scenes highlight the revelatory nature of God's address to Jacob on the eve of his descent to Egypt. For further discussion of the Burning Bush and its significance as a moment of revelation, see essay 3.

A Passover Haggadah: Go Forth and Learn

וַיָּשִׂימוּ עָלָיו שָׂרֵי מִסִּים לְמַעַן עַנֹּתוֹ בְּסִבְלֹתָם וַיִּבֶן עָרֵי מִסְכְּנוֹת לְפַרְעֹה אֶת פִּתֹם
וְאֶת רַעַמְסֵס: וְכַאֲשֶׁר יְעַנּוּ אֹתוֹ כֵּן יִרְבֶּה וְכֵן יִפְרֹץ וַיָּקֻצוּ מִפְּנֵי בְּנֵי יִשְׂרָאֵל:

And they set over them forced-labor foremen so as to abuse them with their burdens, and they built store cities for Pharaoh: Pithom and Ramses. And as they abused them, so did they multiply and so did they spread, and they came to loathe the Israelites. (Exod. 1:11–12)

And in subsequent verses, the root ע-ב-ד appears five times:

וַיַּעֲבִדוּ מִצְרַיִם אֶת בְּנֵי יִשְׂרָאֵל בְּפָרֶךְ: וַיְמָרְרוּ אֶת חַיֵּיהֶם בַּעֲבֹדָה קָשָׁה בְּחֹמֶר
וּבִלְבֵנִים וּבְכָל עֲבֹדָה בַּשָּׂדֶה אֵת כָּל עֲבֹדָתָם אֲשֶׁר עָבְדוּ בָהֶם בְּפָרֶךְ:

And the Egyptians put the Israelites to work at crushing labor, and they made their lives bitter with hard work with mortar and bricks and every work in the field—all their crushing work that they performed. (Exod. 1:13–14)

But *gerut* is not mentioned in Exodus 1.

Gerut appears in chapter 2 following Moses' flight to Midian, his marriage to Jethro's daughter Zipporah, and the birth of their firstborn son, whom he names Gershom in a play on the Hebrew word for sojourning:

וַתֵּלֶד בֵּן וַיִּקְרָא אֶת שְׁמוֹ גֵּרְשֹׁם כִּי אָמַר גֵּר הָיִיתִי בְּאֶרֶץ נָכְרִיָּה:

And she bore a son, and he called his name Gershom, for he said, "A sojourner have I been in a foreign land." (Exod. 2:22)

Although Moses does not specify which land he is referring to as foreign, he seems to be alluding to Egypt (thanks to the new perspective he has acquired) and not Midian.[36] Like Jacob, who was able to recognize his own alienation only after he had left Laban's home, it is specifically in Midian that

---

[36] Later in the narrative, the meaning of Gershom's name is more ambiguous. In Exod. 18:3–4 the Torah reintroduces Moses' children as they arrive in the desert with Jethro. At that juncture, the Torah seems to be focused on Moses' dissociation from his father-in-law, and it therefore seems likely that the "foreign land" alluded to is Midian. For further discussion, see essay 3.

Moses is able to identify his own experience and the experience of his brethren as *gerut*. The enslaved Israelites are too enmeshed in suffering to comprehend their estrangement; but with physical and psychological distance from the conditions of slavery, Moses is able to acknowledge this element of the Egypt experience as well.[37] And although only Moses is able to articulate the experience of *gerut*, he does so on behalf of the people, who suffer *innuy* and *avdut*.[38]

To demonstrate that in naming his child, Moses has satisfied the terms of the covenantal formula, the ensuing verses invoke the divine covenant explicitly:

וַיְהִי בַיָּמִים הָרַבִּים הָהֵם וַיָּמָת מֶלֶךְ מִצְרַיִם וַיֵּאָנְחוּ בְנֵי יִשְׂרָאֵל מִן הָעֲבֹדָה וַיִּזְעָקוּ
וַתַּעַל שַׁוְעָתָם אֶל הָאֱלֹהִים מִן הָעֲבֹדָה: וַיִּשְׁמַע אֱלֹהִים אֶת נַאֲקָתָם וַיִּזְכֹּר אֱלֹהִים
אֶת בְּרִיתוֹ אֶת אַבְרָהָם אֶת יִצְחָק וְאֶת יַעֲקֹב: וַיַּרְא אֱלֹהִים אֶת בְּנֵי יִשְׂרָאֵל וַיֵּדַע
אֱלֹהִים:

And it happened when a long time had passed that the king of Egypt died, and the Israelites groaned from the bondage and cried out, and their plea from the bondage went up to God. And God heard their moaning, and God remembered His covenant with Abraham, with Isaac, and with Jacob. And God saw the Israelites, and God knew. (Exod. 2:23–25)

The final words of chapter 2—"and God knew"—reinforce the association with *Berit bein ha-Betarim* by echoing the opening line of God's original promise to Abraham (Gen. 15:13).[39]

---

[37] In addition to his sojourn in Midian, Moses' sheltered upbringing in Pharaoh's palace positioned him uniquely for this mission; for further discussion of Moses' role as leader and national symbol, see essay 3.

[38] As noted, in the covenant with Abraham at *Berit bein ha-Betarim*, *gerut* is mentioned first, then *avdut*, and finally *innuy*; being a stranger is what allows all the other terrible things to happen. The order is the same in the story of Abraham and Sarah in Egypt as well as in the story of Hagar (where *innuy* is the heart of the story). Nonetheless, in both the Jacob and the Exodus narratives, *avdut* and *innuy* precede *gerut*, a self-awareness that is attained only after having achieved distance from the situation. The difference between these two narratives is that in the Jacob story, *avdut* precedes *innuy*, whereas in the Exodus story, the opposite is true. Deut. 26 echoes the Egypt model, citing *innuy* before *avdut*.

[39] The word *avodah* also appears twice in this description of Egyptian slavery, reminding the reader of God's original promise to Abraham at *Berit bein ha-Betarim*: "But upon the nation for whom they slave [*ya'avodu*] I will bring judgment..." (Gen. 15:14).

But the reader knows what Moses does not. Although the process of redemption has been set into motion, Moses himself will not live to experience its fulfillment. The Torah emphasizes that slavery began only after Joseph and the members of his generation died (Exod. 1:6,8), indicating that Moses son of Amram son of Kehat, himself the son of Joseph's brother Levi, was born into the third generation of bondage. Yet at *Berit bein ha-Betarim* God predicted that "in the fourth generation they shall return here" (Gen. 15:16), meaning that by the terms of the covenant, Moses and the generation that left Egypt would not make it to the Promised Land.[40]

Hagar: Rejection of the Covenant

As noted earlier, the significance of Abraham and Jacob's acceptance of God's covenant—which was subsequently accepted by the People of Israel as well—can be demonstrated by briefly considering another Genesis narrative that pivots on the *gerut, avdut, innuy* theme: the story of Sarah and Hagar. At the beginning of Genesis 16, we are told that Sarah owns an Egyptian slave woman whose name is Hagar (הגר), a homonym to the Hebrew term for "stranger." When Sarah fails to conceive, she convinces Abraham to mate with her slave woman, in the hope that she might build a family through her. Hagar becomes pregnant and consequently scorns her mistress, and Sarah receives permission from Abraham to treat the slave woman as she sees fit. The Torah describes Sarah's discipline as a form of *innuy*:

וַתְּעַנֶּהָ שָׂרַי וַתִּבְרַח מִפָּנֶיהָ:

And Sarai harassed her and she fled from her. (Gen. 16:6)

The fact that Sarah, who herself had endured affliction during her sojourn in Egypt, subsequently inflicted *innuy* upon someone else suggests that she

---

[40]Later on, the Torah goes out of its way to demonstrate that the final terms of God's covenant have been fulfilled. In Num. 21:21–35, after the deaths of Moses' siblings, Aaron and Miriam, the Torah reports that the (fourth-generation) Israelites' first successful conquest of land was from Sihon, king of the Amorites.

GERUT, AVDUT, INNUY: THE COVENANTAL FORMULA

had not internalized the meaning of her experience.[41] Sarah's actions made room for Hagar to assume the role of Abraham's covenantal as well as sexual partner.

Hagar, however, does not accept the covenantal role. The angel of God who appears to Hagar in the desert instructs her to return to Sarah and to her afflictions:

וַיֹּאמֶר לָהּ מַלְאַךְ יהוה שׁוּבִי אֶל גְּבִרְתֵּךְ וְהִתְעַנִּי תַּחַת יָדֶיהָ:

And the LORD's messenger said to her, "Return to your mistress and suffer abuse at her hand." (Gen. 16:9)

But Hagar does not respond. The biblical text emphasizes her silence by prefacing the angel's next words with an additional *va-yomer* (and he said), as though the angel has stopped to wait for her response and begins to speak again only after realizing that she will not offer one.[42] This time God's messenger attempts to entice her with the promise of many descendants, another component of the covenantal promise (Gen. 16:10).

When Hagar still does not respond, the angel finally seems to acknowledge her rejection of the covenantal role, and only afterward does Hagar speak:

וַיֹּאמֶר לָהּ מַלְאַךְ יהוה הִנָּךְ הָרָה וְיֹלַדְתְּ בֵּן וְקָרָאת שְׁמוֹ יִשְׁמָעֵאל כִּי שָׁמַע יהוה אֶל עָנְיֵךְ: וְהוּא יִהְיֶה פֶּרֶא אָדָם יָדוֹ בַכֹּל וְיַד כֹּל בּוֹ וְעַל פְּנֵי כָל אֶחָיו יִשְׁכֹּן: וַתִּקְרָא שֵׁם יהוה הַדֹּבֵר אֵלֶיהָ אַתָּה אֵל רֳאִי כִּי אָמְרָה הֲגַם הֲלֹם רָאִיתִי אַחֲרֵי רֹאִי:

And the LORD's messenger said to her, "Look, you have conceived and will bear a son and you will call his name Ishmael, for the LORD has heeded your suffering. And he will be a wild ass of a man—his

---

[41] Although many of the classical commentators attempted to whitewash, or at least rationalize, Sarah's behavior, both Ramban and R. David Kimhi (Radak) contended that Sarah's treatment of Hagar was sinful; see their commentaries on Gen. 16:6.

[42] The Midrash proposes that the triple repetition of *va-yomer* (Gen. 16:9,10,11) indicates that a different angel delivered each statement; see Gen. Rabbah 45:7, also cited in Rashi's commentary on 16:9, *Va-yomer lah malakh*.

A Passover Haggadah: Go Forth and Learn

*hand against all, the hand of all against him, he will encamp in despite
of all his kin." And she called the name of the L*ORD *who had addressed
her, "El-Roi," for she said, "Did not I go on seeing here after He saw
me?"* (Gen. 16:11–13)

By designating Hagar as the one who will name the child, the angel signaled
to Hagar that the child would be hers entirely and not part of Abraham's
family. Furthermore, by assuring her that God had heard her suffering—in the
past tense—the angel indicated that the affliction would cease, and that she
would no longer be subject to *innuy*.

But Hagar's rejection of the covenantal terms is more than a refusal to subject
herself to further affliction. Hagar is not willing or able to see beyond the
present; she is not prepared to sacrifice for the sake of the future. Jacob, in
contrast, understands the difficult terms of God's covenant—indeed he himself has already endured them—but nonetheless he embraces his destiny, thus
bequeathing the covenantal promise to his descendants.

Parashat Mishpatim: The Covenant in Legal Form

The *gerut, avdut, innuy* formula makes another striking appearance in the
legal portion of Exodus (chapters 21–23), which the Torah itself calls
Sefer ha-Berit (The Book of the Covenant) (Exod. 24:7). This section begins
with the laws of Hebrew servitude: a male serves for six years and is released in
the seventh (21:2–6), while a female is either wedded to her master with all
the rights of a free woman or discharged (21:7–11). Fundamentally, the
Torah seems to be engaged in a process of redefining slavery. In subsequent
verses and chapters, the Torah presents a wide range of statutes, the majority
of which pertain to the establishment and implementation of a fair and just
social order. In this context, the prohibition to oppress the stranger features
twice, showcasing the concepts of both *gerut* and *innuy*.

In Exodus 22, the Torah attributes this directive to the Israelites' own historical experience, citing Egypt as a lesson by way of contrast:

וְגֵר לֹא תוֹנֶה וְלֹא תִלְחָצֶנּוּ כִּי גֵרִים הֱיִיתֶם בְּאֶרֶץ מִצְרָיִם: כָּל אַלְמָנָה וְיָתוֹם לֹא תְעַנּוּן: אִם עַנֵּה תְעַנֶּה אֹתוֹ כִּי אִם צָעֹק יִצְעַק אֵלַי שָׁמֹעַ אֶשְׁמַע צַעֲקָתוֹ: וְחָרָה אַפִּי וְהָרַגְתִּי אֶתְכֶם בֶּחָרֶב וְהָיוּ נְשֵׁיכֶם אַלְמָנוֹת וּבְנֵיכֶם יְתֹמִים:

You shall not cheat a sojourner and you shall not oppress him, for you were sojourners in the land of Egypt. No widow nor orphan shall you abuse. If you indeed abuse them, when they cry out to Me, I will surely hear their outcry. And My wrath shall flare up and I will kill you by the sword, and your wives shall be widows and your children orphans. (Exod. 22:20–23)

The allusion to God's anger in the final verse of this passage is arresting, and its distinctiveness is magnified by the emphatic forms of the verbs in the previous verse: עַנֵּה תְעַנֶּה (to abuse), צָעֹק יִצְעַק (to cry out), שָׁמֹעַ אֶשְׁמַע (to hear). This language and imagery constitute a break from the standard tone of the legal sections of the Torah, which are typically straightforward and dispassionate. It seems clear that the Torah wants to mark these directives as uniquely significant.

In chapter 23, just before the end of the civil laws of *Sefer ha-Berit*, the Torah again instructs:

וְגֵר לֹא תִלְחָץ וְאַתֶּם יְדַעְתֶּם אֶת נֶפֶשׁ הַגֵּר כִּי גֵרִים הֱיִיתֶם בְּאֶרֶץ מִצְרָיִם:

No sojourner shall you oppress, for you know the sojourner's heart, since you were sojourners in the land of Egypt. (Exod. 23:9)

This formulation of the prohibition to oppress the stranger is even more personal than the previous one. It suggests that one purpose of the Egypt experience was to sensitize the People of Israel to the suffering of others, to teach them what it means to be alienated and oppressed, so that when they set up their own society, they will be sure not to impose such suffering on others. The presentation of these laws draws upon a distinct historical and psychological experience, suggesting that if the lessons of that experience were not internalized, it would all be for naught.

Conclusion

In alluding to the terms of God's covenant with Abraham and his descendants, Deuteronomy speaks first of *gerut*, then of *innuy*, and finally of *avdut*. As in the other passages we have examined, the ordering of these terms is significant. By opening with *gerut*, Deuteronomy 26 echoes the formulation of *Berit bein ha-Betarim* in which exile is presented as the basis for subsequent enslavement and affliction. In Deuteronomy, *gerut* comes first because in contrast to both Jacob and the People of Israel, who were not capable of identifying their own alienation while enmeshed in the experience, the pilgrim who recites these verses when bringing first-fruits to the Temple many years after the events described, has attained the necessary distance and perspective to recognize this condition. The allusion to *innuy* before *avdut* follows the order of the Exodus narrative, intimating that this national experience (rather than Abraham's and Jacob's individual stories) was the ultimate instantiation of God's covenant with Israel. Thus it is no surprise that the Egyptian enslavement and the Exodus are evoked with such frequency as the inspiration for codes of social engagement, ritual practice, and religious faith.

The Haggadah itself posits that history is cyclical. Every generation faces an oppressor, and every generation is dependent on God's salvation. The reiteration of God's covenant with Abraham and his descendants throughout the books of Genesis and Exodus speaks not only to the eternal nature of the relationship between human and divine, but also to its conditionality. Those who accept their destiny, along with the suffering entailed, will merit redemption, perhaps because they will have learned the principles for building an ideal society. Those who reject God's terms will not.

3

Exodus:
An Individual and Collective Coming of Age

The Hebrew title for the book of Exodus is *Shemot*—"Names"—and the creation and realization of identity is indeed a theme central to this biblical text. Yet the opening chapters of the book are populated by nameless individuals, and even Moses—arguably the main character of the Exodus story—is born anonymously. Moses' education and development of self ultimately allow him to assist the People of Israel in recovering their own selves; moreover, the Torah presents Moses' experience as emblematic of the Israelite experience, and his coming of age denotes the nation's coming of age. Thus, although Moses is not mentioned in the Haggadah, it is meaningful to consider early events in his life and his first encounters with God as a lens through which to view the creation of Israel's national identity.[43]

Early Influences

God's first revelation to Moses follows an extended narrative about Moses' early life that comprises most of Exodus 2 and takes the reader from Moses' birth to his arrival and integration in Midian. It is striking that none of the characters in the first half of the chapter have personal names: we hear only of "a man from the house of Levi," "the daughter of Levi," "the child," "the mother of the child," "the child's sister," and "the daughter of Pharaoh." Moses is the first one in the story to be named; but although his name refers to an early moment in the narrative—"for from the water I drew him out" (*ki min ha-mayim meshitihu*)—it is not bestowed until the end of the vignette. This is significant because it highlights the process whereby Moses' identity is formed.

---

[43] For a discussion that focuses on the psychological effects of Moses' "adoption" on his identity formation, see Caroline Peyser, "The Book of Exodus: A Search for Identity," in *Torah of the Mothers*, ed. Ora Wiskind Elper and Susan Handelman (Jerusalem: Urim, 2000), 379–97.

A Passover Haggadah: Go Forth and Learn

From infancy, Moses is a child with two mothers: the daughter of Levi, his biological mother, and the daughter of Pharaoh, his adoptive mother. According to the narrative, each woman plays a critical parental role: Moses' biological mother nurses him, while his adoptive mother names him.[44] Nursing is the most primal act of motherhood, but the creation of identity inherent in naming a child is also a defining act of parenting. Moses' name, a variation on the Hebrew root מ-ש-ה (to extract), not only tells of his past but also reflects the person he will become: his major role in life will be to draw the People of Israel out of bondage and exile. Yet the tale is orchestrated so that the act of nursing, which in addition to providing physical sustenance represents nurturing and the inculcation of values, precedes the act of naming.[45] The Torah seems to be emphasizing that although Moses spent most of his childhood with Egyptian royalty, *Bat Levi* and not *Bat Par'oh* was his primary mother.

Moses' early identity is a function of his two mothers, but it is also the product of another influence. Following the story of Moses' birth and adoption, the Torah records a classic coming-of-age episode:

וַיְהִי בַּיָּמִים הָהֵם וַיִּגְדַּל מֹשֶׁה וַיֵּצֵא אֶל אֶחָיו וַיַּרְא בְּסִבְלֹתָם וַיַּרְא אִישׁ מִצְרִי מַכֶּה אִישׁ עִבְרִי מֵאֶחָיו: וַיִּפֶן כֹּה וָכֹה וַיַּרְא כִּי אֵין אִישׁ וַיַּךְ אֶת הַמִּצְרִי וַיִּטְמְנֵהוּ בַּחוֹל:

And it happened at that time that Moses grew and went out to his brothers and saw their burdens. And he saw an Egyptian man striking a Hebrew man of his brothers. And he turned this way and that and saw that there was no man about, and he struck down the Egyptian and buried him in the sand. (Exod. 2:11–12)

---

[44] According to one of the opinions cited by the medieval commentator Hizkuni on Exod. 2:10, Pharaoh's daughter did not actually call the child Moses, a Hebrew name; the verse merely reflects her approval of the name given to him by Jochebed, his biological mother. However, this claim does not accord with a simple reading of the verse, or with various midrashim that consider the Torah's use of Moses' "Egyptian" name to be a reward to Pharaoh's daughter for saving and raising him; see Exod. Rabbah 1:31.

[45] Similarly, Hannah, whose quest for a child is based upon the Moses narrative, nurses her son before she gives him to the priest Eli, who is to become his substitute parent (1 Sam. 1:20–28).

The word that stands out in this passage is *ehav* (his brothers). Moses has chosen to side with "his brothers," the Hebrews that is, with those who suffer rather than with those who impose suffering. One might argue that this choice was a free choice, a balanced decision: Moses had two mothers, was equally connected to both sides of the struggle, and consciously chose to affiliate with the afflicted. This may, in fact, be the image of Moses that the Torah wants us to educe from the narrative. But the reiteration of the word *ehav* suggests that there was another influence behind the scene. In addition to his two mothers, there was a third character who exerted control over Moses' early life: his sister. The text implies that Moses' concern for and identification with "his brothers" is, in large part, a function of the concern that had been bestowed upon him by his sister, who watched over and took care of him from afar.[46] As in Genesis, at the beginning of Exodus the sibling relationship is pivotal.

Yet the figure who is conspicuously absent from Moses' life until this point is a father. His biological father is anonymous, and seemingly inconsequential. No adoptive father is mentioned; and although Moses is drawn to Reu'el/Jethro upon his arrival in Midian, this character becomes a sort of substitute father but never a real one. In summary, Moses' early life has been characterized simultaneously by an overabundance of parental figures and by the lack of a clear influence. Thus, when God approaches Moses for the first time at the Burning Bush, Moses is as yet a man in search of identity.

A Nameless, Indistinct Nation

Moses' protracted process of self-definition reflects the general state of anonymity and incoherence that the Torah ascribes to the nation's period of slavery in Egypt. Although the book of Exodus begins with a detailed listing of the individuals who arrived in Egypt along with Jacob

---

[46]The image of Moses' sister watching the crying child from afar elicits another biblical scene: Hagar watching Ishmael crying from a distance, "for she thought, 'Let me not see when the child dies'" (Gen. 21:16). There are numerous parallels between these stories; above all, the comparison serves to highlight the contrast between Hagar's abandonment of her child and the sister's ongoing involvement with her brother.

A Passover Haggadah: Go Forth and Learn

(Exod. 1:1–5), immediately thereafter the text notes that Jacob's children themselves had died, signaling a significant change in circumstances—namely, unchecked population growth (Exod. 1:6–7). The subsequent verses introduce Pharaoh and his enslavement plan and, as noted, the remainder of chapter 1 and the majority of chapter 2 are populated by anonymous characters, suggesting that disproportionate growth and the ensuing persecution were responsible for a pointed loss of the identities with which Jacob and his family had arrived in Egypt.[47]

The Torah indicates that a third factor, assimilation, was also responsible for the fledgling nation's lack of distinctiveness. The taking on of Egyptian identity is best demonstrated in the context of Moses' attempt to prevent a violent *ish Ivri* (Hebrew man) from injuring a fellow slave with whom he is scuffling. The episode follows immediately on the heels of Moses' killing of an Egyptian who had struck an Israelite slave. It is obvious that in juxtaposing the two scenes, the Torah—and indeed Moses himself—intends to equate the behavior of the Hebrew man with that of the Egyptian oppressor, suggesting that the slave's identification with his master is stronger than his identification with his fellow Israelites. The words used by the *ish Ivri* to dismiss Moses are even more telling:

וַיֹּאמֶר מִי שָׂמְךָ לְאִישׁ שַׂר וְשֹׁפֵט עָלֵינוּ הַלְהָרְגֵנִי אַתָּה אֹמֵר כַּאֲשֶׁר הָרַגְתָּ אֶת הַמִּצְרִי...

And he said, "Who set you as a man prince and judge over us? Is it to kill me that you mean as you killed the Egyptian?" . . . (Exod. 2:14)

These words echo the accusation leveled at Lot by the people of Sodom when he did not agree to hand over his guests as ordered:

...וַיֹּאמְרוּ הָאֶחָד בָּא לָגוּר וַיִּשְׁפֹּט שָׁפוֹט עַתָּה נָרַע לְךָ מֵהֶם...

. . . and they said, "This person came as a sojourner, and he sets himself up to judge! Now we'll do more harm to you than to them . . ." (Gen. 19:9)

---

[47] The two midwives, Shiphrah and Puah, who are pointedly named in the text (Exod. 1:15), are the exception that proves the rule: they represent women's unique role in the Exodus story, which hinges on their ability to maintain identity in spite of the circumstances.

By placing the words of the Sodomites—words that express a complete rejection of law and justice—in the mouth of the *ish Ivri*, the Torah signifies that the People of Israel had assumed the values and the persona of their adversaries. They had actually become their own enemies.[48]

The Herculean task facing Moses—who, like Lot, was branded an outsider—was to guide these people on their journey to regain a distinct identity. Growing up in Pharaoh's palace, removed from the debilitating effects of slavery, presumably gave Moses an advantage; but before he could assume his mission, he needed to appreciate and understand the significance of his own roots. Empathizing with his subjugated brethren was a first declaration of identity; running to Midian and naming his eldest son Gershom in recognition of the foreignness (*gerut*) of his life in Egypt was a second.[49] But it is his first encounter with God that compels Moses to confront the still-missing pieces of his own heritage.

The Burning Bush: God Chooses Moses

At the end of Exodus 2, the Torah interrupts the narrative of Moses' life to provide an update on the fate of the nation in Egypt:

וַיְהִי בַיָּמִים הָרַבִּים הָהֵם וַיָּמָת מֶלֶךְ מִצְרַיִם וַיֵּאָנְחוּ בְנֵי יִשְׂרָאֵל מִן הָעֲבֹדָה וַיִּזְעָקוּ
וַתַּעַל שַׁוְעָתָם אֶל הָאֱלֹהִים מִן הָעֲבֹדָה: וַיִּשְׁמַע אֱלֹהִים אֶת נַאֲקָתָם וַיִּזְכֹּר אֱלֹהִים
אֶת בְּרִיתוֹ אֶת אַבְרָהָם אֶת יִצְחָק וְאֶת יַעֲקֹב: וַיַּרְא אֱלֹהִים אֶת בְּנֵי יִשְׂרָאֵל וַיֵּדַע
אֱלֹהִים:

And it happened when a long time had passed that the king of Egypt died, and the Israelites groaned from the bondage and cried out, and their plea from the bondage went up to God. And God heard their

---

[48] For a more extensive discussion of this point, see essay 6.

[49] See Exod. 2:22. Although Moses does not specify which land he is referring to as foreign, I would argue that at this point he is referencing Egypt (thanks to the new perspective he has acquired) and not Midian. For a more expansive treatment of this point, see essay 2.

moaning, and God remembered His covenant with Abraham, with Isaac, and with Jacob. And God saw the Israelites, and God knew. (Exod. 2:23–25)[50]

The placement of this passage in the middle of the Moses narrative suggests that immediately upon determining that the time for salvation is at hand, God searches for an individual who is capable of carrying out the promise. Moses' ability to identify his own alienation and to articulate that experience in the naming of his child sets him apart from the rest of the Israelites and deems him worthy of serving as their representative.

Moses' encounter at the Burning Bush is not only the first time that God speaks to him; it is also the first time that God speaks at all in the book of Exodus. Indeed, it is the first time that God has spoken since Israel went into exile. God's voice has been entirely absent from the biblical narrative from the moment of Jacob's departure from the land of Canaan in Genesis 46.[51] But although God has been silent, God has not disappeared. The small, flaming bush that draws Moses to the mountain of God—the same spot where God will eventually descend in fire and smoke to give the Torah to Israel[52]—represents God's muted but never fully extinguished presence.

In the opening lines of chapter 3, Moses, shepherding his father-in-law's flocks in the wilderness, approaches the mountain Horeb, where he sees a flaming bush that is not consumed. Intrigued, Moses approaches the *sneh* (bush); God calls to him from the blaze and, in classic fashion, Moses responds, "*hineni*" ("I am present"). With this utterance, which connects him to Abraham and to Jacob, the previous bearers of the covenant, Moses

---

[50] Four verbs are used to describe God's response to Israel's suffering: *va-yishma* (and God heard); *va-yizkor* (and God remembered); *va-yar* (and God saw); and *va-yeda* (and God knew). Each of the four verbs that depict God's reaction to the intensified enslavement is followed in the text by God's name, as if to underscore that God alone was hearing, seeing, remembering, and knowing. In the words of the Haggadah, this was the moment at which God calculated the fulfillment of the promise he had made at *Berit bein ha-Betarim* (*hishev et ha-ketz*): once Abraham's descendants fulfilled their part of the covenant that had been established, God was bound to fulfill God's part.

[51] For further discussion, see essay 2.

[52] According to the Midrash, this mountain was later called Sinai because of God's revelation to Moses from within the *sneh*; see *Pirkei de-Rabbi Eliezer*, chap. 41.

EXODUS: AN INDIVIDUAL AND COLLECTIVE COMING OF AGE

implicitly agrees to do God's bidding.[53] Although the next chapter and a half of the biblical text record extended negotiations as to the terms of the mission, with the *hineni* declaration Moses has fundamentally accepted the calling. Moses is then told not to draw too close and to remove his shoes, for the land upon which he is standing is sacred ground.

Before conveying the content of God's message to Moses, God invokes the previous bearers of the covenant:

וַיֹּאמֶר אָנֹכִי אֱלֹהֵי אָבִיךָ אֱלֹהֵי אַבְרָהָם אֱלֹהֵי יִצְחָק וֵאלֹהֵי יַעֲקֹב וַיַּסְתֵּר מֹשֶׁה פָּנָיו
כִּי יָרֵא מֵהַבִּיט אֶל הָאֱלֹהִים:

And He said, "I am the God of your father, the God of Abraham, the God of Isaac, and the God of Jacob." And Moses hid his face, for he was afraid to look upon God. (Exod. 3:6)

God identifies neither as the God of Moses' biological father nor of Reu'el, the priest of Midian, his father-in-law, but as the God of his covenantal fathers, Abraham, Isaac, and Jacob. Given what we know about Moses' background, it seems clear that in referencing the forefathers, God is not only designating Moses as the savior of Israel but also providing Moses with the missing pieces of his own identity. God's opening statement to Moses—"I am the God of your father"—addresses not only who God is, but also who Moses is. God says to Moses, in effect, you have a father: you are the child of Abraham, Isaac, and Jacob.

At the same time, Moses is made to understand that, like his ancestors, he too has been singled out for communication with God. Revelation was the defining property of the forefathers. What distinguished Abraham, Isaac, and Jacob from their wives as well as from later biblical characters such as Joseph and Judah was that God spoke to them, and they to God. To underscore Moses' association with his forefathers, the Torah presents God's message to him in words that evoke God's communication with Jacob on his

---

[53] Both Abraham and Jacob respond with *hineni* at critical moments in their respective relationships with God; for extended discussion of the covenantal significance of this response, see essay 2.

A PASSOVER HAGGADAH: GO FORTH AND LEARN

way down to Egypt. God appeared to Jacob in a nighttime vision in Beer-sheba, saying:

וַיֹּאמֶר יַעֲקֹב יַעֲקֹב וַיֹּאמֶר הִנֵּנִי: וַיֹּאמֶר אָנֹכִי הָאֵל אֱלֹהֵי אָבִיךָ אַל תִּירָא מֵרְדָה מִצְרַיְמָה כִּי לְגוֹי גָּדוֹל אֲשִׂימְךָ שָׁם: אָנֹכִי אֵרֵד עִמְּךָ מִצְרַיְמָה וְאָנֹכִי אַעַלְךָ גַם עָלֹה וְיוֹסֵף יָשִׁית יָדוֹ עַל עֵינֶיךָ:

. . . "Jacob, Jacob," and he said, "Here I am." And He said, "I am the god, God of your father. Fear not to go down to Egypt, for a great nation I will make you there. I Myself will go down with you to Egypt and I Myself will surely bring you back up as well, and Joseph shall lay his hand on your eyes." (Gen. 46:2–4)

The repeated calling of Jacob's name, the allusion to the "God of your father," the use of the emphatic *anokhi* (I Myself), and the imagery of going down and bringing up all have parallels in God's words to Moses at the Burning Bush:

וַיֹּאמֶר מֹשֶׁה מֹשֶׁה וַיֹּאמֶר הִנֵּנִי . . . וַיֹּאמֶר אָנֹכִי אֱלֹהֵי אָבִיךָ אֱלֹהֵי אַבְרָהָם אֱלֹהֵי יִצְחָק וֵאלֹהֵי יַעֲקֹב וַיַּסְתֵּר מֹשֶׁה פָּנָיו כִּי יָרֵא מֵהַבִּיט אֶל הָאֱלֹהִים . . . וָאֵרֵד לְהַצִּילוֹ מִיַּד מִצְרַיִם וּלְהַעֲלֹתוֹ מִן הָאָרֶץ הַהִוא אֶל אֶרֶץ טוֹבָה וּרְחָבָה אֶל אֶרֶץ זָבַת חָלָב וּדְבָשׁ . . .

. . . "Moses, Moses," and he said, "Here I am." . . . And He said, "I am the God of your father, the God of Abraham, the God of Isaac, and the God of Jacob." And Moses hid his face, for he was afraid to look upon God. ". . . And I have come down to rescue it from the hand of Egypt and to bring it up from that land to a goodly and spacious land, to a land flowing with milk and honey . . ." (Exod. 3:4–8)[54]

By framing Moses' initiation in this manner, the Torah emphasizes that before Moses can assume a leadership role that entails reconnecting the nation to its heritage and destiny, his own identity must crystallize.

---

[54] For further discussion of this connection, see essay 2.

Moses Leaves Midian to Reunite with His Brothers

The depth of Moses' growing identification with his own people is reflected in the weakening of his relationship with his father-in-law. Moses' departure from Midian to reconnect with his "brothers" in Egypt following the revelation at the Burning Bush prefigures his dismissal of Jethro later in the narrative, also out of a sense of obligation to his people.[55]

Moses' connection to Jethro was forged at their first meeting, after Moses has run away from Egypt and Reu'el/Jethro invites him into his home in Midian. The hospitality that Jethro extends is represented in the biblical text by his offer of bread (Exod. 2:20). The significance of eating bread together is emphasized again when Jethro comes to meet Moses in the desert, several chapters later, after the Exodus. He offers a sacrifice, and Aaron and the elders join him in eating bread "before God" (18:12). The eating together symbolizes the extent to which Moses and Jethro were in complete consonance with one another in terms of belief system and ethical outlook.[56] They were beloved to one another because they shared an affinity for the weak and the oppressed.

Nonetheless, Moses does not tell Jethro the truth about why he must leave Midian and return to Egypt. What he tells him is only that he is going to visit his kin:

---

[55] Following the Exodus, Jethro comes to the desert to reconnect with Moses, his daughter Zipporah, and their children. The reunion is a meaningful one, but ultimately Moses sends his father-in-law away. From the beginning, the Torah intimates that this will be the outcome. For one thing, the Torah refers to Moses' father-in-law in this instance as *Yitro* (Jethro), a name that comes from the root י-ת-ר (extraneous). Second, the text here names both of Moses' sons, providing explanations that highlight Moses' deep affiliation with his Israelite identity (Exod. 18:3–4). In this context, as opposed to chap. 2, the "foreign land" that inspired Gershom's name could be understood equally as Egypt or Midian, emphasizing Moses' lack of connection with the homeland of Jethro; and the "God of my fathers" who inspired Eliezer's name distances Moses from his father-in-law even further.

[56] This point is made in reverse in the Joseph narratives: the few barriers that Joseph was not able to cross in his quest to become an Egyptian were marked with bread. At the beginning of Joseph's career, Potiphar granted him unlimited access to everything in his household, except for his bread, which functioned as a symbolic boundary (Gen. 39:6). Later, even after Joseph had become the second-ranking official in the land, the Egyptians refused to eat bread with his family, and apparently even with Joseph himself (Gen. 43:32). The Egyptians' exclusion of Joseph, who controlled all the bread in the country, from breaking bread with them is a powerful statement about Joseph's ultimate inability to be truly Egyptian. (See Ibn Ezra's commentary on Gen. 39:6.)

וַיֵּלֶךְ מֹשֶׁה וַיָּשׇׁב אֶל יֶתֶר חֹתְנוֹ וַיֹּאמֶר לוֹ אֵלְכָה נָּא וְאָשׁוּבָה אֶל אַחַי אֲשֶׁר בְּמִצְרַיִם
וְאֶרְאֶה הַעוֹדָם חַיִּים וַיֹּאמֶר יִתְרוֹ לְמֹשֶׁה לֵךְ לְשָׁלוֹם:

*And Moses went and returned to Jether his father-in-law, and he said
to him, "Let me go, pray, and return to my brothers who are in Egypt
that I may see whether they still live." (Exod. 4:18)*

Yet with these words, Moses intimates the truth: that he must give up his
relationship with his confidant and kindred spirit in order to reconnect with
his brothers, who in fact reject him and do not accept him as a brother at all.
The words that Moses employs to explain his departure recall Joseph's words
to his own brothers— "הֲשָׁלוֹם אֲבִיכֶם הַזָּקֵן אֲשֶׁר אֲמַרְתֶּם הַעוֹדֶנּוּ חָי" / "Is all well
with your aged father of whom you spoke? Is he still alive?" (Gen. 43:27).
The allusion suggests that Moses, like Joseph, was entangled in a complicated
family dynamic. Moses' choice to return to Egypt in spite of the personal price
he must pay underscores the strength of his identification with and commitment to his people.

The Covenant Is Revealed to Moses

In God's address to Moses at the Burning Bush, the Torah employs three
primary verbs to explain why God has chosen this moment for revelation:
seeing, hearing, and knowing:

וַיֹּאמֶר יהוה רָאֹה רָאִיתִי אֶת עֳנִי עַמִּי אֲשֶׁר בְּמִצְרַיִם וְאֶת צַעֲקָתָם שָׁמַעְתִּי מִפְּנֵי
נֹגְשָׂיו כִּי יָדַעְתִּי אֶת מַכְאֹבָיו...

*And the LORD said, "I indeed have seen the abuse of My people that is
in Egypt, and its outcry because of its taskmasters. I have heard, for
I know its pain . . ." (Exod. 3:7)*

Not coincidentally, these are the same words that were used to describe God's
reaction to the people's suffering at the end of chapter 2. But in contrast to
chapter 2, the verb "to remember" is noticeably absent. Although God's
address at the Burning Bush begins by invoking the forefathers, there is no
mention of the covenant with Abraham, Isaac, and Jacob that God has presumably remembered.

EXODUS: AN INDIVIDUAL AND COLLECTIVE COMING OF AGE

In fact, God does not mention the covenant to Moses directly until after he has gone back to Egypt, confronted Pharaoh, and experienced rejection. Only in chapter 6, after Moses returns to God, complaining that his mission has failed, does God explain the role of the *berit* in the redemption plan:

וַיְדַבֵּר אֱלֹהִים אֶל מֹשֶׁה וַיֹּאמֶר אֵלָיו אֲנִי יהוה: וָאֵרָא אֶל אַבְרָהָם אֶל יִצְחָק וְאֶל
יַעֲקֹב בְּאֵל שַׁדָּי וּשְׁמִי יהוה לֹא נוֹדַעְתִּי לָהֶם: וְגַם הֲקִמֹתִי אֶת בְּרִיתִי אִתָּם לָתֵת
לָהֶם אֶת אֶרֶץ כְּנָעַן אֵת אֶרֶץ מְגֻרֵיהֶם אֲשֶׁר גָּרוּ בָהּ:

And God spoke to Moses and said to him, "I am the LORD. And I appeared to Abraham, to Isaac, and to Jacob as El Shaddai, but in My name the LORD I was not known to them. And I also established My covenant with them to give them the land of Canaan, the land of their sojournings in which they sojourned. (Exod. 6:2–4)

At the Burning Bush, Moses was not ready to hear about the covenant. But in chapter 6, after Moses has experienced failure, God is able to deliver the other part of the message: the Exodus Moses has been sent to facilitate is part of a covenantal promise.

At the Burning Bush, God invoked the forefathers primarily to indicate to Moses that he was experiencing a moment of revelation. In chapter 6, when Moses turns to God in despair, God invokes Abraham, Isaac, and Jacob in a different manner, as if to say: now you can appreciate what it means to be the inheritor of these men, who were the beneficiaries of a divine promise but did not personally experience redemption. They were never privileged to see the fulfillment of the covenant they had entered. At this moment of failure, God recalls the forefathers to reassure Moses that he is working toward a long-term goal, that he is but one link in a long chain. At this point in Moses' development as a leader, God presents the covenant to him, for now he can understand what it means to be covenantal.[57]

---

[57] In order to highlight Moses' ongoing development, the Torah goes out of its way to distinguish between God's communications with him in chap. 3 and chap. 6. In both passages, God promises to bring the people to the Land; but the description of the Land in each case is distinct. In chap. 3, the

Unlike his ancestors, Moses will live to see redemption; but he too will experience setbacks, and he too will be denied the ultimate fulfillment of God's promise: entry into the Land. At the Burning Bush, Moses was not yet ready to accept the full implications of this new role. But by chapter 6, Moses is ready and God conveys to him that to be covenantal means to enter into an eternal, but personally circumscribed, relationship with the Divine.

Acquiring a Name

Following the conversation between God and Moses in chapter 6, the Torah indicates that an important transition has occurred by recording a genealogy with fairly unusual features. It begins with a brief listing of the families of Reuben and Simeon and then provides an exceptionally detailed description of the tribe of Levi, striking for its inclusion of women as well as men. Several of the people mentioned in this genealogy are the same individuals alluded to anonymously in chapter 2; but whereas chapter 2 was exceptional for its abstraction, chapter 6 is remarkable for its overabundance of detail. Moses himself is named pointedly in this chapter; indeed the conclusion of the passage emphasizes that the main objective of this foray into family history is to account for his (and Aaron's) background:

focus is on the land of Canaan as a broad, safe haven, in contrast to the constricted, menacing nature of Egypt (Exod. 3:8–9). This depiction of the Land is consistent with the portrait of Moses that has been painted in chap. 2: Moses is an individual who is concerned with social justice, with standing up for the weak and disadvantaged. In this first address to Moses, God presents the mission in terms that will resonate with him at this point in his development. But the description of the Land in chap. 6 is radically different. In contrast to flowing milk and honey, chap. 6 cites the covenant by which God committed to bringing the people to "the land of their sojourning." Now the Land is portrayed as one that was given under oath. The land of Canaan is the land where God is present, specifically the land where God speaks. (As noted, God never speaks in Egypt except to instruct the people to leave: from the moment Jacob and his children descend to Egypt until the encounter with Moses at the Burning Bush, God is silent.) In chap. 6, the covenantal Land, the Land of sojourning, the Land of God's name, functions primarily as the mediating agent that allows the relationship with God to unfold. In consonance with Moses' own developing identity, the expression of God's commitment to the people has been reformulated.

EXODUS: AN INDIVIDUAL AND COLLECTIVE COMING OF AGE

הוּא אַהֲרֹן וּמֹשֶׁה אֲשֶׁר אָמַר יהוה לָהֶם הוֹצִיאוּ אֶת בְּנֵי יִשְׂרָאֵל מֵאֶרֶץ מִצְרַיִם עַל
צִבְאֹתָם: הֵם הַמְדַבְּרִים אֶל פַּרְעֹה מֶלֶךְ מִצְרַיִם לְהוֹצִיא אֶת בְּנֵי יִשְׂרָאֵל מִמִּצְרָיִם
הוּא מֹשֶׁה וְאַהֲרֹן:

It was the very Aaron and Moses to whom the LORD *said, "Bring out*
the Israelites from the land of Egypt in their battalions." It was they
who were speaking to Pharaoh king of Egypt to bring out the Israelites
from Egypt, the very Moses and Aaron. (Exod. 6:26–27)

Not coincidentally, Moses' lineage is presented to us just after the covenant
with God has been revealed. In other words, Moses receives a name and a
pedigree the moment he understands who he himself actually is: the inheritor
of Abraham, Isaac, and Jacob.[58] This identity was already revealed at the
Burning Bush, but there the connection between Moses and the forefathers
was drawn on the basis of their common experience of revelation. Now the
connection derives from an acceptance of the meaning and terms of the divine covenant. After Moses has come into his own character, he is able to
approach the People of Israel as a peer and a leader and offer them a sense of
their common history and destiny.

Conclusion

Over the course of this first section of Exodus, Moses undergoes a
personal odyssey that takes him from anonymous birth to distinguished
lineage; from adoption as a foundling to leadership of a nation; from
"heaviness of mouth and heaviness of speech" to triumphant, exalted song.
In various ways Moses' personal life experiences serve as symbols for the
experiences of the nation and for the collective transformation that will
transpire over the course of the entire book of Exodus. Although Jacob and
his children came to Egypt as distinct households, with a clear sense of ances-
try and familial affiliation, slavery deprived the nascent nation of identity and

---

[58]The reader understands immediately that Moses, like Abraham, Isaac, and Jacob, is himself not
going to inherit the Land. Like the forefathers, Moses is the recipient of a promise, and he enables
the fulfillment of the promise, but he will not get to actualize it.

left the People of Israel bereft of connectedness and of purpose—much as Moses' own childhood and adolescence were characterized by ambiguous ties and unclear goals. Just as Moses needed to flee Egypt in order to gain the perspective that allowed him to recognize his own alienation, the Israelites must be taken forcibly out of Egypt in order to become an independent people; and just as Moses' experience at the Burning Bush and his subsequent encounters with God instilled him with a sense of mission and destiny, it is ultimately the revelation at Sinai and the nation's ongoing experience of God in the *Mishkan* that makes them a nation.

4
Elu Eser Makot:
Rereading the Plagues

The Ten Plagues that God inflicted upon the Egyptians before they agreed to release the Israelites from bondage are an essential feature of the biblical Exodus story and also play a central role in the Haggadah. While the plagues passages are often read as straightforward depictions of increasingly harsh divine punishment, their complex literary presentation and links to other biblical stories captured the attention of the Midrash and later commentators. The Haggadah itself employs a range of midrashic tools for creatively reading and interpreting the plagues. Counting, a seemingly simple technique, is foremost among them. The Haggadah puts forward various proposals for grouping the plagues—one by one, two by two, three by three, and five by five—and each of these combinations sheds light on different themes inherent in the biblical narrative. But in its quest to tease meaning out of the text, the Haggadah uses other literary strategies as well. Let us first review the groupings of the Ten Plagues and then consider one particularly evocative intertextual reading to demonstrate the way in which the Haggadah employs midrash to convey educational and theological messages.

Grouping the Plagues

The first time it references the plagues directly, the Haggadah (citing an early midrash) proposes reading them into the words of Deuteronomy 26:8, the final verse of the *Arami oved avi* passage discussed in essay 1. The verse itself, which concludes the brief historical narrative that serves as the core text of *Maggid*, reads:

וַיּוֹצִאֵנוּ יהוה מִמִּצְרַיִם בְּיָד חֲזָקָה וּבִזְרֹעַ נְטוּיָה וּבְמֹרָא גָּדֹל וּבְאֹתוֹת וּבְמֹפְתִים:

And the LORD brought us out from Egypt with a strong hand and with an outstretched arm and with great terror and with signs and with portents. (Deut. 26:8)

The Haggadah suggests the following interpretation:

בְּיָד חֲזָקָה — שְׁתַּיִם, וּבִזְרֹעַ נְטוּיָה — שְׁתַּיִם, וּבְמֹרָא גָּדֹל — שְׁתַּיִם, וּבְאֹתוֹת — שְׁתַּיִם, וּבְמֹפְתִים — שְׁתַּיִם. אֵלוּ עֶשֶׂר מַכּוֹת שֶׁהֵבִיא הַקָּדוֹשׁ בָּרוּךְ הוּא עַל הַמִּצְרִים בְּמִצְרָיִם.

With a strong hand—two; with an outstretched arm—two; and with great terror—two; and with signs—two; and with portents—two. These are the Ten Plagues that the Blessed Holy One brought upon the Egyptions in Egypt.

This explication is sensitive to both the double-worded phrases ("strong hand," "outstretched arm," "great terror") and to the plural form of the words in the verse ("signs," "portents"). The plurality, according to this midrash, teaches that God afflicted the Egyptians with "pairs" of wonders. In fact, the pairing of plagues one and two, three and four, five and six, seven and eight, and nine and ten is a highly reasonable division: blood (*dam*) and frogs (*tzefarde'a*) both involve water; lice (*kinim*) and swarming creatures (*arov*) both arrive in hordes;[59] pestilence (*dever*) and boils (*shekhin*) are diseases; hail (*barad*) and locusts (*arov*) are blights that destroy crops; and darkness (*hoshekh*) and the Plague of the Firstborn (*bekhorot*) represent the final and ultimate destruction.[60]

Another method of grouping the plagues is presented in the Haggadah's brief statement:

רַבִּי יְהוּדָה הָיָה נוֹתֵן בָּהֶם סִמָּנִים: דְּצַ"ךְ עַדַ"שׁ בְּאַחַ"ב.

R. Judah referred to them by a mnemonic: *detzakh, adash, be-ahav.*

It is possible that R. Judah offered these acronyms as a simple mnemonic device; indeed, he is cited elsewhere providing such initials, apparently for

---

[59] Some commentators claim that the fourth plague, *arov*, was another form of insect, rendering it even more similar to lice (*kinim*).

[60] The pairing of these two plagues is reminiscent of the manner in which God destroyed Sodom as well: first by blinding the people, then by obliterating the place (Gen. 19). For further comparison of the destruction of Egypt and the destruction of Sodom, see essay 6.

memorization purposes.[61] But since it is not that difficult to remember ten items, it seems likely that R. Judah's acronyms were intended to highlight something more profound about the nature of the various plagues, or at least about their presentation in the biblical text.

As Nahum Sarna and other scholars have pointed out, there is a striking literary character to the Ten Plagues passages in the Torah, which exhibit a structure based on threes.[62] The first two plagues—blood and frogs—are each accompanied by a warning, whereas the third plague—lice—comes about with no prior notification. This pattern repeats itself for the next two sets of three: the fourth plague, swarming creatures, and the fifth plague, pestilence, are forewarned, while the sixth, boils, is not; likewise, Pharaoh is alerted before the seventh and eighth plagues—hail and locusts—but not before the ninth, darkness.[63] Similarly, the time at which the warning took place is specified as morning for the first plague in each set of three (i.e., the first, the fourth, and the seventh plagues); whereas the timing of the warning for the second, fifth, and eighth plagues is not given at all. Furthermore, the first two plagues in each set of three are focused on specific locales: the first and the second plagues revolve around the water (specifically, the Nile River); the fourth and fifth plagues relate to the land; and the seventh and eighth, plagues come from the sky.

This grouping seems to be echoed in Psalm 78, which, along with Psalm 105, provides an alternative listing of the plagues. Sarna claims that in contrast to the book of Exodus, which lists ten plagues, each of the psalms lists only seven. (In truth, counting the plagues in these psalms is not simple, given their impressionistic rendering.) In Psalm 78, the order of the plagues seems to be: blood, swarming creatures, frogs, locusts, hail, pestilence, and firstborn. Assuming this list is accurate, missing from Psalm 78 are plagues three, six, and nine—lice, boils, and darkness—the same three plagues that, as noted, arrive without forewarning. Read in this way, it seems that Psalm 78 records a

---

[61] See M. Men. 11:4 and the commentary of R. Ovadia me-Bartenura.

[62] Nahum M. Sarna, *Exploring Exodus: The Heritage of Biblical Israel* (New York: Schocken Books, 1986), 73–78.

[63] See the commentary of Hizkuni on Exod. 8:15, *Va-yehezak lev Par'o*, where he explicitly connects this pattern with R. Judah's mnemonics.

tradition that counts seven plagues as a derivative of the Torah's Ten Plague tradition, excising from the record those plagues that were experienced as continuations of the previous ones (in other words, responses to Pharaoh's refusal to heed God's earlier threats).

Finally, the Haggadah suggests dividing the plagues into two groups of five, or at least alludes to such a division, again in the context of the midrash on Deuteronomy 26:5–8. In an alternative interpretation to that which produced the 2/2/2/2/2 division, the Haggadah proposes reading Deuteronomy 26:8 as a reference to the fifth and tenth plagues, pestilence and the Plague of the Firstborn:

בְּיָד חֲזָקָה—זוֹ הַדֶּבֶר, כְּמָה שֶׁנֶּאֱמַר: הִנֵּה יַד יהוה הוֹיָה בְּמִקְנְךָ אֲשֶׁר בַּשָּׂדֶה, בַּסּוּסִים, בַּחֲמֹרִים, בַּגְּמַלִּים, בַּבָּקָר וּבַצֹּאן, דֶּבֶר כָּבֵד מְאֹד.
וּבִזְרֹעַ נְטוּיָה—זוֹ הַחֶרֶב, כְּמָה שֶׁנֶּאֱמַר: וְחַרְבּוֹ שְׁלוּפָה בְּיָדוֹ, נְטוּיָה עַל יְרוּשָׁלָיִם.

With a strong hand (Deut. 26:8)—this is the pestilence, as it says: *Look, the hand of the LORD is about to be against your livestock which is in the field, against the horses, against the donkeys, against the camels, against the cattle, and against the sheep—a very heavy pestilence* (Exod. 9:3).

And with an outstretched arm—this is the sword, as it says: *With a drawn sword in his hand stretched over*[64] *Jerusalem* (1 Chron. 21:16).

The phrase "a strong hand" is associated with pestilence because the Torah itself describes the fifth plague as the work of God's hand. The phrase "an outstretched arm" is read as an allusion to God's sword because it evokes a similarly worded verse in Chronicles that depicts God's angel with a drawn weapon. The Torah does not explicitly invoke a sword in its description of the tenth plague, but it does repeatedly refer to God's smiting of the Egyptian firstborn (Exod. 12:12,14,29).

---

[64]Translation has been emended; the original reads: "directed against Jerusalem."

The Haggadah's allusion to the plagues that God wrought upon the Egyptians via the symbols of pestilence and sword is consonant with the Torah's first allusion to the punishment and affliction that would result from defiance of God's will. When Moses and Aaron approach Pharaoh for the first time in chapter 5, requesting permission to worship in the desert, Pharaoh refuses with the assertion that he does not recognize the God of the Israelites. In response to Pharaoh's rebuff, Moses and Aaron declare:

וַיֹּאמְרוּ אֱלֹהֵי הָעִבְרִים נִקְרָא עָלֵינוּ נֵלֲכָה נָּא דֶּרֶךְ שְׁלֹשֶׁת יָמִים בַּמִּדְבָּר וְנִזְבְּחָה
לַיהוה אֱלֹהֵינוּ פֶּן יִפְגָּעֵנוּ בַּדֶּבֶר אוֹ בֶחָרֶב:

. . . "The God of the Hebrews happened upon us. Let us go, pray, a three day's journey into the wilderness, that we may sacrifice to the Lord *our God, lest He hit us with pestilence or sword." (Exod. 5:3)*

Although the threat seems to be directed at the Israelites for failing to fulfill God's command, it includes, by implication, those who prevent them from so doing.[65] Thus "pestilence" and "sword" function as shorthand for all the plagues that God later wreaks.

Undoing Creation

In addition to highlighting particular literary features of the biblical text, the Haggadah's various divisions of the plagues are an attempt to draw attention to the underlying messages that the plagues convey. The Torah is fairly obvious about presenting the Ten Plagues as a counterpoint to Creation. The organization of the plagues into a 3/3/3 division plays off the tripartite description of Creation in Genesis 1. Days one and four focus on the sky; days two and five, on the water; days three and six, on the land. Similarly, plagues one and two are about the waters; four and five are about the land;

---

[65] This is the understanding of Ibn Ezra, Sforno, and Hizkuni; see their commentaries on Exod. 5:3, *Pen yifga'enu*. Other commentators, including Rashi, understood Moses and Aaron's words to be euphemistic and reflective of their subservient stance: what they really meant was that Pharaoh and the Egyptians would be punished.

A Passover Haggadah: Go Forth and Learn

and seven and eight are about the sky. These lead up to the ninth plague, darkness, evocative of the world prior to the days of Creation:

$$\text{וְהָאָרֶץ הָיְתָה תֹהוּ וָבֹהוּ וְחֹשֶׁךְ עַל פְּנֵי תְהוֹם} \ldots$$

And the earth then was welter and waste and darkness over the deep . . . (Gen. 1:2)

To further the Genesis association, the Torah emphasizes that the Egyptians were trapped by the darkness and unable to move for three days, whereas the Israelites had light in their homes and moved freely—a contrast that also recalls the first act of Creation, in which God separated light from darkness (Gen. 1:4). Of course, the plagues culminate with the Egyptians drowning in the sea, conjuring up images of the Flood, God's first undoing of Creation.

Psalm 105, whose listing of the plagues does not accord precisely with the Torah's, seems to demonstrate a similar understanding of the havoc that God wreaked upon Egypt.[66] The psalm includes fewer plagues than the traditional ten and begins with darkness (*hoshekh*), which is the ninth plague in the book of Exodus.[67] Here, *hoshekh* could actually be read as emblematic of all the other plagues, rather than as a plague unto itself. The relevant verse is somewhat cryptic:

$$\text{שָׁלַח חֹשֶׁךְ וַיַּחְשִׁךְ וְלֹא מָרוּ אֶת דבריו (דְּבָרוֹ):}$$

He sent darkness, and it grew dark, yet they did not keep His word. (Ps. 105:28)

Who did not keep God's word? Various interpretations have been offered. I would suggest that *hoshekh* is the most likely subject of the verb *maru*

---

[66] The list begins with darkness and goes on to list blood, frogs, swarming creatures, lice, hail, locusts, and firstborn. Pestilence and boils, plagues five and six in the Torah, are entirely absent from Ps. 105. These two plagues are the "disease pair" in the 2/2/2/2/2 division discussed previously. It is possible that the Psalmist omitted them because they are more naturally occurring and thus less awe inspiring than the others.

[67] Sarna counts seven plagues in Ps. 105, but in point of fact there are eight. Sarna arrives at seven because he assumes v. 31 to refer to a single plague; however, since the Torah counts swarming creatures and lice separately, there is no reason to assume they are one in the book of Psalms.

(rebelled), although its singular form does not match the plural of the verb. It is *hoshekh* itself, or the plagues represented by *hoshekh*, that did not rebel against or deviate from God's word, fulfilling God's mission of destruction without protest. In Genesis, light was the first thing that God created—with words. In Egypt, the word of God created not light, but darkness; the plagues were a reversal of Creation. Read this way, the plagues are meant to teach that those who oppose God, who deny God, are reduced to darkness; they cannot be a part of Creation.

Knowing God

The division of the plagues into groups of three highlights another theme: that the plagues were designed to bring knowledge of God to the world.[68] This is made clear by the explanation or rationale that God offers before each "group" of three plagues. Before the first plague, God instructs Moses to tell Pharaoh:

כֹּה אָמַר יהוה בְּזֹאת תֵּדַע כִּי אֲנִי יהוה הִנֵּה אָנֹכִי מַכֶּה בַּמַּטֶּה אֲשֶׁר בְּיָדִי עַל הַמַּיִם אֲשֶׁר בַּיְאֹר וְנֶהֶפְכוּ לְדָם:

Thus said the LORD, By this shall you know that I am the LORD: Look, I am about to strike with the staff in my hand on the water that is in the Nile and it will turn into blood. (Exod. 7:17)

Before the fourth plague, God similarly instructs Moses to tell Pharaoh:

וְהִפְלֵיתִי בַיּוֹם הַהוּא אֶת אֶרֶץ גֹּשֶׁן אֲשֶׁר עַמִּי עֹמֵד עָלֶיהָ לְבִלְתִּי הֱיוֹת שָׁם עָרֹב לְמַעַן תֵּדַע כִּי אֲנִי יהוה בְּקֶרֶב הָאָרֶץ:

But I shall set apart on that day the land of Goshen upon which My people stands so that no horde will be there, that you may know that I am the LORD in the midst of the land. (Exod. 8:18)

---

[68] See Nehama Leibowitz, *Studies in Shemot* (Jerusalem: The World Zionist Organization, 1976), 170–77.

And before the seventh plague, God instructs Moses to tell Pharaoh one last time:

כִּי בַּפַּעַם הַזֹּאת אֲנִי שֹׁלֵחַ אֶת כָּל מַגֵּפֹתַי אֶל לִבְּךָ וּבַעֲבָדֶיךָ וּבְעַמֶּךָ בַּעֲבוּר תֵּדַע כִּי אֵין כָּמֹנִי בְּכָל הָאָרֶץ:

For this time I am about to send all My scourges to your heart and against your servants and against your people, so that you may know that there is none like Me in all the earth. (Exod. 9:14)

Each of these statements suggests that the purpose of the plagues is not merely to punish Pharaoh and the Egyptians for their refusal to heed God's commands or to enable the Israelites to leave their bonds of slavery, but to demonstrate God's presence and involvement in the world.[69]

This type of knowing represents what is arguably the central idea of Exodus. On the one hand, the book begins with the rise of a new Egyptian king "who knew not Joseph" (Exod. 1:8), the same Pharaoh who later declares that he does not "know God" (5:2). Pharaoh's "not knowing" carries with it a sense of ingratitude, as Joseph was the savior of his nation; it also suggests callousness and a lack of sensitivity, and the Torah implies that it is not just an intellectual lapse but a moral deficiency. God's response to the one who does not know is that he will come to know, by force if necessary. He will come to recognize God through the plagues, which were designed to let him know that God exists.

On the other hand, the bond between Israel and God reflects mutual knowledge. First the Torah introduces God into the Exodus story by reporting that God has heard the cries of the suffering Israelites, has remembered the covenant with their forefathers, and "knows" (Exod. 2:24–25). And later the Torah declares that the Israelites' knowledge of God is the objective of their relationship with the Divine (6:7). Similarly, Moses' prayers following the sin of the Golden Calf and the breaking of the tablets pay tribute to God's familiarity with Israel and constitute Moses' plea, as a human being, to know God more intimately:

---

[69] Indeed, Jethro later declares that hearing of the Israelites' redemption from Egypt has led him to "know" God (Exod. 18:10–11).

וַיֹּאמֶר מֹשֶׁה אֶל יהוה...וְאַתָּה אָמַרְתָּ יְדַעְתִּיךָ בְשֵׁם וְגַם מָצָאתָ חֵן בְּעֵינָי: וְעַתָּה
אִם נָא מָצָאתִי חֵן בְּעֵינֶיךָ הוֹדִעֵנִי נָא אֶת דְּרָכֶךָ וְאֵדָעֲךָ לְמַעַן אֶמְצָא חֵן בְּעֵינֶיךָ
וּרְאֵה כִּי עַמְּךָ הַגּוֹי הַזֶּה...וּבַמֶּה יִוָּדַע אֵפוֹא כִּי מָצָאתִי חֵן בְּעֵינֶיךָ אֲנִי וְעַמֶּךָ...

*And Moses said to the LORD, ". . . And You, You have said, 'I know
you by name, and you have also found favor in My eyes.' And now,
if, pray, I have found favor in Your eyes, let me know, pray, Your
ways, that I may know You, so that I may find favor in Your eyes.
And see, for this nation is Your people" . . . "And how, then, will it be
known that I have found favor in Your eyes, I and Your people? . . ."*
(Exod. 33:12–16)

Knowing God is God's own stated goal for the People of Israel as they become
a nation. Following the seventh plague, hail, God explains that Pharaoh's
heart was hardened so that Moses and the Israelites might see the wonders
and signs and come to know God (Exod. 10:2). And after the Exodus, God
commands the building of the *Mishkan* for the purpose of allowing the people
to know God (29: 43–46).[70] All this suggests that God's redemption of the
Israelites from Egypt is not simply a utilitarian action but serves primarily to
magnify the Divine Presence in the world.

"So that you may know" is God's ultimate rationale for the plagues, and it
also connects the plagues to a broader theme that runs through the book of
Exodus. Exodus is a story about the quest for human freedom; but it is one in
which God plays a central role. The purpose of the Exodus is to relieve the
people of their suffering and to grant them independence; but it is also to
magnify the Divine Presence in the world and to enable the people to serve
God. The דצ״ך עד״ש באח״ב division of the plagues emphasizes that the book of
Exodus is not only Israel's story but God's story as well.

---

[70] The *Mishkan* conveys knowledge of God in several ways: (1) the *Mishkan* does not represent
intellectual cognizance, but rather the knowledge derived from the experience of being in God's
presence; (2) as "God's house," the *Mishkan* and its vessels provide a material sense of who God is,
what God is like, and what God's values are; and (3) the *Mishkan* is the place where God speaks, the
site from which God's voice emanates—thus the kinds of communications and commands that issue
from the *Mishkan* enable the People of Israel to understand something about God.

A PASSOVER HAGGADAH: GO FORTH AND LEARN

Becoming Egypt

We noted earlier that in one of its variations on the plagues' groupings, the Haggadah represents God smiting the Egyptians with an allusion to the plagues of *dever* and *herev*, ostensibly the fifth and tenth plagues of the Exodus narrative. To support its understanding of the phrase "an outstretched arm" (*zero'a netuyah*) as an allusion to God's sword, the Haggadah cites a verse from Chronicles 21 drawn from the episode in which David is castigated for taking a census of the people. This is apparently a grievous sin, and the prophet Gad presents David with a choice of three punishments. David abstains from deciding, but the punishment that is meted out is pestilence (*dever*). In the Chronicles version of the story, David then sees an angel with a sword in hand, "stretched out" over Jerusalem (*netuyah al Yerushalayim*). The appearance of the word *netuyah* (stretched out) here is the basis for the Haggadah's citation of this verse to elaborate on the imagery of Exodus.

But in drawing our attention to the story in Chronicles and, by extension, to its parallel account in the book of Samuel, the Haggadah highlights more than just the linguistic association. A close reading of these passages reveals that their authors borrowed themes and motifs from the Exodus story and particularly from God's confrontation with Pharaoh during the plagues to depict David's sin and punishment. For the Haggadah, that intertextuality is highly significant.

The final chapter of Samuel opens with a cryptic statement that is troubling for theological as well as textual reasons:

וַיֹּסֶף אַף יהוה לַחֲרוֹת בְּיִשְׂרָאֵל וַיָּסֶת אֶת דָּוִד בָּהֶם לֵאמֹר לֵךְ מְנֵה אֶת יִשְׂרָאֵל וְאֶת יְהוּדָה:

The anger of the LORD *again flared up against Israel; and He incited David against them, saying, "Go and number Israel and Judah."* (2 Sam. 24:1)

God's unexplained anger and provocation is so baffling that the medieval commentator Rashi writes only, "I do not know its cause."[71] Following God's incitement, David instructs his general Joab ben Zeruiah to count the people. Joab is initially reluctant to do so, but David insists, and Joab obeys. After Joab has carried out the census, David is struck with remorse and confesses his sin in calling for a census and begs God for forgiveness:

‫...וַיֹּאמֶר דָּוִד אֶל יהוה חָטָאתִי מְאֹד אֲשֶׁר עָשִׂיתִי וְעַתָּה יהוה הַעֲבֶר נָא אֶת עֲוֹן‬
‫עַבְדְּךָ כִּי נִסְכַּלְתִּי מְאֹד:‬

...And David said to the LORD, "I have sinned grievously in what I have done. Please, O LORD, remit the guilt of Your servant, for I have acted foolishly." (2 Sam. 24:10)

The intensity of David's confession is arresting, particularly when contrasted with the wording of his legendary admission after the sin with Bathsheba. There David says *"hatati"* ("I have sinned"); here, he says *"hatati me'od"* ("I have sinned greatly"). Why is counting the people a more severe sin in David's mind than the affair that entailed adultery, murder, and conspiracy?

An explanation of both the troubling first verse and David's puzzling confession lies in an understanding of this story's function within the book of Samuel as a whole. God's anger is directed to the core conflict in the book, namely, the establishment of a monarchy amid concerns about the corrosive nature of power and fear that kingship will lead human beings to supplant God. Samuel objects to the people's initial request for a king, possibly upset by their expressed desire to be like all the nations. He argues that a king would take advantage of his position and make excessive demands on the nation (1 Sam. 8:4–22). Samuel's deeper objection, however, is that kingship itself is a form of heresy, as it challenges God's dominion. In this last chapter, the author returns to that fundamental debate concerning the merits of monarchy. God's anger is not initially directed at David, but at the people. Yet David, the ideal king, is portrayed as acting in a manner that directly contravenes God's kingship. The book of Exodus makes clear that a census is

---

[71] See Rashi on 2 Sam. 24:1, *Va-yosef af.*

A PASSOVER HAGGADAH: GO FORTH AND LEARN

to be taken via the *Mishkan*, for it is only in God's presence that the people are a nation. But David counts the people of his own volition, without direction from God and without the appropriate framework; he circumvents God and claims the people as his own. David's exaggerated remorse suggests that he realizes the implication of his violation, and thus its gravity.

When presented with a choice of punishment—seven years of famine, three years of war, or three days of pestilence, David attempts to demonstrate that he has learned his lesson, that God alone is arbiter of the world—by abstaining from making a decision. But it is clear which of the three options is the most fitting. First, the book of Exodus states clearly that the goal of counting the people via the half-shekel donation to the *Mishkan* is to avoid punishment by plague (Exod. 30:12). (The *negef* plague of this verse and the *dever* plague that God offers David are presumably one and the same.) Second, the nation just recently has suffered a famine (2 Sam. 21:1), and David himself was pursued by enemies and involved in wars throughout his life, so that pestilence is the one tribulation that he has not yet experienced. Furthermore, the writer uses wordplay in the prophet Gad's speech to David to intimate that *dever* will be the ultimate choice:

וּדְבַר יהוה הָיָה אֶל גָּד הַנָּבִיא חֹזֵה דָוִד לֵאמֹר: הָלוֹךְ וְדִבַּרְתָּ אֶל דָּוִד כֹּה אָמַר
יהוה שָׁלֹשׁ אָנֹכִי נוֹטֵל עָלֶיךָ ... עַתָּה דַּע וּרְאֵה מָה אָשִׁיב שֹׁלְחִי דָבָר:

...the word (davar) of the LORD had come to the prophet Gad, David's seer: "Go and tell (ve-dibarta el) David, "Thus said the LORD: I hold three things over you ... Now consider carefully what reply [davar] I shall take back to Him who sent me." (2 Sam. 24:11–13)[72]

In describing David's behavior in this chapter as well as the punishment that is meted out, the author borrows language from the Torah's portrayal of Pharaoh's interactions with Moses and from its account of the fifth plague. By adopting Pharaoh's language to depict David, the narrator seems to suggest that in this story, David has become Pharaoh! At the beginning of the

---

[72]The word *davar* appears in Joab's initial objection to the census as well; see 2 Sam. 24:3.

ELU ESER MAKOT: REREADING THE PLAGUES

narrative, the phrasing of David's insistence that the census be carried out despite Joab's objection recalls the refrain of Pharaoh's repeated refusals to let the Israelites out of bondage:

וַיֶּחֱזַק דְּבַר הַמֶּלֶךְ אֶל יוֹאָב וְעַל שָׂרֵי הֶחָיִל...

However, the king's command to Joab and to the officers of the army remained firm (va-yehezak)... (2 Sam. 24:4)

In the context of the first five plagues, Pharaoh hardens his own heart; but after each of the second five, the Torah indicates that God has caused Pharaoh's reaction. Similarly, 2 Samuel 24 begins by noting that God either "incites" David to call for the census or prevails upon his heart. (However, as the continuation of the story indicates, God's incitement does not absolve David of responsibility for his sin, just as it did not absolve Pharaoh.) When presented with a choice of punishment, David tells the prophet Gad that he would rather fall into "the hand of the LORD" than the hands of man (2 Sam. 24:13), recalling the Torah's designation of the fifth plague as the work of "God's hand" (Exod. 9:3). And in describing the implementation of David's punishment, the book of Samuel again seems to evoke words from Exodus:

וַיִּתֵּן יהוה דֶּבֶר בְּיִשְׂרָאֵל מֵהַבֹּקֶר וְעַד עֵת מוֹעֵד...

The LORD sent a pestilence upon Israel from morning until the set time... (2 Sam. 24:15)

This phrasing is strikingly similar to God's warning regarding the implementation of the fifth plague:

וַיָּשֶׂם יהוה מוֹעֵד לֵאמֹר מָחָר יַעֲשֶׂה יהוה הַדָּבָר הַזֶּה בָּאָרֶץ:

And the LORD set a fixed time, saying, "Tomorrow the LORD will do this thing in the land." (Exod. 9:5)

So too does the previously noted *dever/davar* wordplay in the Samuel story call to mind a similar phenomenon in the Exodus narrative:

A PASSOVER HAGGADAH: GO FORTH AND LEARN

הִנֵּה יַד יהוה הוֹיָה בְּמִקְנְךָ אֲשֶׁר בַּשָּׂדֶה בַּסּוּסִים בַּחֲמֹרִים בַּגְּמַלִּים בַּבָּקָר וּבַצֹּאן דֶּבֶר כָּבֵד מְאֹד: וְהִפְלָה יהוה בֵּין מִקְנֵה יִשְׂרָאֵל וּבֵין מִקְנֵה מִצְרָיִם וְלֹא יָמוּת מִכָּל לִבְנֵי יִשְׂרָאֵל דָּבָר: וַיָּשֶׂם יהוה מוֹעֵד לֵאמֹר מָחָר יַעֲשֶׂה יהוה הַדָּבָר הַזֶּה בָּאָרֶץ: וַיַּעַשׂ יהוה אֶת הַדָּבָר הַזֶּה מִמָּחֳרָת וַיָּמָת כֹּל מִקְנֵה מִצְרָיִם ...

"Look, the hand of the LORD *is about to be against your livestock which is in the field, against the horses, against the donkeys, against the camels, against the cattle, and against the sheep—a very heavy pestilence (dever). And the* LORD *will set apart the livestock of Israel from the livestock of Egypt, and nothing (davar) of the Israelites' will die." And the* LORD *set a fixed time, saying, "Tomorrow the* LORD *will do this thing (ha-davar) in the land." And the* LORD *did this thing (ha-davar) on the next day, and all the livestock of Egypt died . . .* (Exod. 9:3–6)

Finally, the angel who carries out God's punishment against the People of Israel in the book of Samuel is depicted in terms that recall the messenger of God who executes the Plague of the Firstborn:

וַיִּשְׁלַח יָדוֹ הַמַּלְאָךְ יְרוּשָׁלַ͏ִם לְשַׁחֲתָהּ וַיִּנָּחֶם יהוה אֶל הָרָעָה וַיֹּאמֶר לַמַּלְאָךְ הַמַּשְׁחִית בָּעָם רַב עַתָּה הֶרֶף יָדֶךָ ...

But when the angel extended his hand against Jerusalem to destroy it, the LORD *renounced further punishment and said to the angel who was destroying the people, "Enough! Stay your hand!" . . .* (2 Sam. 24:16)

The numerous linguistic and conceptual parallels between the Samuel and Exodus stories suggest that the prophetic author consciously chose to paint David in Pharaoh-like colors, challenging and defying God. The message is clear: every king who presumes that he has ultimate power can become God's enemy, including David.

Nonetheless, the conclusion to the book of Samuel restores David to his heroic status, whereas Pharaoh and his people perish. Ultimately, the difference between David and Pharaoh lies in their distinct responses to failure and sin. Pharaoh, like David, utters the *hatati* confession numerous times during the course of the plagues and on several occasions asks Moses to pray

ELU ESER MAKOT: REREADING THE PLAGUES

for him; however, each time the afflictions abate, he retracts his promises and refuses to allow the Israelites to make their pilgrimage or to offer sacrifices to God. David, on the other hand, confesses his sin (2 Sam. 24:10); refrains from choosing a punishment to express his surrender to God's will (24:14); declares that his own actions have stripped him of the moral authority to be king (24:17); and builds an altar, offering *olot u-zevahim* (24:25), the very sacrifices that Pharaoh denies the Israelites. Once David has demonstrated his genuine contrition, God stops the plague:

... וַיֵּעָתֵר יהוה לָאָרֶץ וַתֵּעָצַר הַמַּגֵּפָה מֵעַל יִשְׂרָאֵל:

> *. . . The* LORD *responded to the plea for the land, and the plague against Israel was checked.* (2 Sam. 24:25)

The language used to denote God's response is also borrowed from the Pharaoh story: *va-ye'etar* (was entreated) is the word that Pharaoh uses no less than eight times in asking Moses to pray on his behalf. But in this case, the common language highlights the contrast between the two rulers: unlike Pharaoh, who consistently makes gestures and then retreats, David's atonement is authentic. Thus, in contrast to Pharaoh's demise, David merits the privilege of identifying and establishing sacred space (i.e., the Temple Mount) and thereby confirms his own status as the eternal king.

David himself does not choose the sacred place; he merely recognizes the site by virtue of the angel hovering above (in fact, the angel, particularly in the Chronicles version, is depicted as preventing David from entering Goren Aravna/Jerusalem). But because David accepts responsibility and recognizes the limitations of his role, he merits not only encountering God but setting up the eternal place of encounter, the Temple Mount. In a sense, David's atonement for the sin of counting the people is buying the threshing floor from Aravna. Although Aravna wants to give the land to David for free, David insists on paying for it, because he has learned that people, land, and the world's resources do not belong to him but to God alone.

This, then, is the reason that the Haggadah cites the David narrative as a means of explicating the verse from Deuteronomy. In the cyclical pattern of history, we are not only in danger of experiencing another Egypt, but also of becoming an Egypt ourselves.

A PASSOVER HAGGADAH: GO FORTH AND LEARN

Conclusion

The Midrash employs many techniques that push the limits of the biblical text, allowing it to speak to different audiences in multifaceted manners. In accordance with Mishnah *Pesahim*, which deems midrashic exegesis to be one of the core seder activities, the Haggadah engages these types of reading strategies to expand the repertoire of messages that the biblical text yields. The Torah's account of the Ten Plagues provides particularly fertile ground for engaging the minds of seder participants and making the Exodus story meaningful in countless ways.

5

Korban Pesah:
The Sacrifice That Shaped a Nation

According to Rabbinic tradition, the ancient seder was a rite that consisted primarily of interweaving the eating of the Passover offering with the telling of the Exodus story. Following the destruction of the Temple, the Rabbis debated appropriate ways to commemorate this sacrificial meal: some advocated eating a roasted lamb in lieu of the original sacrifice, while others forbade such a practice, which they deemed confusing and improper.[73] Today, the Passover offering informs the organization of seder-night ritual primarily on a symbolic level (as, for example, with the *korekh* sandwich and the *afikoman*). Nonetheless, to appreciate the significance of this commemoration, it is instructive to examine the role that the original Passover sacrifice assumed in the biblical narrative. There, on the brink of the Exodus from Egypt, the offering functioned in four primary capacities, each of which played a key role in the formation of the nascent nation.

National Awakening

In Exodus 12, just after Moses announces the onset of the tenth plague, the Torah interrupts the central narrative to present God's instructions to the People of Israel concerning the preparation and offering of their first Passover sacrifice. The verses also recount the implementation of these directives and serve as the primary biblical account of what the Rabbis call *Pesah Mitzrayim*, the Egyptian Passover.[74] However, this is not the Torah's first reference to a

---

[73] For the sources and discussion of this debate, see Kulp, *Schechter Haggadah* , 238–40. In most communities today, the practice is to avoid eating roasted meat; see the commentary of R. David ha-Levi Segal (TaZ) on the Shulhan Arukh, *Orah Hayyim* 473:4.

[74] In various ways, the Torah distinguishes between the celebration of Pesah in Egypt on the eve of the Exodus (*Pesah Mitzrayim*) and the celebration of Pesah in subsequent years and generations (*Pesah Dorot*). This essay will focus primarily on the original *korban Pesah* that was brought in Egypt, as described in Exod. 12:3–13, 21–23, 43–50. These passages may be contrasted with the description of the *korban Pesah* "for the generations" in Deut. 16.

communal offering, and one essential feature of the Passover sacrifice emerges from earlier passages.

The first time Moses and Aaron approach Pharaoh, in chapter 5, they do not ask for blanket permission to leave the bonds of slavery, but only for a three-day respite to allow the people to journey into the desert and sacrifice to their God (Exod. 5:1,3).[75] Implicit in Moses and Aaron's request is that the sacrifice which God demands cannot be offered in the land of Egypt. Indeed, later in the narrative, while the fourth plague, *arov* (swarming creatures), rages, Pharaoh calls for Moses and Aaron, offering them permission to sacrifice to God in Egypt; but Moses reiterates the need for a journey into the desert, pointing out that the Egyptians would not allow the Hebrews to sacrifice "the abomination of Egypt" before their eyes (8:21–23). In both instances, the reader is left wondering: What if Pharaoh had allowed the pilgrimage to take place? Would Moses have sufficed with a three-day excursion? Would the people have returned to Egypt after their religious holiday?

The most plausible reading of the biblical narrative is that Moses did intend to return after worshiping in the desert, because he understood God to be commanding a sacrificial pilgrimage that was a prerequisite to the ultimate redemption. Thus, when Pharaoh finally agrees to the excursion, insisting only that they not wander too far, Moses appears to accept the offer and its condition (Exod. 8:24–25). Moses' acquiescence suggests that, to his mind, the demand for a three-day excursion was not a trick to enable mass escape but precisely what it claimed to be: a brief journey that would take the people away from their place of bondage so that they might worship God undeterred. Moses believed the sacrificial service to be essential to forming a national identity, in itself a necessary precursor to the Exodus. But this worship could not be performed in the land of Egypt, whose people considered the sacrifice an abomination and would not suffer such an act on the part of their slaves (8:22).

---

[75] This was in accordance with God's own directive to Moses; see Exod. 3:18.

KORBAN PESAH: THE SACRIFICE THAT SHAPED A NATION

While it is true that the Passover sacrifice ultimately is offered in Egypt, that fact does not detract from the basic point regarding its purpose and significance. By the time God instructs the people to prepare the paschal lamb, the Israelites have been transformed and their physical presence in Egypt is no longer an impediment to achieving the goal of collective, identity-building worship.[76] The plagues have considerably shifted the balance of power, destroying Egyptian unity and identity and according the People of Israel a status that allows for national awakening, even in their place of bondage.[77] There in Egypt, the Passover offering functions as both a catalyst and a symbol for the forging of national consciousness and identification.

Reestablishment of Community

Exodus 12 focuses on the role of the home in the original Passover offering in Egypt: according to God's instructions, the sacrifice is to be brought by the people of the house, physically displayed on the house, and eaten

---

[76] In fact, commentators have puzzled for generations over the seemingly extraneous statement that opens Exod. 12: "And the LORD said to Moses and to Aaron in the land of Egypt, saying". Why does the Torah specify at this point that God spoke to Moses and Aaron in Egypt, where the plot has already been focused for several chapters? Where else would God have spoken to them? The simplest answer is that the Torah wishes to draw attention to the transformation that has occurred by highlighting the location of God's command regarding the Passover offering.

[77] The Torah illustrates this development in several stages. First, the sixth plague, *shehin* (boils), isolated Pharaoh from the *hartumim*, his magician advisors, who were struck down by the epidemic along with the Egyptian people (Exod. 9:10–11). Then the advent of the seventh plague, *barad* (hail), resulted in divisiveness among the Egyptian people themselves, some of whom heeded Moses' warning and removed their property from the fields, while others did not (Exod. 9:20–21). Finally, in response to the threat of an eighth plague, *arbeh* (locusts), Pharaoh's servants challenged him openly, demanding that he bring back Moses and Aaron and accede to their request (Exod. 10:7). At this stage, the dissent in Pharaoh's court was strong enough to force his hand, and Pharaoh did capitulate, though he subsequently retracted his consent. Following the ninth plague, *hoshekh* (darkness), God instructed the Israelites to request gold and silver ornaments from their Egyptian neighbors, and the Egyptians' cooperation provides further evidence that their regard for their own leadership was shifting to the People of Israel. The Torah reports that by this point, the Egyptian masses held both the People of Israel and Moses in high esteem (Exod. 11:3). And in warning Pharaoh of events to come, Moses similarly describes the veneration that will be accorded him by the Egyptians after the Plague of the Firstborn (Exod. 11:8). The Israelites' change of status in the eyes of the Egyptians, from despised slaves to the elect of a mighty deity, presumably affected their own self-perception as well.

exclusively in the house.[78] The word *bayit* (house) appears numerous times throughout the passage to emphasize this point:

דַּבְּרוּ אֶל כָּל עֲדַת יִשְׂרָאֵל לֵאמֹר בֶּעָשֹׂר לַחֹדֶשׁ הַזֶּה וְיִקְחוּ לָהֶם אִישׁ שֶׂה לְבֵית אָבֹת שֶׂה לַבָּיִת: וְאִם יִמְעַט הַבַּיִת מִהְיוֹת מִשֶּׂה וְלָקַח הוּא וּשְׁכֵנוֹ הַקָּרֹב אֶל בֵּיתוֹ בְּמִכְסַת נְפָשֹׁת אִישׁ לְפִי אָכְלוֹ תָּכֹסּוּ עַל הַשֶּׂה... וְלָקְחוּ מִן הַדָּם וְנָתְנוּ עַל שְׁתֵּי הַמְּזוּזֹת וְעַל הַמַּשְׁקוֹף עַל הַבָּתִּים אֲשֶׁר יֹאכְלוּ אֹתוֹ בָּהֶם:

Speak to all the community of Israel, saying: "On the tenth of this month, let every man take a lamb for a father's house, a lamb for a household. And should a household be too small to have a lamb, it must take together with its neighbor who is close to its house, in proportion to the persons, each man according to what he eats shall take his portion of the lamb . . . And they shall take from the blood and put it on the two doorposts and on the lintel, on the houses in which they will eat it." (Exod. 12:3–7)

When Moses conveys God's instructions to the people several verses later, he too emphasizes the role of the house:

וּלְקַחְתֶּם אֲגֻדַּת אֵזוֹב וּטְבַלְתֶּם בַּדָּם אֲשֶׁר בַּסַּף וְהִגַּעְתֶּם אֶל הַמַּשְׁקוֹף וְאֶל שְׁתֵּי הַמְּזוּזֹת מִן הַדָּם אֲשֶׁר בַּסָּף וְאַתֶּם לֹא תֵצְאוּ אִישׁ מִפֶּתַח בֵּיתוֹ עַד בֹּקֶר:

And you shall take a bundle of hyssop and you shall dip it in the blood that is in the basin and you shall touch the blood that is in the basin to the lintel and to the two doorposts, and as for you, none of you shall go out from the entrance of his house till morning" (Exod. 12:22)[79]

---

[78] This description contrasts with the presentation of the Passover offering in Deuteronomy: there, sheep and cattle are mentioned, as opposed to sheep alone; the offering is cooked, as opposed to broiled; and the sacrifice is slaughtered and eaten at a central site of worship, as opposed to in the house (in fact, it is specifically forbidden to offer the sacrifice "within one of your gates"; see Deut. 16:2,5–7). The resolution to this contradiction, as suggested by the Mishnah, is that the subject of Deuteronomy is not the Passover or Pesah, sacrifice itself, but a quasi-*Pesah*, the *Hagigah* offering (see M. Pes. 6:3–5). The *Hagigah* serves as the main meal of the seder, whereas the *Pesah* is the dessert eaten at the end of the seder, nowadays represented by the *afikoman*.

[79] This, of course, echoes an additional facet of God's instructions, that the blood on the doorposts will be a sign on the Israelite houses indicating to the "Destroyer" to pass over them during the Plague of the Firstborn (Exod. 12:13).

Korban Pesah: The Sacrifice That Shaped a Nation

And the house features similarly in the concluding verses of the chapter, which continue the instructions for this sacrifice:

וַיֹּאמֶר יהוה אֶל מֹשֶׁה וְאַהֲרֹן זֹאת חֻקַּת הַפָּסַח . . . בְּבַיִת אֶחָד יֵאָכֵל לֹא תוֹצִיא מִן הַבַּיִת מִן הַבָּשָׂר חוּצָה וְעֶצֶם לֹא תִשְׁבְּרוּ בוֹ . . .

And the LORD *said to Moses and Aaron, "This is the statute of the Passover offering . . . In one house shall it be eaten, you shall not take out any meat from the house, and no bone shall you break in it . . ."* (Exod. 12:43–46)

The term *bayit,* or house, has various meanings, but in Exodus 12 it refers to an inclusive structure or setting. This is the sense in which *bayit* is used in the Jacob narrative as well. Running away from his brother Esau, Jacob declares that if God takes care of him on his journey and returns him safely to his parents' home, the God of his fathers will become distinctly his own, and the stone that he has erected as a monument will be designated a house of God (Gen. 28:22). Jacob's vow is not to be understood as a negotiating ploy. What he means is that the mark of his success will be the uniqueness of his relationship with God. Although on a literal level Jacob refers to a physical structure, metaphorically the "house of God" that Jacob declares he will establish is a legacy of faith imparted to all his descendants.[80] By the end of his life, Jacob indeed manages to create a community in which every one of his sons is included: all receive blessings and all are deemed covenantal, in contrast to what happened in the families of Abraham and Isaac.

The book of Exodus begins with a reference to the houses, or households, of Jacob's children, suggesting that they came down to Egypt as a close-knit clan:

וְאֵלֶּה שְׁמוֹת בְּנֵי יִשְׂרָאֵל הַבָּאִים מִצְרָיְמָה אֵת יַעֲקֹב אִישׁ וּבֵיתוֹ בָּאוּ:

And these are the names of the sons of Israel who came to Egypt with Jacob, each man with his household they came. (Exod. 1:1)

---

[80] Jacob refers to his family as his *bayit* on several occasions; see Gen. 30:29–30 and 34:30.

A PASSOVER HAGGADAH: GO FORTH AND LEARN

But although Jacob and his family arrived in Egypt in cohesive units, slavery soon destroyed that sense of association, and as the Exodus narrative unfolds, the People of Israel seem hardly to identify with one another. In a key scene in Exodus 2, Moses intervenes to separate two scuffling Hebrews. The aggressor responds to Moses dismissively, asking who had given him the authority to judge them (2:14). The man's bitter words echo the brothers' response to Joseph's dreams and recall the deep rifts that divide family members in Genesis.[81]

Beit Yisrael—the house, or community, of Israel—is re-created in Egypt by way of the Passover sacrifice. The rebuilding begins with individual families; consequently one sacrifice does not suffice for the entire people, as with a typical *korban tzibbur* (communal offering); rather, every household must bring its own offering. Nonetheless, Moses demands of Pharaoh that the entire nation, including babies and old people, be freed to participate in the ritual (Exod. 10:8–11), and the verses of chapter 12 emphasize that the sacrifice must be offered by "the whole congregation of the community of Israel" (12:6; see also 12:47). The Passover sacrifice underscores the People of Israel's transition from a group of families to a national collective.

Curiously, the passage in chapter 12 describing the Passover sacrifice is preceded by the designation of the month in which the Exodus will occur as the "head month," or the first month of the year:

וַיֹּאמֶר יהוה אֶל מֹשֶׁה וְאֶל אַהֲרֹן בְּאֶרֶץ מִצְרַיִם לֵאמֹר: הַחֹדֶשׁ הַזֶּה לָכֶם רֹאשׁ חֳדָשִׁים רִאשׁוֹן הוּא לָכֶם לְחָדְשֵׁי הַשָּׁנָה:

And the Lord *said to Moses and to Aaron in the land of Egypt, saying, "This month is for you head of months, it is the first for you of the months of the year." (Exod. 12:1–2)*

In alluding to a new year and a new beginning, it is possible that the Torah intends to recall one of the opening lines of Exodus, which describes the onset of persecution and slavery as a new era, marked by the ascension of a new king:

---

[81] Compare Exod. 2:14 and Gen. 37:8.

Korban Pesah: The Sacrifice That Shaped a Nation

וַיָּקָם מֶלֶךְ חָדָשׁ עַל מִצְרָיִם אֲשֶׁר לֹא יָדַע אֶת יוֹסֵף:

And a new king arose over Egypt who knew not Joseph. (Exod. 1:8)

In contrast to the beginning of Exodus, which depicts the dissolution of households and the loss of names and identities, chapter 12 represents the dawning of a new age, characterized by the building of community, in which the Passover sacrifice plays an essential role.

Sacrificial Protection

Aside from being a great unifier, the Passover offering is, above all, a sacrifice, which is why the Torah emphasizes the roles of throwing the blood and of eating the animal, both central acts of sacrificial worship (Exod. 12:7–10).[82] A primary function of animal sacrifice in the Torah is to serve as a proxy for human beings—whether to stand in for the sinner who should have been punished or to mediate a dangerous encounter with God.[83] Nadab and Abihu die when they bring "strange fire" in the *Mishkan* (Lev. 10:1–2) because that fire is not sufficient to protect them at the moment of revelation. That is why, following their deaths, God specifically instructs Aaron to enter the "Holy," i.e., the inner sanctuary of the *Mishkan*, with a sacrifice on hand (Lev. 16:1–3).

Similarly, God's presence overwhelms the Egyptians and endangers them: when God finally appears in Egypt to carry out the Plague of the Firstborn, the Egyptian people themselves rise up to drive out the Israelites, for they cannot withstand God's force. But the blood of the *korban Pesah* protects the Israelites from the dangerous power and intensity of the Divine encounter

---

[82] In this case, the house functions as a sort of vertical altar, symbolized by the lintel and two doorposts.

[83] Jacob alludes to this sort of danger when he expresses relief after his encounter with the unknown "man" at the river Jabbok (Gen. 32:31). And it is fear of this danger that the People of Israel express when begging Moses to speak to them in place of God at Sinai (Deut. 5:21–23). Rashbam suggests that this was also the function of the sacrifices brought by Gideon and Manoah after their encounters with angels of God (Judg. 6:24 and 13:19); see his commentary on Exod. 4:25, *Va-tikhrot.*

A PASSOVER HAGGADAH: GO FORTH AND LEARN

and prevents the "Destroyer" sent by God from entering their homes.[84] This facet of the Passover sacrifice is reflected in the *Mekhilta*, which provides an alternative rendering of the term וּפָסַחְתִּי עֲלֵכֶם in Exodus 12:13; instead of the usual "and I will pass over you," the Midrash suggests reading "and I will protect you" on the basis of a verse from Isaiah:

> אין פסיחה אלא חייס, שנאמר: כְּצִפֳּרִים עָפוֹת כֵּן יָגֵן יהוה צְבָאוֹת עַל יְרוּשָׁלַָם גָּנוֹן וְהִצִּיל פָּסֹחַ וְהִמְלִיט.

> *Pesihah* means nothing other than protection, as it is said: *Like the birds that fly, even so will the* LORD *of Hosts shield Jerusalem, shielding and saving, protecting and rescuing* (Isa. 31:5). (Mekhilta de-Rabbi Yishmael, Bo 7 and 11)

Comparison with the pivotal sacrifice in Genesis—the ram that Abraham offers on the altar he had prepared for Isaac—highlights this protective aspect of the *korban Pesah*. Both the ram and the *korban Pesah* serve as proxies for those who should have been sacrificed: Isaac and the firstborn of the Israelites. Genesis emphasizes that Abraham offered the ram *tahat beno*, in lieu of his son (Gen. 22:13). Similarly, the blood of the Passover offering displayed on the doorposts is not merely a flag indicating that the house is an Israelite one: it is a sacrifice that is offered in place of the person who should have been taken. But the ram and the *korban Pesah* also mediate the linking of generations: the ram allows Abraham to connect with Isaac and pass God's covenant to him, and, as we will see, the Passover sacrifice similarly underscores the bond between parents and children.

Linking of Generations

As noted, Exodus 12 emphasizes the role of the Passover sacrifice in protecting the Israelite homes from the destructive forces let loose upon Egypt during the Plague of the Firstborn. Ostensibly, the blood that the Israelites smeared on their lintels and doorposts as a sign to God to pass over their

---

[84] For analysis of the Rabbinic texts that refer to the sacrifice's function as a "guardian" or protector of Israel, see Aharon Shemesh, "*Pesah zeh 'al shum mah?,*" *AJS Review* 21, no. 2 (1996): 1–17.

houses served to protect those individuals who were in immediate danger: their own firstborn children. The Torah celebrates this particular deliverance with the commandment to consecrate every firstborn human and animal to God (Exod. 13:1–2). However, the language of Exodus 12 seems to indicate that it was actually the homes that were in peril and that the blood of the sacrifice was intended primarily to safeguard them:

וְהָיָה כִּי יֹאמְרוּ אֲלֵיכֶם בְּנֵיכֶם מָה הָעֲבֹדָה הַזֹּאת לָכֶם: וַאֲמַרְתֶּם זֶבַח פֶּסַח הוּא לַיהוה אֲשֶׁר פָּסַח עַל בָּתֵּי בְנֵי יִשְׂרָאֵל בְּמִצְרַיִם בְּנָגְפּוֹ אֶת מִצְרַיִם וְאֶת בָּתֵּינוּ הִצִּיל ...

And so should your sons ask you, "What is this service to you?" you shall say, "A Passover sacrifice to the LORD, who passed over the houses of the Israelites in Egypt when He scourged Egypt and our houses[85] He rescued" . . . (Exod. 12:26–27)

As argued earlier, the "homes" in this narrative are primarily symbolic edifices that represent the family. But why this emphasis?

The opening lines of Exodus imply that the beginning of the persecution in Egypt coincided with the death of Joseph and his generation (1:6–14). If the Egyptian enslavement is calculated from this juncture, then Moses and most of the adults whom he led out of Egypt were third-generation slaves.[86] God's promise to Abraham at the Covenant between the Pieces (Gen. 15:13–16) was that the fourth generation would return to the Land; thus, the fulfillment of God's covenant hinges on the children of those who experienced the Exodus.[87] At stake, then, during the Plague of the First-born are not only individual children but the inheritors of the covenant: the next generation. The collective as well as the personal fate of the people who leave Egypt is wholly dependent on their descendants. This may explain the Torah's focus on educational interaction between parent and child in

---

[85] Translation has been emended; the original reads "households."
[86] Moses was the son of Amram; Amram was the son of Kehat; Kehat was the son of Levi, brother of Joseph.
[87] For an extensive analysis of the terms of God's covenant with Abraham and his descendants, see essay 2.

A PASSOVER HAGGADAH: GO FORTH AND LEARN

the context of the Passover offering, which the Haggadah adopts in its Four Children midrash.[88]

The bond of dependency between parents and children, a central theme in the Exodus narrative, is introduced prior to the Passover sacrifice by the enigmatic anecdote concerning a near-death encounter as Moses makes his way back to Egypt after his sojourn in Midian:

וַיְהִי בַדֶּרֶךְ בַּמָּלוֹן וַיִּפְגְּשֵׁהוּ יהוה וַיְבַקֵּשׁ הֲמִיתוֹ: וַתִּקַּח צִפֹּרָה צֹר וַתִּכְרֹת אֶת עָרְלַת בְּנָהּ וַתַּגַּע לְרַגְלָיו וַתֹּאמֶר כִּי חֲתַן דָּמִים אַתָּה לִי: וַיִּרֶף מִמֶּנּוּ אָז אָמְרָה חֲתַן דָּמִים לַמּוּלֹת:

And it happened on the way at the night camp that the LORD *encountered him and sought to put him to death. And Zipporah took a flint and cut off her son's foreskin and touched it to his feet, and she said, "Yes, a bridegroom of blood you are to me." And He let him go. Then did she say, "A bridegroom of blood by the circumcising."* (Exod. 4:24–26)

The precise nature of the event is unclear, and scholars have long debated the details; however, the simplest understanding is that God sought to kill Moses, who was saved by Zipporah's hasty circumcision of their son.[89] Read in this manner, the *hatan damim* (bridegroom of blood) story foreshadows the Plague of the Firstborn. In the first episode, Moses the parent is saved by virtue of his child's blood, which has a sacrificial cast. The blood of circumcision is "touched to his feet," and thus the danger is averted. In the second episode, the firstborn children and their entire households are saved by way of the

---

[88] In its depictions of three of the four children, the Haggadah quotes verses in which the Israelites are commanded to instruct their children about the Passover sacrifice; see Exod. 12:26–27, 13:8, 13:14.

[89] This is the explanation of Rashi and Rashbam on Exod. 4:24–25; for alternative explanations, see Rabbenu Hananel and Ibn Ezra. This reading is supported by the verses that precede the episode, in which God instructs Moses that he is to warn Pharaoh, well in advance, of the impending death of his own son (Exod. 4:22–23). The inclusion of such a warning at this stage of the narrative is puzzling: God has already conveyed the content of the message that Moses is to bring to Pharaoh, and the Plague of the Firstborn is still far in the future. It seems that the threat was intended not only for Pharaoh, but also for Moses, who was reluctant to carry out his mission—to remind him that one who defies God will pay the price.

KORBAN PESAH: THE SACRIFICE THAT SHAPED A NATION

sacrificial blood. The blood of the Passover offering is "touched" to the lintel and doorposts, and thus destruction is avoided.[90] In both cases, blood is taken in lieu of life; and in both cases, the Torah emphasizes the linking of the two generations.

This linking of generations is a theme central to the Passover seder, in terms of its emphasis both on intergenerational dialogue and engagement and on the obligation to imagine oneself personally experiencing the Exodus, as though one's own identity were bound with that of earlier generations. This lesson corresponds to the premise of God's covenant with the People of Israel, as conveyed to the forefathers and to Moses: that no single generation can both receive God's promise and witness its fulfillment.[91] In the biblical narrative, the Passover sacrifice serves to reinforce this message of intergenerational dependence.

Conclusion

Ultimately, the collective experience of God is what made the People of Israel a nation. Over the course of the book of Exodus, their identity is bound up in moments of joint revelation: the Exodus itself, the Splitting of the Sea, the manna, Sinai, and the *Mishkan*. The Passover sacrifice marked, and enabled, the first collective encounter with the Divine, and thus, the birth of a nation. In a deep sense, then, the Passover seder is a reliving of the *korban Pesah* experience. It brings together families and households, encouraging participants to reconsider what it means to be a community through a series of rituals that foster kinship. In the context of a communal meal, we pay tribute to God and celebrate our ancient and ongoing redemption.

---

[90] For additional analyses of the connections between these passages, see Yoel Bin-Nun, "*Hametz* and *Matzah* on the Festivals of Pesah, Shavuot, and in the Bread Offerings" (in Hebrew), *Megadim* 13 (Adar 5751): 40–41; and Zeev Weitman, "My Firstborn Son Israel" (in Hebrew), *Megadim* 48 (Iyar 5768): 37–46.

[91] For further development of this theme, see essay 2.

A PASSOVER HAGGADAH: GO FORTH AND LEARN

6
Lot and the Destruction of Sodom: A Prefiguring of Exodus

The destruction of Sodom, as recounted in Genesis 18 and 19, is an important anecdote in the narrative of Abraham's developing relationship with God; but on its own, the tale appears to have minimal bearing on later events in the Torah. Yet the medieval commentator Rashi offers a famously anachronistic interpretation of the episode, which suggests that Sodom's destruction may be more significant than it seems. Noting the unusual food that Abraham's nephew Lot prepares for the two heavenly messengers who arrive at his home—namely, matzah—Rashi comments: "It was Passover."[92] On the surface, Rashi's remark is nonsensical: this story is set hundreds of years before the Exodus when the holiday of Passover did not exist! But Rashi and the midrashim that he drew upon point us in an important direction: in considering this seemingly absurd claim, it is worth noting that the story of Sodom bears many linguistic and thematic similarities to the Exodus narrative.[93] The various textual parallels suggest that the destruction of Sodom was meant to prefigure the devastation of Egypt and that Lot in some sense represents the split character of the Israelites who were redeemed. A close reading of the Genesis passage will shed light on the Exodus story and on the messages of the Haggadah.

Sodom and Egypt

Introducing Sodom for the first time through the eyes of Lot, the Torah explicitly compares the city to the land of Egypt. Following the famine that sends Abraham and his family south in search of sustenance and their

---

[92] Rashi on Gen. 19:3, *U-Matzot afah va-yokhelu.*

[93] Some of these parallels have been noted by others; see Gershon Hepner, "Lot's Exodus from Sodom Foreshadows That of the Israelites from Egypt and the Passover Laws," *Zeitschrift für Altorientalische und Biblische Rechtsgeschichte* 9 (2003): 129–64; and Jeffrey C. Geoghegan, "The Abrahamic Passover," *Le-David Maskil* , ed. R. E. Friedman and W. H. C. Propp, 47–62 (Winona Lake, In.: Eisenbrauns, 2004).

ensuing encounter with Pharaoh, they return to Canaan in Genesis 13 with newly acquired wealth, only to discover in short order that they can no longer live together.[94] Heeding his uncle's suggestion that they part ways amicably, Lot searches for a new home and is drawn to the cities of the Jordan River valley, presumably because their fertility reminds him of the lush and fruitful land he recently departed:

וַיִּשָּׂא לוֹט אֶת עֵינָיו וַיַּרְא אֶת כָּל כִּכַּר הַיַּרְדֵּן כִּי כֻלָּהּ מַשְׁקֶה לִפְנֵי שַׁחֵת יהוה אֶת סְדֹם וְאֶת עֲמֹרָה כְּגַן יהוה כְּאֶרֶץ מִצְרַיִם בֹּאֲכָה צֹעַר:

And Lot raised his eyes and saw the whole plain of the Jordan, saw that all of it was well watered, before the LORD's destruction of Sodom and Gomorrah, like the garden of the LORD, like the land of Egypt, till you come to Zoar. (Gen. 13:10)

It is not clear whether Lot, following his gaze, is aware of Sodom's wicked ways when he chooses to live there, although the Torah suggests that this was common knowledge (Gen. 13:13). Regardless, the Torah emphasizes that in moving to Sodom, Lot journeyed eastward, which in light of Adam's banishment from Eden, also to the east, signifies exile.[95] Yet, despite these clearly negative connotations, Lot is actually taking Abraham's lead in choosing Sodom, a fertile but evil place. Although Abraham had a reason for descending to Egypt, namely the famine, he too chose to bring his family to a land of immorality, and profited from this decision. Here and elsewhere, Lot serves as a foil for Abraham, a point to which we will return.

A less explicit but no less striking comparison between Sodom and Egypt is made by the Torah in its use of parallel language and imagery to describe God's attention to both places. In Genesis 18, following the arrival of three messengers to inform Abraham and Sarah of Isaac's impending conception, God reveals to Abraham the decision to destroy Sodom, whose cries have reached the heavens:

---

[94] The Torah indicates the growing distance between Abraham and his nephew Lot in the very description of their return from Egypt: in contrast to Gen. 12:4, which singles out Lot as the primary relative accompanying Abraham to Canaan (despite listing him after Sarah in 12:5), in 13:1, Lot merits mention only after the material possessions!

[95] Compare Gen. 13:11 with 3:24. For further discussion, see Steinmetz, *From Father to Son.*

A PASSOVER HAGGADAH: GO FORTH AND LEARN

וַיֹּאמֶר יהוה זַעֲקַת סְדֹם וַעֲמֹרָה כִּי רָבָּה וְחַטָּאתָם כִּי כָבְדָה מְאֹד: אֵרְדָה נָּא
וְאֶרְאֶה הַכְּצַעֲקָתָהּ הַבָּאָה אֵלַי עָשׂוּ כָּלָה וְאִם לֹא אֵדָעָה:

And the LORD *said, "The outcry of Sodom and Gomorrah, how great! Their offense is very grave. Let Me go down and see whether as the outcry that has come to Me they have dealt destruction, and if not, I shall know." (Gen. 18:20–21)*

What God perceives to be emerging from Sodom is strikingly similar to what God later experiences as emerging from Egypt. Both places reverberate with the cries of the oppressed. At the beginning of Exodus, it is the Israelites' cries that compel God to see, to know, and to begin the process of redemption:

... וַיֵּאָנְחוּ בְנֵי יִשְׂרָאֵל מִן הָעֲבֹדָה וַיִּזְעָקוּ וַתַּעַל שַׁוְעָתָם אֶל הָאֱלֹהִים מִן הָעֲבֹדָה:
וַיִּשְׁמַע אֱלֹהִים אֶת נַאֲקָתָם וַיִּזְכֹּר אֱלֹהִים אֶת בְּרִיתוֹ אֶת אַבְרָהָם אֶת יִצְחָק וְאֶת
יַעֲקֹב: וַיַּרְא אֱלֹהִים אֶת בְּנֵי יִשְׂרָאֵל וַיֵּדַע אֱלֹהִים:

... and the Israelites groaned from the bondage and cried out, and their plea from the bondage went up to God. And God heard their moaning, and God remembered His covenant with Abraham, with Isaac, and with Jacob. And God saw the Israelites, and God knew. (Exod. 2:23–25)

Similarly, God's determination to "go down" and verify the meaning of the cries that have "come to" God from Sodom parallels the later assertion that God will "go down" to save the People of Israel, whose cries have "come to" God from Egypt:

וָאֵרֵד לְהַצִּילוֹ מִיַּד מִצְרַיִם וּלְהַעֲלֹתוֹ מִן הָאָרֶץ הַהִוא אֶל אֶרֶץ טוֹבָה וּרְחָבָה אֶל
אֶרֶץ זָבַת חָלָב וּדְבָשׁ ... וְעַתָּה הִנֵּה צַעֲקַת בְּנֵי יִשְׂרָאֵל בָּאָה אֵלַי וְגַם רָאִיתִי אֶת
הַלַּחַץ אֲשֶׁר מִצְרַיִם לֹחֲצִים אֹתָם:

And I have come down to rescue it from the hand of Egypt and to bring it up from that land to a goodly and spacious land, to a land flowing with milk and honey ... And now, look, the outcry of the Israelites has come to me and I have also seen the oppression with which the Egyptians oppress them. (Exod. 3:8–9)

Even the two messengers whom God sends to save Lot and destroy Sodom recur in Egypt in the persons of Moses and Aaron.[96]

The mores of Egypt are also presented by the Torah as implicitly, if not explicitly, comparable to the notoriously evil culture of Sodom. The beginning of Exodus depicts the new Pharaoh instilling fear of the outsider amid his people, convincing them that the descendants of Jacob are likely to join with their enemies and rise against them (1:9–10). Sodom too is a place that hates outsiders: the residents express their resentment of Lot as a relative newcomer and intend to abuse his visitors (Gen. 19:4–5,9).[97] The opening chapters of Exodus emphasize the violence of the Egyptians, who abuse their slaves with crushing labor (1:11–14), kill babies by flinging them into the river (1:16,22), and strike other human beings (2:11). The people of Sodom are similarly characterized by their aggressive and sadistic behavior: they demand that Lot turn over his guests so that they might "know" them (Gen. 19:5), an unequivocal allusion to sexual abuse;[98] they threaten to harm Lot himself (19:9); and they push against Lot, attempting to break down the door of his home (19:9). Finally, the Torah characterizes Pharaoh as one "who did not know Joseph," implying willful lack of recognition and base ingratitude for the person who had been the savior of his nation (Exod. 1:8). In rejecting Lot, the people of Sodom display a similar trait: Lot was the one responsible for the continued existence of their city, as Abraham had battled the four kings and liberated Sodom with the single-minded intention of saving his nephew (Gen. 14:13–16).[99]

---

[96] Although Aaron's inclusion in the mission to Pharaoh as seems initially to be an afterthought, merely to assuage Moses' concerns, the Torah later presents him as an equal partner; see Exod. 6:26.

[97] The xenophobia of Sodom's citizens becomes a focus of later midrashim; see B.T. Sanh. 109a–b, Gen. Rabbah 49:6 and 51:5 *Pirkei de-Rabbi Eliezer* 25 and others.

[98] See Gen. Rabbah 50:5; and Rashi on Gen. 19:5, *Ve-nede'ah otam*. Sexual abuse and sexual perversion are also traits that the Torah associates with Egypt, though not explicitly in the Exodus context; see Lev. 18, which begins its list of forbidden sexual behaviors with the admonition not to do "like the deeds of the land of Egypt in which you dwelt" (Lev. 18:3).

[99] The Midrash suggests that Abraham's battle to save Lot, which he fought in the middle of the night (Gen. 14:15), was the impetus for God's battle on behalf of the Israelites in Egypt, which also occurred in the middle of the night (Exod. 11:4; 12:29); see Gen. Rabbah 43:3.

A PASSOVER HAGGADAH: GO FORTH AND LEARN

Lot and the People of Israel

At the beginning of Genesis 19, Lot is represented as being like Abraham, seeking guests in a place where no one else welcomes strangers. The two messengers of God arrive at Sodom in the evening, and Lot, who is sitting at the gate, rises to greet them. He invites them to his home, offering them a place to sleep and to wash their feet. The messengers decline the invitation, claiming they would rather spend the night in the street; however, Lot insists, and they agree to go with him. Upon arriving at his home, Lot prepares a meal and bakes them matzot (Gen. 19:3).

The Torah's description of Lot's hospitality is clearly modeled on the account of Abraham's interactions with the same guests one chapter earlier.[100] Nonetheless, as compared to Abraham's generosity and ceaseless activity, Lot's hospitality falls short. Abraham ran to greet the strangers, whereas Lot merely stands. Abraham fed the messengers a complete meal, whereas Lot offers a paltry selection. Abraham rallied both Sarah and the *na'ar* (servant) to help him, including the members of his household in his acts of kindness, whereas Lot operates alone, suggesting that the positive traits he possesses fail to influence those around him. (In fact, the name "Lot" probably means "hiddenness" or "isolation.")[101] It is significant that Lot offers matzah to his guests instead of a meal because it represents his tenuous link with the messengers of God, in contrast to Abraham's deep connection. The messengers don't initially want to enter Lot's home, and when they finally agree to come, they eat with Lot, but only matzah, not bread. In the Torah, the eating of bread often has a covenantal cast, reflecting identification and intimacy; in contrast, Lot's matzah represents a half-baked relationship, an incomplete bond.[102]

---

[100] The Midrash makes this point explicitly; see Tanhuma Yashan, Va-yera 16 and 21, and Tanhuma, Va-yera 11.

[101] See 1 Sam. 21:10, "The priest said, 'There is the sword of Goliath the Philistine whom you slew in the valley of Elah; it is over there, wrapped in a cloth [*lutah ba-simlah*], behind the ephod'"; and 1 Kings 19:13, "When Elijah heard it, he wrapped his mantle about his face [*va-yalet panav be-adarto*]."

[102] This is true of Moses' relationship with his father-in-law, Jethro, and in the negative, of Joseph's relationship with the Egyptians; see essay 3 for more details.

Although Lot does exhibit Abraham-like behavior, he also chooses to ally himself with the people of Sodom, and even when confronting them, his behavior betrays Sodom-like characteristics. Lot invites the messengers to spend the night in his home, but, as noted, before they go to sleep, the townspeople surround the house and demand that Lot hand over his guests. (Earlier, in response to Abraham's pleas to spare the righteous, God agreed to verify the prevalence of reported abuses in Sodom; therefore the Torah emphasizes that the entire population participated in the siege on Lot's home, from young to old.) Lot goes out to reason with the people and suggests that in lieu of his guests, they take his two virgin daughters. The people of the town are not placated and try to break down the door, whereupon the messengers draw Lot into the house and strike the people outside with blindness. Although danger is averted, the reader is left with a sense of deep unease regarding Lot's behavior: how could he have offered his daughters to the mob? Lot's sense of responsibility toward his guests was certainly commendable, but his readiness to hand over his daughters to be abused indicates that he was not much better than the Sodomites himself. Lot is a character caught between the two halves of his identity, and in this respect, he is a model for the Israelites in Egypt.

On the cusp of the Exodus and through their early years in the desert, the People of Israel seem torn between their role as God's chosen and their identity as former slaves. When Moses and Aaron first arrive with their message of redemption, the people are quick to express their belief in God and to celebrate their election (Exod. 4:29–31). But these same people identify deeply with Egyptian values and mores,[103] as demonstrated by the violent *ish Ivri* (Hebrew man), whose fight with a fellow Hebrew Moses attempts to interrupt (Exod. 2:13–14). The Torah presents this scene of aggression between two Israelites immediately following one in which an Egyptian strikes

---

[103] The Midrash makes this point in a homily on Deut. 4:34, which adopts the phrase "a nation from within a nation" to describe the manner in which God redeems Israel from Egypt. According to the Midrash, the Torah refers to both Israel and Egypt with the same word—*goy* (nation)—to emphasize their essential equivalence at the moment of the Exodus: "These were uncircumcised and those were uncircumcised; these grew their hair in gentile fashion and those grew their hair in gentile fashion; these wore mixed fibers and those wore mixed fibers…" See Lev. Rabbah 23:2.

an Israelite (2:11–12), implicitly comparing the behavior of the Hebrew man with that of the Egyptian. The depiction of the slave taking up the abusive role of his master suggests that his identification with his oppressor is stronger than his identification with his own people. Strikingly, this Egyptianized Hebrew accuses Moses of arrogance in language that echoes the Sodomites' response to Lot:

וַיֹּאמֶר מִי שָׂמְךָ לְאִישׁ שַׂר וְשֹׁפֵט עָלֵינוּ הַלְהָרְגֵנִי אַתָּה אֹמֵר כַּאֲשֶׁר הָרַגְתָּ אֶת הַמִּצְרִי...

And he said, "Who set you as a man prince and judge over us? Is it to kill me that you mean as you killed the Egyptian?" . . . (Exod. 2:14)

וַיֹּאמְרוּ הָאֶחָד בָּא לָגוּר וַיִּשְׁפֹּט שָׁפוֹט עַתָּה נָרַע לְךָ מֵהֶם...

And they said, "This person came as a sojourner and he sets himself up to judge! Now we'll do more harm to you than to them" . . . (Gen. 19:9)

We have noted the resemblance between the ethos of Egypt and that of Sodom; thus the placing of Sodomite words in the mouth of a Hebrew slave is a powerful representation of the extent to which the Israelites identify with the dominant culture, albeit the culture of their oppressors.[104]

This identification is not easily shed, and the desire to return to Egypt becomes a refrain that repeats itself over the course of the Israelites' wanderings. Lot is admonished not to look back toward Sodom (Gen. 19:17), and his wife is famously punished for doing just that (19:26). But the Israelites figuratively "look back" toward Egypt constantly, expressing a misplaced longing for their lives there and a paradoxical attachment to the place of their oppression and suffering (Exod. 14:11–12, 16:3; Num. 11:4–6, 14:2–4, 20:3–5).

---

[104] For further discussion of this incident, see essay 3.

The Destruction of Sodom and the Destruction of Egypt

Lot's rescue and the subsequent destruction of Sodom also bear distinct similarities to events in the book of Exodus. When the people of Sodom demand that Lot hand over his visitors and begin to threaten him, Lot takes refuge in his house in much in the same way that the Israelites are protected by their homes during the Plague of the Firstborn. The verses in Genesis 19 focus particularly on the opening and closing of the door and on the attempts and failure of the Sodomites to break down the door and reach the entrance; in the Exodus story, the doorframe is smeared with blood and the people are instructed not to go through the entrance, over which the "Destroyer" will pass. The Sodomites outside Lot's house are smitten with blindness, then presumably killed in the city's destruction—much as the Egyptians are stricken with the penultimate plague, darkness, and then by the Plague of the First-born (which visits death and destruction upon the Egyptians, even if not all are killed).

The messengers instruct Lot to gather his family members and take them out of the city because they are about to obliterate the place. The root ש-ח-ת (to destroy), which has already been used several times in chapter 18 in connection with God's plan for Sodom,[105] recurs an additional three times in chapter 19:

וַיֹּאמְרוּ הָאֲנָשִׁים אֶל לוֹט עֹד מִי לְךָ פֹה חָתָן וּבָנֶיךָ וּבְנֹתֶיךָ וְכֹל אֲשֶׁר לְךָ בָּעִיר הוֹצֵא מִן הַמָּקוֹם: כִּי מַשְׁחִתִים אֲנַחְנוּ אֶת הַמָּקוֹם הַזֶּה כִּי גָדְלָה צַעֲקָתָם אֶת פְּנֵי יהוה וַיְשַׁלְּחֵנוּ יהוה לְשַׁחֲתָהּ: וַיֵּצֵא לוֹט וַיְדַבֵּר אֶל חֲתָנָיו לֹקְחֵי בְנֹתָיו וַיֹּאמֶר קוּמוּ צְּאוּ מִן הַמָּקוֹם הַזֶּה כִּי מַשְׁחִית יהוה אֶת הָעִיר וַיְהִי כִמְצַחֵק בְּעֵינֵי חֲתָנָיו:

And the men said to Lot, "Whom do you still have here? Your sons and your daughters and whomever you have in the city take out of the place. For we are about to destroy this place because the outcry against them has grown great before the LORD and the LORD has sent us to destroy it." And Lot went out and spoke to his sons-in-law who had

---

[105] Gen. 18:28,31,32 as well as 19:29.

A PASSOVER HAGGADAH: GO FORTH AND LEARN

married his daughters and he said, "Rise, get out of this place, for the
LORD *is about to destroy the city." And he seemed to his sons-in-law*
to be joking. (Gen. 19:12–14)

The destruction God wreaks upon Sodom is echoed in the Torah's description of the "Destroyer" who will smite the Egyptian firstborn:

וְהָיָה הַדָּם לָכֶם לְאֹת עַל הַבָּתִּים אֲשֶׁר אַתֶּם שָׁם וְרָאִיתִי אֶת הַדָּם וּפָסַחְתִּי עֲלֵכֶם
וְלֹא יִהְיֶה בָכֶם נֶגֶף לְמַשְׁחִית בְּהַכֹּתִי בְּאֶרֶץ מִצְרָיִם:

And the blood will be a sign for you upon the houses in which you are,
and I will see the blood and I will pass over you, and no scourge shall
become a Destroyer amongst you when I strike in the land of Egypt.
(Exod. 12:13)[106]

With the breaking of dawn, the messengers urge Lot to leave the city lest he
be caught in the impending devastation, but Lot tarries until they forcibly
remove him:

וַיִּתְמַהְמָהּ וַיַּחֲזִקוּ הָאֲנָשִׁים בְּיָדוֹ וּבְיַד אִשְׁתּוֹ וּבְיַד שְׁתֵּי בְנֹתָיו בְּחֶמְלַת יהוה עָלָיו
וַיֹּצִאֻהוּ וַיַּנִּחֻהוּ מִחוּץ לָעִיר:

And he lingered, and the men seized his hand and his wife's hand and
the hands of his two daughters in the LORD's *compassion for him and*
led him outside the city. (Gen. 19:16)

Both the term for the messengers' coercion (*va-yahaziku*) and the term for
Lot's lingering (*va-yitmahmah*) reverberate in the Exodus story. As the Plague
of the Firstborn rages, the Egyptians push the Israelites out in a similarly
forcible manner:

וַתֶּחֱזַק מִצְרַיִם עַל הָעָם לְמַהֵר לְשַׁלְּחָם מִן הָאֶרֶץ כִּי אָמְרוּ כֻּלָּנוּ מֵתִים:

And Egypt bore down (va-tehezak) on the people to hurry to send them
off from the land, for they said, "We are all dead men." (Exod. 12:33)

---

[106] See also Exod. 12:23.

And in describing the hasty departure that resulted in the baking of unleavened bread, the Torah portrays the Israelites as unable to linger the way Lot did—suggesting that if it had been possible, they would have done so:

וַיֹּאפוּ אֶת הַבָּצֵק אֲשֶׁר הוֹצִיאוּ מִמִּצְרַיִם עֻגֹת מַצּוֹת כִּי לֹא חָמֵץ כִּי גֹרְשׁוּ מִמִּצְרַיִם
וְלֹא יָכְלוּ לְהִתְמַהְמֵהַּ וְגַם צֵדָה לֹא עָשׂוּ לָהֶם:

And they baked the dough that they had brought out of Egypt in rounds of flatbread, for it had not leavened, since they had been driven out of Egypt and could not tarry (le-hitmahmeha), *and provisions, too, they could not make for themselves.* (Exod. 12:39)

Both Lot and the people who left Egypt are instructed to go directly to a specific place, and both fail to attain that objective. The messengers deposit Lot outside the city and order him to head for the mountains, but Lot beseeches them to allow him a different destination, claiming that he is afraid of evil and death overtaking him in the highlands. The messengers agree, and Lot takes refuge in the town of Zoar (Gen. 19:17–22).[107] In the Exodus story too the people's initial destination is modified; and the Torah cites God's concern that a violent encounter with the nations living in Canaan so soon after leaving slavery would scare the people into returning to Egypt (Exod. 13:17).

The very manner in which God destroys Sodom prefigures the destruction of Egypt: fire and brimstone rain down upon the city and level it, much as the hail of the seventh plague, which is laced with fire, rains down upon the fields of Egypt and devastates them:

וַיהוה הִמְטִיר עַל סְדֹם וְעַל עֲמֹרָה גׇּפְרִית וָאֵשׁ מֵאֵת יהוה מִן הַשָּׁמָיִם: וַיַּהֲפֹךְ אֶת
הֶעָרִים הָאֵל וְאֵת כָּל הַכִּכָּר וְאֵת כָּל יֹשְׁבֵי הֶעָרִים וְצֶמַח הָאֲדָמָה:

---

[107] Following the destruction of Sodom, Lot is afraid to remain in Zoar, and he does ultimately head for the hills, where he and his daughters take refuge in a cave; but it is not clear that these are the same mountains the angels originally intended.

A Passover Haggadah: Go Forth and Learn

And the LORD rained upon Sodom and Gomorrah brimstone and fire from the LORD from the heavens. And He overthrew all those cities and all the plain and all the inhabitants of the cities and what grew in the soil. (Gen. 19:24–25)

וַיֵּט מֹשֶׁה אֶת מַטֵּהוּ עַל הַשָּׁמַיִם וַיהוה נָתַן קֹלֹת וּבָרָד וַתִּהֲלַךְ אֵשׁ אָרְצָה וַיַּמְטֵר יהוה בָּרָד עַל אֶרֶץ מִצְרָיִם: וַיְהִי בָרָד וְאֵשׁ מִתְלַקַּחַת בְּתוֹךְ הַבָּרָד כָּבֵד מְאֹד אֲשֶׁר לֹא הָיָה כָמֹהוּ בְּכָל אֶרֶץ מִצְרַיִם מֵאָז הָיְתָה לְגוֹי: וַיַּךְ הַבָּרָד בְּכָל אֶרֶץ מִצְרַיִם אֵת כָּל אֲשֶׁר בַּשָּׂדֶה מֵאָדָם וְעַד בְּהֵמָה וְאֵת כָּל עֵשֶׂב הַשָּׂדֶה הִכָּה הַבָּרָד וְאֶת כָּל עֵץ הַשָּׂדֶה שִׁבֵּר:

And Moses stretched out his staff over the heavens, and the LORD let loose thunder and hail, and fire went along earthward, and the LORD rained hail on the land of Egypt. And there was very heavy hail, with fire flashing in the midst of the hail, the like of which there had not been in all the land of Egypt from the time it became a nation. And the hail struck through all the land of Egypt whatever was in the field, from man to beast, and all the grass of the field did the hail strike, and every tree of the field did it smash. (Exod. 9:23–25)

In both cases, the scorching deluge destroys everything in its path: land, humans and animals, and growing things.

The destruction of Sodom is bookended by descriptions of the messengers and of Abraham himself observing the city from afar. Before they embark on their mission, the messengers gaze upon Sodom as they take leave of Abraham (Gen. 18:16). And after they have rescued Lot and God has released the fire and brimstone that obliterate the city, Abraham himself gazes upon Sodom (19:28). In both cases, the term used is (va-yashkef) (and he looked out), a relatively uncommon word that resonates in the Exodus story as well. There too the gazing is paired with destruction:[108] God "looks upon" (va-yashkef) the Egyptians as they rush after the Israelites into the split sea, moments before the waters close over them (Exod. 14:24). However, an altered form

---

[108] The root שׁ-ק-ף seems most often to assume a negative connotation: see Gen. 26:8 and Judg. 5:28. Deut. 26:15 is, of course, an exception.

of the word also appears in the Exodus context with a nearly opposite connotation: (*mashkof*) is the lintel upon which the Israelites are instructed to smear the blood of the paschal sacrifice, to protect themselves from the "Destroyer" (12:7 and 12:22).

At this point in the Sodom narrative, God clarifies that Lot was saved primarily because of his association with Abraham:

וַיְהִי בְּשַׁחֵת אֱלֹהִים אֶת עָרֵי הַכִּכָּר וַיִּזְכֹּר אֱלֹהִים אֶת אַבְרָהָם וַיְשַׁלַּח אֶת לוֹט מִתּוֹךְ הַהֲפֵכָה בַּהֲפֹךְ אֶת הֶעָרִים אֲשֶׁר יָשַׁב בָּהֵן לוֹט:

And it happened when God destroyed the cities of the plain that God remembered Abraham and sent Lot out of the upheaval as the cities in which Lot dwelled were overthrown. (Gen. 19:29)

God's decision to save Lot after he remembers Abraham recalls God's decision to redeem the People of Israel upon remembering the covenant forged with their forefathers:

וַיִּשְׁמַע אֱלֹהִים אֶת נַאֲקָתָם וַיִּזְכֹּר אֱלֹהִים אֶת בְּרִיתוֹ אֶת אַבְרָהָם אֶת יִצְחָק וְאֶת יַעֲקֹב: וַיַּרְא אֱלֹהִים אֶת בְּנֵי יִשְׂרָאֵל וַיֵּדַע אֱלֹהִים:

And God heard their moaning, and God remembered His covenant with Abraham, with Isaac, and with Jacob. And God saw the Israelites, and God knew. (Exod. 2:24–25)

Conclusion

As demonstrated, the manner in which the Sodom narrative prefigures the redemption from Egypt lends an additional perspective to the Torah's account of the Exodus. In particular, Lot's conflicted character, torn between his affinity for Abraham and his alliance with the Sodomites, worthy of salvation but unable to free himself completely from the pull of his adopted home, offers an enlightening glimpse into the soul of the Israelites. They too are caught between their covenantal heritage and an ironic but ingrained identification with their oppressors; and they too seem barely to deserve salvation. Nonetheless, God does redeem the Israelites, much as God saved Lot, if only to fulfill the promise made (in both cases) to Abraham.

Lot, however, is not the only paradigm that the Torah conscripts to depict the People of Israel on the eve of redemption, and Lot's story is instructive for the ways in which it contrasts with the Exodus narrative as well as for its parallels. Lot is a character who is exiled and does not return; he survives the destruction of Sodom only to be banished to a cave in the mountains where he is raped by his daughters and never heard from again. In contrast, the generation that experiences the Exodus enters into a covenantal relationship with God, which entails a promise that although they will die in the desert, their children will reach the Land. Lot is alienated from his surroundings and fails to establish a legacy: he has no influence on his neighbors or his sons-in-law; his wife turns back toward Sodom, demonstrating that her strongest loyalties lie beyond her marriage; and his relationship with his remaining daughter takes a perverse turn. In distinction, the People of Israel forge community around their homes, thereby underscoring the family heritage and generational linkages that characterize the covenantal promise. Although there is much similarity between Lot and the Israelites, what ultimately distinguishes the People of Israel is their stake in the divine covenant. Abraham's personal merit suffices to save Lot from the destruction of Sodom, but nothing more; however, God's covenant with the descendants of Abraham not only provides for their redemption from Egypt but also endows them with post-salvation destiny and purpose.

The shameful fact that the Israelites came to identify with the evil Egyptian environment in which they were enslaved—that they had, in the words of the Zohar, "reached the forty-ninth rung of impurity"[109]—accentuates the detrimental effects of slavery that the Haggadah details, underscoring our debt of gratitude to God for redeeming our ancestors:

---

[109] *Zohar Hadash*, Yitro 31a.

עֲבָדִים הָיִינוּ לְפַרְעֹה בְּמִצְרָיִם, וַיּוֹצִיאֵנוּ יהוה אֱלֹהֵינוּ מִשָּׁם בְּיָד חֲזָקָה וּבִזְרֹעַ נְטוּיָה. וְאִלּוּ לֹא הוֹצִיא הַקָּדוֹשׁ בָּרוּךְ הוּא אֶת אֲבוֹתֵינוּ מִמִּצְרָיִם, הֲרֵי אָנוּ וּבָנֵינוּ וּבְנֵי בָנֵינוּ מְשֻׁעְבָּדִים הָיִינוּ לְפַרְעֹה בְּמִצְרָיִם.

Slaves were we to Pharaoh in Egypt, and the LORD *brought us out* (Deut. 6:21) *from there with a strong hand and an outstretched arm* (Deut. 5:15). *And if the Blessed Holy One had not taken our ancestors out of Egypt, we, our children, and our children's children would (still) be enslaved to Pharaoh in Egypt.*

However, it is the covenantal aspect of redemption that the Haggadah deems critical:

בָּרוּךְ שׁוֹמֵר הַבְטָחָתוֹ לְיִשְׂרָאֵל, בָּרוּךְ הוּא. שֶׁהַקָּדוֹשׁ בָּרוּךְ הוּא חִשַּׁב אֶת הַקֵּץ, לַעֲשׂוֹת כְּמַה שֶּׁאָמַר לְאַבְרָהָם אָבִינוּ בִּבְרִית בֵּין הַבְּתָרִים...

Blessed is He who keeps His promise to Israel, Blessed is He. For the Blessed Holy One calculated the end, to do as He had promised Abraham in the Covenant between the Pieces...

It is somewhat inglorious to consider that the People of Israel were unworthy of liberation; but by focusing on the promise God forged with Abraham, the Haggadah highlights God's historical commitment to his descendants and the eternal efficacy of the covenant between them.

7
Creation Themes
in the Exodus Story

R. Judah bar Shallum said: The world was created for the sake of Israel. "From of old" is not written here (in Gen. 1:1), nor is "from the start" written here, but "*In the beginning.*" What is the meaning of "*In the beginning*"? This is Israel, which is called "Beginning." It is so stated (Jer. 2:3): *Israel is holy to the Lord, the beginning of His harvest.* (Tanhuma 1:3)[110]

The language used at the beginning of Exodus to chronicle the birth of the Jewish nation is unmistakably culled from the Creation narratives of Genesis. Genesis language and motifs also permeate the final chapters of Exodus, culminating in a symbolic "return to Eden" via the construction of the *Mishkan* (Tabernacle). Given that both the opening and closing narratives of Exodus are closely linked to the first book of the Torah, it seems likely that the thematic paradigms of Genesis play a role in other sections of Exodus as well. What is the significance of all these literary loans? Although this is not an exhaustive study, an examination of several ways in which Exodus builds upon the stories and messages of Genesis will illuminate both the structure and the message of the biblical text.

Egyptian Enslavement in Genesis Terms

The beginning of Exodus depicts the rapid and exponential growth of the 70-person clan that descended to Egypt:

וּבְנֵי יִשְׂרָאֵל פָּרוּ וַיִּשְׁרְצוּ וַיִּרְבּוּ וַיַּעַצְמוּ בִּמְאֹד מְאֹד וַתִּמָּלֵא הָאָרֶץ אֹתָם:

And the sons of Israel were fruitful and swarmed and multiplied and grew very vast, and the land was filled with them. (Exod. 1:7)

---

[110] John T. Townsend, *Midrash Tanhuma, Translated into English with Introduction, Indices, and Brief Notes* (Hoboken, NJ: Ktav Publishing House, 1989), 2.

The wording of this description clearly echoes the account of Creation in the first chapter of Genesis (1:20,22,28,31) as well as God's words to Noah when he returns to dry land after the Flood (8:17; 9:1,7). The one exception is the word *va-ya'atzmu* (and they grew very vast), which appears instead in the Torah's narratives concerning both Abraham (18:18) and Isaac (26:16). The depiction of the incongruous population growth that followed the nation's enslavement is similarly evocative:

וְכַאֲשֶׁר יְעַנּוּ אֹתוֹ כֵּן יִרְבֶּה וְכֵן יִפְרֹץ...

And as they abused them, so did they multiply and so did they spread . . . (Exod. 1:12)

Here too the word *yifrotz* (they spread), though not Creation language, echoes the foundational story of Jacob and his family (Gen. 28:14, 30:43).

The account of Moses' birth in chapter 2 also draws upon the language of the Creation narratives. When the daughter of Levi observes the child she has birthed, the Torah recounts:

...וַתֵּרֶא אֹתוֹ כִּי טוֹב הוּא וַתִּצְפְּנֵהוּ שְׁלֹשָׁה יְרָחִים:

. . . and she saw that he was goodly, and she hid him three months. (Exod. 2:2)

This formulation clearly recalls the refrain from Genesis 1, "and God saw . . . that it was good" (Gen. 1:4,10,12,18,21,25,31), which repeats after each act of Creation.[111] After three months have passed and Moses' mother can no longer hide her baby from the Egyptians who would drown him, she places him in an ark and sets him adrift in the reeds at the banks of the Nile River. This twist recalls the other biblical character saved from destruction adrift in

---

[111] In his commentary on Exodus, Rashi also calls the reader's attention to Genesis, albeit indirectly. Moses' mother saw that her child "was goodly;" and Rashi cites a midrash asserting that when Moses was born, the house filled with light, evoking the first act of Creation and the first appearance of the phrase "and God saw . . . that it was good." See Rashi on Exod. 2:2, *Ki tov hu*; the midrash cited appears in B.T. Sot. 12a.

A PASSOVER HAGGADAH: GO FORTH AND LEARN

an ark, namely Noah. Thus, the opening passages of Exodus evoke not only the original Creation story of Genesis but also the account of humanity's re-creation after the Flood.

The Tower of Babel is another foundational Genesis narrative that informs the beginning of Exodus. Here too striking linguistic parallels point to a deeper thematic connection.[112] Just a few generations after the Flood, the people of Shinar decide to build a city with bricks and mortar for the purpose of banding together to "make a name" for themselves and to prevent their dispersion across the land:

וַיֹּאמְרוּ אִישׁ אֶל רֵעֵהוּ הָבָה נִלְבְּנָה לְבֵנִים וְנִשְׂרְפָה לִשְׂרֵפָה וַתְּהִי לָהֶם הַלְּבֵנָה
לְאָבֶן וְהַחֵמָר הָיָה לָהֶם לַחֹמֶר: וַיֹּאמְרוּ הָבָה נִבְנֶה לָּנוּ עִיר וּמִגְדָּל וְרֹאשׁוֹ בַשָּׁמַיִם
וְנַעֲשֶׂה לָּנוּ שֵׁם פֶּן נָפוּץ עַל פְּנֵי כָל הָאָרֶץ:

And they said to each other, "Come, let us bake bricks and burn them hard." And the brick served them as stone, and bitumen served them as mortar. And they said, "Come, let us build us a city and a tower with its top in the heavens, that we may make us a name, lest we be scattered over all the earth." (Gen. 11:3–4)

The very phrasing of their plan, with its unique juxtaposition of the words *havah* (come!) and *pen* (lest), is echoed in Exodus 1, in Pharaoh's appeal to his people to enslave the Israelites and force them to build cities with mortar and bricks, lest they overwhelm the host population and rise up from the land:

וַיֹּאמֶר אֶל עַמּוֹ הִנֵּה עַם בְּנֵי יִשְׂרָאֵל רַב וְעָצוּם מִמֶּנּוּ: הָבָה נִתְחַכְּמָה לוֹ פֶּן יִרְבֶּה
וְהָיָה כִּי תִקְרֶאנָה מִלְחָמָה וְנוֹסַף גַּם הוּא עַל שֹׂנְאֵינוּ וְנִלְחַם בָּנוּ וְעָלָה מִן הָאָרֶץ:
וַיָּשִׂימוּ עָלָיו שָׂרֵי מִסִּים לְמַעַן עַנֹּתוֹ בְּסִבְלֹתָם וַיִּבֶן עָרֵי מִסְכְּנוֹת לְפַרְעֹה אֶת פִּתֹם
וְאֶת רַעַמְסֵס: וְכַאֲשֶׁר יְעַנּוּ אֹתוֹ כֵּן יִרְבֶּה וְכֵן יִפְרֹץ... וַיְמָרְרוּ אֶת חַיֵּיהֶם בַּעֲבֹדָה
קָשָׁה בְּחֹמֶר וּבִלְבֵנִים וּבְכָל עֲבֹדָה בַּשָּׂדֶה אֵת כָּל עֲבֹדָתָם אֲשֶׁר עָבְדוּ בָהֶם בְּפָרֶךְ:

---

[112]For extensive analysis of the relationship between these passages, see Judy Klitsner, *Subversive Sequels in the Bible* (Philadelphia: The Jewish Publication Society, 2009), 31–62.

CREATION THEMES IN THE EXODUS STORY

And he said to his people, "Look, the people of the sons of Israel is more numerous and vaster than we. Come, let us be shrewd with them lest they multiply and then, should war occur, they will actually join our enemies and fight against us and go up from the land." And they set over them forced-labor foremen so as to abuse them with their burdens, and they built store cities for Pharaoh: Pithom and Ramses. And as they abused them, so did they multiply and so did they spread . . . and they made their lives bitter with hard work with mortar and bricks and every work in the field—all their crushing work that they performed. (Exod. 1:9–14)

The Tower of Babel story is followed by a genealogy of Shem's family and the genealogy is followed by the story of Abraham's journey from Ur Kasdim to the land of Canaan. Shortly after arriving in Canaan, the land is beset by famine, and Abraham and his family descend to Egypt, whose people are known to abduct women and kill their men.[113] In Exodus too the description of the Israelites' enslavement in Egypt is followed by Pharaoh's plot to limit the Israelite population by keeping the female children alive while killing the males.

By presenting the enslavement in Egypt as parallel to the Tower of Babel and subsequent Genesis narratives, the Torah casts Pharaoh and the Egyptian people as adversaries not only of the Israelites, but also of God. The birth of the Jewish nation thus becomes an event of cosmic significance.

---

[113] The deep connection between the Tower of Babel tale and the story of Abraham's journey to Canaan is indicated by the use of the homophonous key words *shem* (name) and *sham* (there) in both narratives (compare Gen. 11:2,4,7,8,9 to 12:2,7,8). (These key words also appear in the Binding of Isaac story in Gen. 22, which is the second time God commands Abraham to "Go forth".) Yet the first is a story of punishment and exile, whereas the second is about possessing the Land and inheriting sacred space; thus, it is no coincidence that in the Midrash, Nimrod, who is associated with the first story (see Gen. 8:8–10), is presented as the archenemy of Abraham, who is the hero of the second.

A PASSOVER HAGGADAH: GO FORTH AND LEARN

The *Mishkan*: Human Construction Parallels Divine Creation

Later in the book of Exodus, in describing the *Mishkan* and its construction, the Torah once again draws upon the language and themes of the Creation narratives. Martin Buber pointed to seven points of correspondence between the texts,[114] and in her *Studies in Shemot*, Nehama Leibowitz developed these ideas further.[115] I will cite only the most obvious examples.

Genesis depicts God creating the world over the course of six days and resting on the seventh, which is the primary basis for the weekly observance of the Sabbath. In Exodus, the commandment to observe *Shabbat* following six days of labor is reiterated several times, twice in the context of building the *Mishkan* (31:13–17 and 35:2–3).[116] The Midrash and later commentators suggest various connections between *Shabbat* and the *Mishkan*; for the moment, I will simply note that in linking the two, the Torah implicitly associates human construction with Divine Creation.[117]

Melakhah is the term used most frequently in Exodus to describe the labors involved in constructing the *Mishkan*. This is also the term used in Genesis with reference to the work entailed in the Creation of the world (Gen. 2:1–3). In contrast, the word *melakhah* is never used to describe the slave labor that Pharaoh imposed on the Israelites; there, only the term *avodah* appears. The use of Creation language to depict the building of the *Mishkan* underscores the link between God's formation of the world and the Israelites' fashioning of sacred space. The comparison is reinforced in the penultimate

---

[114]Martin Buber, *The Way of the Bible* (in Hebrew) (Jerusalem: Bialik Institute, 1964), 54–58.

[115]Leibowitz, *Studies in Shemot*, 475–82.

[116]The Torah also utilizes the seven-day Creation model to depict the encounter between God and Moses/Israel at Mount Sinai; see Exod. 24:16. Nehama Leibowitz demonstrates that during this meeting on the mountain God showed Moses precise plans for the *Mishkan*, further reinforcing the association between the seven days of Creation and the construction of the Tabernacle.

[117]See also Shimon Bakon, "Creation, Tabernacle, and Sabbath," *Jewish Bible Quarterly* 25, no. 2 (1997): 79–85; and Tzvi Erlich, "The Garden of Eden Story as Compared to the Encounter at Mount Sinai and the *Mishkan*" (in Hebrew), *Alon shevut le-bogrei Yeshivat Har Etzion* 11 (5758): 17–35; and Liebowitz, *Studies in Shemot* 475–82.

chapter of Exodus, which recounts Moses' response to the completion of the *Mishkan* in language that echoes God's response to the conclusion of Creation (Gen. 1:31–2:3):

וַיַּרְא מֹשֶׁה אֶת כָּל הַמְּלָאכָה וְהִנֵּה עָשׂוּ אֹתָהּ כַּאֲשֶׁר צִוָּה יהוה כֵּן עָשׂוּ וַיְבָרֶךְ אֹתָם מֹשֶׁה:

And Moses saw all the tasks, and, look, they had done it as the LORD had charged, thus they had done it, and Moses blessed them. (Exod. 39:43)[118]

Like God surveying the world at the end of the sixth day (Gen. 1:31, 2:3), Moses sees, evaluates, and blesses. Even the term for completion itself—*va-yekhal*—which appears later in the narrative (Exod. 40:33; see also 39:32) is culled from the Genesis account (2:1–2).

In contrast, the two *keruvim* (cherubs) who feature in the Genesis narrative take on a nearly opposite function in the context of the *Mishkan*. After man and woman sin and are banished from the Garden of Eden, God employs the *keruvim*, along with the "flame of the whirling sword," to block the entrance to the garden and prevent humans from reaching the Tree of Life (Gen. 3:24). In the *Mishkan*, the two golden *keruvim* adorn the cover of the ark that houses the tablets of the covenant and are the very site of ongoing communication with God (Exod. 25:22). Thus the *keruvim*, which in Genesis serve as a barrier between humans and the Divine, function in Exodus to facilitate connection. In Genesis the *keruvim* impede the acquisition of godly attributes, whereas in Exodus, they serve as the centerpiece of the *Mishkan*, whose primary function is to provide humans with access to and knowledge of God (Exod. 29:42–46).

---

[118]Compare also Num. 7:1 and Gen. 2:1–3.

A PASSOVER HAGGADAH: GO FORTH AND LEARN

The Struggle Against Other Gods

One of the most striking aspects of the world's Creation as described in Genesis 1 is that it does not seem to entail effort: it is conducted by an omnipotent God who brings the world into being by acts of speech alone. Unlike the creation myths of various other cultures, the depiction of Creation in Genesis 1 does not portray a clash of forces or a battle of gods; indeed the one, transcendent God seems to be the only preexisting entity and does not appear to encounter any resistance. The 20th-century commentator Umberto Cassuto has argued that the Torah's account of Creation was purposefully designed to counter popular legends of the ancient Near East that describe creation as a great struggle of primordial forces from which one god emerges supreme.[119] To demonstrate this point, Cassuto notes that the only creatures singled out in Genesis 1 are the *tanninim ha-gedolim*, the "great sea monsters," about whom legends abounded in the ancient world, mostly concerning their inherent evil and epic antagonism toward God. According to Cassuto, the Torah highlights God's creation of the *tanninim* (Gen. 1:21) so as to say:

> Far be it from anyone to suppose that the sea monsters were mythological beings opposed to God or in revolt against Him; they were as natural as the rest of the creatures, and were formed in their proper time and in their proper place by the word of the Creator, in order that they might fulfill His will like the other created beings.[120]

Much rings true about Cassuto's claim, and the evidence that he gathers is compelling; but it is not entirely sufficient, because the Torah's second account of Creation points in a different direction.

The second Creation narrative, which encompasses chapters 2 and 3 of Genesis, features not a sea monster but a snake who figures as the enemy

---

[119] Umberto Cassuto, *A Commentary on the Book of Genesis*, p. 1 (Jerusalem: Magnes Press, 1961), 7–12. He notes that echoes of what are possibly earlier Israelite accounts of Creation are preserved in Isa. 40:12,21–22 and Job 38:4–7. He also suggests that Ezek. 28:11–19 preserves an ancient epic tradition regarding the Garden of Eden, from which Genesis digresses; see Cassuto, *Genesis*, 75–83.
[120] Cassuto, *Genesis*, 50–51.

CREATION THEMES IN THE EXODUS STORY

of God.[121] The snake does not challenge God directly but rather attacks God's stewards on earth: man and woman, who were created in God's image and endowed with God's spirit. Ostensibly, the impetus for the snake's enmity is God's pronouncement that the fruit of the trees was designated for the enjoyment of human beings alone, while animals were relegated to eating the produce of the ground (Gen. 1:29–30).[122] The snake does not perceive itself as essentially different from man and woman; indeed they are all described as *arum*.[123] It so deeply resents the imposed distinction that it conceives a plot to seduce the humans into disobeying God's orders and getting thrown out of Eden. Fundamentally, though, the snake seems to have one desire: to defeat God by foiling God's plan for the world. The second narrative of Creation (in contrast to Genesis 1) focuses on the creation of Eden, the unique place God fashioned as a dwelling for the newly created humans. The snake's devious manipulations and ultimate success at driving the humans out of Eden represent a victory over God and the collapse of God's Creation scheme. Thus, the remainder of Genesis is devoted to re-creating the world via the Flood and to reestablishing sacred space via the wanderings of the forefathers and God's covenant with the progenitors of Israel.

The clash between God and the snake—or God and the force of evil—in the Torah's second account of Creation becomes a dominant theme in Exodus. Unlike Genesis 1, in which God creates the world with no resistance, the opening chapters of Exodus narrate a historic showdown between God and Pharaoh, that is, between the God of Israel and the gods of Egypt and the ancient world. In his confrontations with Moses and Aaron, Pharaoh presents himself as God's adversary, initially dismissing God as an unknown entity and

---

[121] In Exodus, the sea monster (*tannin*) and the snake (*nahash*) seem to function interchangeably. In chap. 4, God gives Moses a series of signs to convince the People of Israel that he is indeed God's messenger, and the Torah recounts that Moses threw his staff to the ground and it became a *nahash* (Exod. 4:3). But in chap. 7, when Moses and Aaron approach Pharaoh for the second time and he requests a proof that they bear God's message, Aaron throws his staff to the ground and it becomes a *tannin* (Exod. 7:9,10).

[122] It is not clear why God's first communication with humans contains these seemingly extraneous verses that designate different produce for humans and animals; my suggestion is that the Torah is already setting up the next story, namely the encounter between the snake and the humans.

[123] In the literal sense, *arum* means "naked" in the case of man and woman (Gen. 2:25) and "wily" with reference to the snake (Gen. 3:1); but it is hard to overlook the Torah's use of the same word in these two successive verses.

A PASSOVER HAGGADAH: GO FORTH AND LEARN

answering the Israelites' request for time to worship with an intensification of their workload in service to himself. In response, the Torah emphasizes repeatedly that God has designed the plagues to teach the Egyptians—and by extension Israel and the rest of the nations—that God is the one and only master of the world (Exod. 7:5,17; 8:6,18; 9:14). Indeed, God refers explicitly to the final Plague of the Firstborn as a confrontation with the gods of Egypt:

וְעָבַרְתִּי בְאֶרֶץ מִצְרַיִם בַּלַּיְלָה הַזֶּה וְהִכֵּיתִי כָל בְּכוֹר בְּאֶרֶץ מִצְרַיִם מֵאָדָם וְעַד בְּהֵמָה וּבְכָל אֱלֹהֵי מִצְרַיִם אֶעֱשֶׂה שְׁפָטִים אֲנִי יהוה:

And I will cross through the land of Egypt on this night, and I will strike down every firstborn in the land of Egypt from man to beast, and from all the gods of Egypt I will extract retributions. I am the LORD. (Exod. 12:12)

This battle against Pharaoh and other gods is referenced in the Song at the Sea as well, which celebrates the Exodus and God's redemption of Israel:

יהוה אִישׁ מִלְחָמָה יהוה שְׁמוֹ: מַרְכְּבֹת פַּרְעֹה וְחֵילוֹ יָרָה בַיָּם וּמִבְחַר שָׁלִשָׁיו טֻבְּעוּ בְיַם סוּף ... מִי כָמֹכָה בָּאֵלִם יהוה מִי כָּמֹכָה נֶאְדָּר בַּקֹּדֶשׁ נוֹרָא תְהִלֹּת עֹשֵׂה פֶלֶא:

The LORD is a man of war, the LORD is His name. Pharaoh's chariots and his force He pitched into the sea and the pick of his captains were drowned in the Reed Sea... Who is like You among the gods, O LORD, who is like You, mighty in holiness? Awesome in praise, worker of wonders. (Exod. 15:3–4,11)[124]

The raging waters that drown Pharaoh and his Egyptian armies are, of course, also reminiscent of the Flood and the undoing of Creation in Genesis. As in the case of the Flood, the battle at the sea presents an opportunity for re-creation and for the reestablishment of sacred space, as emphasized in the song's concluding stanzas:

---

[124] The Song at the Sea also references the mythical forces *yam* and *tehom*; see Exod. 15:4–5,8.

CREATION THEMES IN THE EXODUS STORY

תְּבִאֵמוֹ וְתִטָּעֵמוֹ בְּהַר נַחֲלָתְךָ מָכוֹן לְשִׁבְתְּךָ פָּעַלְתָּ יהוה מִקְּדָשׁ אֲדֹנָי כּוֹנְנוּ יָדֶיךָ:
יהוה יִמְלֹךְ לְעֹלָם וָעֶד:

You'll bring them, You'll plant them, on the mount of Your estate,
a firm place for Your dwelling You wrought, O Lord, the sanctum,
O Sovereign, Your hands firmly founded. The Lord shall be king for
all time! (Exod. 15:17–18)

This quest forms the central theme of the second half of Exodus; but before it is realized, another struggle of primeval forces unfolds.

The Battle with Amalek

Shortly after leaving the Sea of Reeds, the People of Israel begin to complain bitterly about food and water; and despite God's provision of *slav* (quail), manna, and water from the rock, they eventually question God's very presence in their midst (Exod. 17:7). Immediately, as if in response, they are waylaid by Amalek at Rephidim. Amalek, condemned in Deuteronomy for attacking Israel at its moment of weakness, is the "snake" of Exodus: God's enemy and evil incarnate.

The Torah describes the encounter with Amalek in some detail, and the language of this description is significant because of its parallels to other texts that appear later in Exodus. Moses instructs Joshua to choose men to take with him to the battlefield; and Moses himself ascends the nearby mountain with Aaron and Hur, his staff in hand. So long as Moses raises his arms, Israel is victorious; but as soon as Moses lowers them, Amalek prevails. Moses' arms become heavy, so Aaron and Hur place a rock beneath him, and he sits while they support his arms, one on either side. Thus Moses' arms remain firm until sunset, and Joshua is able to weaken Amalek by the sword. God instructs Moses to write the incident down as a memory in a book and to tell Joshua that God will wipe Amalek out from under the heavens. Moses builds an altar and declares that there will be a "war for the Lord against Amalek from all time" (Exod. 17:16).

From this standpoint, Amalek embodies the persistent force of evil, the element of Creation that does not accept God's dominion and that God seemingly cannot, or will not, control. After witnessing the ultimate destruction of Egypt at the sea, all the nations fear God (Exod. 15:14–16); yet shortly thereafter Amalek is brazen enough to attack God's people. At the sea, God's stated goal for the People of Israel is to cross over to God's mountain where they will establish God's Temple and God will reign eternal; yet two chapters later, Amalek tries to prevent the accomplishment of this goal and to impede the establishment of God's sovereignty. Thus, in the Song at the Sea, God's hand was described as building God's own sacred dwelling place, whereas in chapter 17, it is with a "hand upon God's throne" that Moses swears to wage an eternal "war for God" against Amalek. But although Amalek is weakened by the sword, they are not obliterated. At least on a symbolic level, Amalek lingers forever. The remainder of Exodus, and of the Torah as a whole, is punctuated by challenging encounters with the adversarial force represented by Amalek.

The Sin of the Golden Calf

The perseverance of Amalek-like antagonism toward God is easily demonstrated through a careful reading of the Golden Calf story. The language of this narrative closely parallels the Torah's description of the confrontation with Amalek at Rephidim, implying that one is meant to inform the other. In addition, a number of suggestive words and phrases link the tale of the Golden Calf to the account of man and woman's transgression in Eden, marking it as another manifestation of human beings' first sin.

In Exodus 32 the people believe Moses to be lingering on the mountain that he has ascended to receive the tablets of the law; and they turn to Aaron, demanding that he fashion for them a god to lead them in place of Moses, whose fate is unknown. The term used to denote Moses' delay, *boshesh*, is distinctive; in fact, its only other appearance in the Torah is with reference to man and woman in the Garden of Eden, just prior to their encounter with the snake:

CREATION THEMES IN THE EXODUS STORY

וַיִּהְיוּ שְׁנֵיהֶם עֲרוּמִּים הָאָדָם וְאִשְׁתּוֹ וְלֹא יִתְבֹּשָׁשׁוּ:

And the two of them were naked, the human and his woman, and they were not ashamed (yitboshashu). (Gen. 2:25)

Although the meaning of the word in the Genesis text is different than in Exodus, its use in the introductory verses to both of these pivotal transgressions intimates a connection between the two narratives, a point to which we will return. Aaron instructs the people to bring him their golden jewelry, which he fashions into a calf that the people proclaim as their god. Aaron then builds an altar and calls for a holiday; and the people arise early the next morning to offer sacrifices, eat, drink, and make merry.[125] In the meantime, God informs Moses of what has happened and commands him to descend the mountain, and God declares that God will destroy the people and establish a new nation from Moses' progeny. Moses beseeches God to contain God's wrath, and God relents. At this point, Moses descends to the camp and encounters those who are worshiping the calf. The description of this encounter is particularly instructive.

The Torah informs us that as Moses comes down the mountain, he carries the tablets of the covenant in his hand, and they are:

...כְּתֻבִים מִשְׁנֵי עֶבְרֵיהֶם מִזֶּה וּמִזֶּה הֵם כְּתֻבִים: וְהַלֻּחֹת מַעֲשֵׂה אֱלֹהִים הֵמָּה וְהַמִּכְתָּב מִכְתַּב אֱלֹהִים הוּא חָרוּת עַל הַלֻּחֹת:

. . . written on both their sides, on the one side and on the other they were written. And the tablets, God's doing they were, and the writing, God's writing it was, inscribed on the tablets. (Exod. 32:15–16)

The vivid depiction of the tablets at this juncture seems misplaced and even extraneous, as they were already described several verses prior as "tablets of stone written by the finger of God" (Exod. 31:18). The reader recalls, however, that the specific phrase, *mi-zeh u-mi-zeh* (on the one side and on the other), was also used in the Amalek story to portray Aaron and Hur, who

---

[125] It is worth noting that both the sin of the Golden Calf and the sin in Eden are associated with eating.

A PASSOVER HAGGADAH: GO FORTH AND LEARN

stood on either side of Moses to support him (17:12). The reappearance of these words here, with reference to the tablets, highlights the absence, indeed desertion, of Moses' supporters: Aaron is down in the camp abetting the people's transgression, and Hur has disappeared (although, according to the Midrash, he was killed by the mob for attempting to forestall them).[126] Moses is left with nothing but the tablets themselves to buttress him against the people and their sin.

When Moses reaches the bottom of the mountain, he encounters Joshua, who reports that he has heard shouting from the camp:

וַיֹּאמֶר אֶל מֹשֶׁה קוֹל מִלְחָמָה בַּמַּחֲנֶה: וַיֹּאמֶר אֵין קוֹל עֲנוֹת גְּבוּרָה וְאֵין קוֹל עֲנוֹת חֲלוּשָׁה קוֹל עֲנוֹת אָנֹכִי שֹׁמֵעַ:

And he said to Moses, "A sound of war in the camp!" And he said, "Not the sound of crying out in triumph, and not the sound of crying out in defeat. A sound of crying out I hear." (Exod. 32:17–18)

It is not entirely clear from the verses whether it is Joshua or Moses himself who clarifies that the noises from the camp are neither triumphant nor distressed. In his commentary Ibn Ezra asserts that it is Moses, and his reading is supported by several passages from the Midrash, which suggest that Moses' words were meant to rebuke his disciple Joshua, who was slated to become the next leader of the nation, yet could not distinguish between the sounds of battle and the sounds of levity.[127] Read this way, the exchange with Joshua reflects the intensification of Moses' alienation from the people, as even his loyal student fails to understand the gravity of what has occurred. The words *gevurah* (triumph) and *halushah* (defeat), which echo the Amalek narrative, emphasize the difference between that episode, in which Israel triumphed against an external enemy, and this episode, in which the deleterious conflict derives from within:

---

[126] Lev. Rabbah 10:3, also cited in Rashi's commentary on Exod. 32:5, *Hag la-ha-shem mahar.*
[127] See J.T. Ta'an. 4:5; Eccles. Rabbah 9:11; Tanhuma, Va'ethannan 2. See also the commentary of Ramban.

CREATION THEMES IN THE EXODUS STORY

וְהָיָה כַּאֲשֶׁר יָרִים מֹשֶׁה יָדוֹ וְגָבַר יִשְׂרָאֵל וְכַאֲשֶׁר יָנִיחַ יָדוֹ וְגָבַר עֲמָלֵק...וַיַּחֲלשׁ
יְהוֹשֻׁעַ אֶת עֲמָלֵק וְאֶת עַמּוֹ לְפִי חָרֶב:

*And so, when Moses would raise his hand, Israel prevailed, and
when he would put down his hand, Amalek prevailed . . . And Joshua
disabled Amalek and its people by the edge of the sword.* (Exod.
17:11,13)[128]

Moses approaches the camp, sees the calf and the dancing, and is so angered
that he flings the tablets from his hands and smashes them at the bottom of
the mountain. He burns the calf in the fire and then grinds its ashes, sprinkles
them in water, and forces the Israelites to drink the concoction. He confronts
Aaron over his role in the affair in terms that resonate with the phrasing of
God's confrontation with the woman in Eden:

וַיֹּאמֶר מֹשֶׁה אֶל אַהֲרֹן מֶה עָשָׂה לְךָ הָעָם הַזֶּה כִּי הֵבֵאתָ עָלָיו חֲטָאָה גְדֹלָה:

*And Moses said to Aaron, "What did this people do to you that you
should have brought upon it great offense?"* (Exod. 32:21)

וַיֹּאמֶר יהוה אֱלֹהִים לָאִשָּׁה מַה זֹּאת עָשִׂית...

And the LORD *God said to the woman, "What is this you have
done?"...* (Gen. 3:13)

Next, Moses gathers the Levites and dispatches them to kill by sword those
who are guilty. Finally, he returns to God to pray for forgiveness on behalf of
the nation. In his appeal to God, Moses declares that if God will not pardon
the people, he himself wishes to be erased from the Torah; but God demurs:

וְעַתָּה אִם תִּשָּׂא חַטָּאתָם וְאִם אַיִן מְחֵנִי נָא מִסִּפְרְךָ אֲשֶׁר כָּתָבְתָּ: וַיֹּאמֶר יהוה אֶל
מֹשֶׁה מִי אֲשֶׁר חָטָא לִי אֶמְחֶנּוּ מִסִּפְרִי:

*"And now, if You would bear their offense . . . and if not, wipe me
out, pray, from Your book which You have written." And the* LORD
*said to Moses, "He who has offended against me, I shall wipe out from
my book."* (Exod. 32:32–33)

---

[128]The Midrash also notes the common language employed by the Torah in these two narratives;
see Exod. Rabbah 41:1.

A PASSOVER HAGGADAH: GO FORTH AND LEARN

Given the connection that has been established between the story of the Golden Calf and the story of Amalek, the wording of Moses' appeal is striking, because it is the inverse of what God instructs him to do following the battle at Rephidim:

וַיֹּאמֶר יהוה אֶל מֹשֶׁה כְּתֹב זֹאת זִכָּרוֹן בַּסֵּפֶר וְשִׂים בְּאָזְנֵי יְהוֹשֻׁעַ כִּי מָחֹה אֶמְחֶה אֶת זֵכֶר עֲמָלֵק מִתַּחַת הַשָּׁמָיִם:

And the LORD *said to Moses, "Write this down as a remembrance in a record, and put it in Joshua's hearing, that I will surely wipe out the name of Amalek from under the heavens."* (Exod. 17:14)

Following Moses' appeal, God instructs Moses to continue journeying with the people toward the Land that was promised to Abraham, Isaac, and Jacob; and God pledges to send a messenger to lead them and to drive out the nations who currently occupy the Land. But God declares that God will not accompany the Israelites:

כִּי לֹא אֶעֱלֶה בְּקִרְבְּךָ כִּי עַם קְשֵׁה עֹרֶף אַתָּה פֶּן אֲכֶלְךָ בַּדָּרֶךְ:

But I shall not go up in your midst, for you are a stiff-necked people, lest I put an end to you on the way. (Exod. 33:3)

The phrasing of God's declaration is familiar from the Torah's prologue to the Amalek story, another literary effect that links the two stories:

וַיִּקְרָא שֵׁם הַמָּקוֹם מַסָּה וּמְרִיבָה עַל רִיב בְּנֵי יִשְׂרָאֵל וְעַל נַסֹּתָם אֶת יהוה לֵאמֹר הֲיֵשׁ יהוה בְּקִרְבֵּנוּ אִם אָיִן:

And he called the name of the place Massah and Meribah (Testing and Dispute), for the disputation of the Israelites, and for their testing the LORD, *saying, "Is the* LORD *in our midst or not?"* (Exod. 17:7)[129]

---

[129] The phrase *im ayin* (or not) that appears in this verse functions as another linguistic connection between the Amalek and Golden Calf narratives: the same phrase appears in Moses' appeal to God for forgiveness following the sin (Exod. 32:32).

CREATION THEMES IN THE EXODUS STORY

The resistance and rejection of God on display in the Golden Calf story do not originate from an external enemy but come from the People of Israel themselves, from their own internalization of the qualities of Amalek. Like the snake in Genesis, who brings about the expulsion from Eden, this antagonism toward God in Exodus, whether in the form of an actual Amalek or by way of an internalization of Amalek's qualities, is the force that threatens the possibility of God's dwelling together with the people. Following the sin of the Golden Calf, God declines to remain in the people's midst. The tablets, which were the work of God, were to have been God's primary contribution to the *Mishkan*, which was otherwise a human construction; but the tablets are broken.

For the story of Exodus to come to a successful conclusion, Moses and the people must find a way to nonetheless build the *Mishkan*. Having sinned, having rejected God, it is up to them to enable a return to Eden by re-creating sacred space. The manner in which this is ultimately achieved draws upon another Creation narrative from Genesis, that is, the story of the Flood and the world's subsequent re-creation via Noah and his family.[130]

Noah and the (Re)building of the *Mishkan*

The Torah's conscription of the Flood narrative to tell the story of God's reconciliation with the People of Israel, which in turn allows for construction of the *Mishkan* at the end of Exodus, is reflected first and foremost in the borrowing of words and phrases from the Genesis passages. In Exodus 32 God informs Moses, up on the mountain, that the people have sinned, saying:

לֶךְ רֵד כִּי שִׁחֵת עַמְּךָ אֲשֶׁר הֶעֱלֵיתָ מֵאֶרֶץ מִצְרָיִם:

Quick, go down, for your people that I brought up from Egypt has acted ruinously. (Exod. 32:7)

---

[130] As noted earlier, Creation language and motifs also feature prominently in the description of the *Mishkan*'s construction. The Flood theme is co-opted specifically to highlight the reconciliation with God that preceded it.

A PASSOVER HAGGADAH: GO FORTH AND LEARN

Genesis uses very similar terminology to describe the corruption of the world that preceded the Flood:

וַתִּשָּׁחֵת הָאָרֶץ לִפְנֵי הָאֱלֹהִים וַתִּמָּלֵא הָאָרֶץ חָמָס: וַיַּרְא אֱלֹהִים אֶת הָאָרֶץ וְהִנֵּה נִשְׁחָתָה כִּי הִשְׁחִית כָּל בָּשָׂר אֶת דַּרְכּוֹ עַל הָאָרֶץ:

And the earth was corrupt before God and the earth was filled with outrage. And God saw the earth and, look, it was corrupt, for all flesh had corrupted its ways on the earth. (Gen. 6:11–12)

When Moses, still on the mountain, makes his initial appeal to God not to destroy the people, the Torah uses a fairly uncommon word to denote his petition:

וַיְחַל מֹשֶׁה אֶת פְּנֵי יהוה אֱלֹהָיו וַיֹּאמֶר לָמָה יהוה יֶחֱרֶה אַפְּךָ בְּעַמֶּךָ אֲשֶׁר הוֹצֵאתָ מֵאֶרֶץ מִצְרַיִם בְּכֹחַ גָּדוֹל וּבְיָד חֲזָקָה:

And Moses implored the presence of the LORD *his God and said, "Why, O* LORD, *should your wrath flare against Your people that You brought out from the land of Egypt with great power and with a strong hand?"* (Exod. 32:11)

Interestingly, this four-letter combination, ויחל, which appears a total of four times in the Torah, is used twice in the story of Noah. Although each of the words seems to derive from a different Hebrew root, the appearance of this unusual letter arrangement creates at least a visual connection between the passages.[131] When the dove that Noah releases from a window of the ark forty days after the Flood returns, having found no dry land upon which to alight, the Torah reports:

וַיָּחֶל עוֹד שִׁבְעַת יָמִים אֲחֵרִים וַיֹּסֶף שַׁלַּח אֶת הַיּוֹנָה מִן הַתֵּבָה:

Then he waited another seven days and again sent the dove out from the ark. (Gen. 8:10)

---

[131] According to F. Brown, S. R. Driver, and C. A. Briggs, *A Hebrew and English Lexicon of the Old Testament* (Oxford: Clarendon Press, 1907), the word in Exod. 32:11 derives from the root ח-ל-ה; in Gen 8:10, from the root י-ח-ל; and in Gen. 9:20, from the root ח-ל-ל.

CREATION THEMES IN THE EXODUS STORY

And later, after the waters have receded, and Noah has left the ark:

וַיָּחֶל נֹחַ אִישׁ הָאֲדָמָה וַיִּטַּע כָּרֶם:

And Noah, a man of the soil, was the first to plant a vineyard. (Gen. 9:20)

On a more substantive level, God's threat to destroy the People of Israel and remake the nation through the descendants of Moses is, in fact, precisely God's solution to the corruption of the world in Genesis: God annihilates the human race in the Flood and repopulates the world with the descendants of Noah. But here the two stories diverge: whereas Noah complied with God's plan, Moses challenges God and refuses to accept God's decision. God actually seems to invite Moses' appeal, whereas the text does not indicate that the same was true of God's attitude toward Noah.[132]

Two additional key words from the Flood narrative reappear in the story of the Golden Calf and suggest further associations between the stories: the words *nahem* and *hen*. When Noah is born, his father Lemekh names him by saying:

זֶה יְנַחֲמֵנוּ מִמַּעֲשֵׂנוּ וּמֵעִצְּבוֹן יָדֵינוּ מִן הָאֲדָמָה אֲשֶׁר אֵרְרָהּ יהוה:

This one will console us for the pain of our hands' work from the soil which the LORD cursed. (Gen. 5:29)

And when God subsequently recognizes the evil inherent in humankind and decides to destroy the world, the Torah recounts:

וַיִּנָּחֶם יהוה כִּי עָשָׂה אֶת הָאָדָם בָּאָרֶץ וַיִּתְעַצֵּב אֶל לִבּוֹ: וַיֹּאמֶר יהוה אֶמְחֶה אֶת הָאָדָם אֲשֶׁר בָּרָאתִי מֵעַל פְּנֵי הָאֲדָמָה מֵאָדָם עַד בְּהֵמָה עַד רֶמֶשׂ וְעַד עוֹף הַשָּׁמָיִם כִּי נִחַמְתִּי כִּי עֲשִׂיתִם:

---

[132] God in fact stymies Noah's opportunity to pray by telling him explicitly that he is the only righteous one in his generation (Gen. 7:1). In other words, God says to Noah: there is no point in appealing My decision, because there is no one else worth saving. This contrasts with the opportunities to appeal that God implicitly extends to both Abraham regarding the destruction of Sodom and Moses regarding the destruction of Israel.

A PASSOVER HAGGADAH: GO FORTH AND LEARN

And the LORD *regretted having made the human on earth and was grieved to the heart. And the* LORD *said, "I will wipe out the human race I created from the face of the earth, from human to cattle to crawling thing to the fowl of the heavens, for I regret that I have made them." (Gen. 6:6–7)*

This same term is used in the story of the Golden Calf to indicate that Moses' initial intervention has succeeded:

וַיִּנָּחֶם יהוה עַל הָרָעָה אֲשֶׁר דִּבֶּר לַעֲשׂוֹת לְעַמּוֹ:

And the LORD *relented from the evil that He had spoken to do to His people. (Exod. 32:14)*[133]

The word *hen* (favor) appears in the Noah story as the primary explanation for God's selection of Noah, who "found favor in the eyes of the LORD" (Gen. 6:8). The same term appears repeatedly throughout Exodus 33 to depict the relationship between God and Moses that is challenged and intensified following the sin of the calf.

In the second half of Exodus, the Torah enlists the Flood/re-Creation narrative from Genesis to illuminate the significance of building the *Mishkan* after the near rupture between the people and God occasioned by the sin of the Golden Calf. In the Genesis story, Noah ensures the future of the world by building an ark cubit by cubit, according to God's precise specifications. At the end of the Exodus narrative, Moses and the People of Israel similarly construct a wooden edifice according to precise specifications, and this structure is meant to redeem the world by establishing the space for an ongoing encounter between God and humans.

---

[133] This is after Moses has beseeched God to respond in just this manner; see Exod. 32:11–12.

CREATION THEMES IN THE EXODUS STORY

Conclusion

The Genesis narrative emphasizes the role of God as the sole Creator of the world. Human beings are charged with serving God and the world insofar as they are placed in Eden *le-avdah u-le-shomrah*, "to till it and watch it." But in Genesis, humans are not partners in creation.

The book of Exodus conscripts Genesis language and motifs to depict the birth of Israel in cosmic terms, and the Passover story is thus elevated to a place of great prominence in the history of the world. Exodus emphasizes that like the first human beings in Genesis, the newly formed nation is destined to serve God's will. But in contrast to the limited role of humans in the original Creation story, in the Exodus narrative humans are endowed with creative powers. The People of Israel initially fail in their mission; but the process of atonement and reconciliation ultimately leads to a reconceptualization of their relationship with God. In Exodus, freedom coupled with service allows humans to partner with God in the ongoing process of creation.

A PASSOVER HAGGADAH: GO FORTH AND LEARN

8
Hallel at the Seder:
A Song of Redemption

According to the final chapter of Mishnah *Pesahim*, *Maggid*, the story-telling section of the Passover seder, is to conclude with the recitation of *Hallel*.[134] However, the Mishnah records a dispute between the School of Shammai (*Beit Shammai*) and the School of Hillel (*Beit Hillel*) concerning the specific psalms that are to be included in this recitation:

עד היכן הוא אומר? בית שמאי אומרים: עד אם הבנים שמחה; ובית הלל
אומרים: עד חלמיש למעינו מים.

> Until where does he recite? The School of Shammai says: Until
> *A happy mother of sons* (Ps. 113:9); and the School of Hillel says:
> Until *Flint to a spring of water* (Ps. 114:8). (M. Pes. 10:6)

Both schools seem to share the conviction that a narration of events is not, in and of itself, a sufficient prelude to eating the Passover sacrifice (or the symbolic Passover meal) and must be accompanied by a formal expression of thanksgiving. The dispute between the two tannaitic schools pivots on the number of passages to be read at this point in the evening's ritual: the School of Shammai requires reading only one of the six chapters that are included in the standard *Hallel*, whereas the School of Hillel requires reciting the first two.

Without explanation, the authors of the Haggadah ruled in accordance with *Beit Hillel*, and at the traditional seder, *Maggid* concludes with the recitation of Psalms 113 and 114, while Psalms 115 through 118 are recited after the meal. But what is the logic behind each of the positions? A close reading of the *Hallel* text will allow us to consider the deeper significance of the different divisions.

---

[134] See M. Pes. 10:5. The text reads simply, "And we shall say before Him [i.e., God], Hallelujah!"

Psalm 113: The Position of *Beit Shammai*

I t is possible that *Beit Shammai* confined the pre-meal recitation to a single psalm to accentuate the purely symbolic significance of reciting some portion of the thanksgiving prayer before the celebratory feast. However, in so ruling, *Beit Shammai* also succeeded in highlighting the thematic connection between Psalm 113 and the storytelling section of the Haggadah: the psalm itself tells a story of redemption that alludes richly, if not explicitly, to the Exodus.

Psalm 113 begins by instructing God's servants to give thanks:

הַלְלוּיָהּ הַלְלוּ עַבְדֵי יהוה הַלְלוּ אֶת שֵׁם יהוה:

> *Hallelujah. Praise, O servants of the* LORD, *praise the* LORD*'s name.*
> (Ps. 113:1)

This reference to the People of Israel as "servants of the Lord" resonates with a central theme in the Exodus narrative: the Israelites' transition from Egyptian slaves to servants of God. Indeed, the Exodus narrative plays off the dual connotation of the root ע-ב-ד, which means, in one sense, to serve as a slave, but in another, to serve or worship God. The main purpose of redemption is expressed by way of God's multiple commands to Moses to approach Pharaoh and demand that he release the People of Israel "that they may worship Me" (Exod. 7:16,26; 8:16–17; 9:1,13; 10:3–4). Similarly, during the exchange at the Burning Bush, God tells Moses that after he brings the people out of Egypt, they will return to that very mountain to worship (3:12). Repeatedly, God's words imply that the goal of the Exodus is to enable the People of Israel to serve the Divine.

Whereas the book of Exodus begins with the descent to Egypt and the infliction of slavery, it ends with the construction of the *Mishkan* (Tabernacle), the site of worshiping God. Because the deliverance from Egypt is consummated with service to God, the story of Israel's redemption is not complete until the *Mishkan* is built. By emphasizing repeatedly that the donations to the *Mishkan* are voluntary and that the givers are *nedivei lev* (urged by their hearts),[135] the Torah underscores the relationship between the Exodus and the Tabernacle: the same people who were slaves at the beginning of the book—individuals who, by definition, own nothing of their own—have become *nedivim*, voluntary gift givers, by its conclusion. The significance of this conversion from slavery to service of God is highlighted by the structure of the biblical text. The first part of Exodus is devoted to the story of redemption and concludes with the Song at the Sea, which itself ends with an allusion to the building of the Temple (Exod. 15:17). The second part of the book opens with the Israelites walking through the desert; and it too concludes with the construction of a temporary temple.

The poetry of Psalm 113 reflects perfectly the transformation from slavery to service. After ordering the servants of God to praise their master, the Psalmist goes on to exalt God, who is enthroned in the heavens but is nonetheless concerned with earthly matters and raises lowly people to the heights of greatness:

מְקִימִי מֵעָפָר דָּל מֵאַשְׁפֹּת יָרִים אֶבְיוֹן: לְהוֹשִׁיבִי עִם נְדִיבִים עִם נְדִיבֵי עַמּוֹ:

He raises the poor from the dust, from the dungheap lifts the needy,
to seat him among princes, among the princes of his people. (Ps.
113:7–8)

This is precisely the story of the book of Exodus. Just as Exodus begins with the descent to Egypt and ends with the construction of the *Mishkan*, so too Psalm 113 depicts the downtrodden uplifted among *nedivim* (princes). Thus, although Egypt is not explicitly mentioned, *Beit Shammai* seems to have perceived in Psalm 113 an organic connection to the Exodus story recounted in *Maggid*, that is, a poetic expression of redemption inspired by Israel's historical experience.

---

[135] See Exod. 5:2, 35:22, and 36:3.

Psalm 114: The Position of *Beit Hillel*

I n Rabbinic texts, the six-psalm *Hallel* recited at the seder is occasionally called *Hallel ha-Mitzri*, the Egyptian *Hallel*,[136] and the opening lines of Psalm 114 may explain why:

בְּצֵאת יִשְׂרָאֵל מִמִּצְרָיִם בֵּית יַעֲקֹב מֵעַם לֹעֵז: הָיְתָה יְהוּדָה לְקָדְשׁוֹ יִשְׂרָאֵל מַמְשְׁלוֹתָיו:

When Israel came out of Egypt, the house of Jacob from a barbarous-tongued folk, Judah became His sanctuary, Israel His dominion. (Ps. 114:1–2)

This verse reflects what is presumably the closest thematic connection between the *Hallel* psalms and the Passover ritual; and it seems to be the simplest explanation for *Beit Hillel*'s inclusion of Psalm 114 in the initial *Hallel* recitation at the end of *Maggid*.

However, Psalm 114 is connected to the seder in an even deeper way: the Psalm is based on a section of *Shirat ha-Yam*, the song that Moses and the People of Israel sing when they witness the defeat and destruction of the Egyptian army at the Sea of Reeds. Specifically, Psalm 114 highlights and appropriates three themes that dominate the end of the Song at the Sea: God's dominion (Exod. 15:11–13, 17–18), the achievement or establishment of holiness (15:13), and the nations' terror at Israel's deliverance (15:14–16). However, instead of describing Israel's experiences following the Exodus, the Psalmist associates these motifs with the moment of redemption itself. The first two themes appear in the opening verses of the Psalm, as cited. The third theme from *Shirat ha-Yam* appears in slightly altered form: in Exodus, the nations of the world shook and trembled, but in Psalm 114, it is the mountains and the waters that are fearful.[137]

---

[136] See, for example, B.T. Ber. 56a and Rashi's commentary on the words *Hallela mitzra'a*.

[137] In the context of Ps. 114, the term *huli aretz* clearly connotes fear. This is its meaning in *Shirat ha-Yam* (Song at the Sea) as well, where the "trembling [*hil*]" that "seized Philistia's dwellers" (Exod. 15:14) is one of the seven terms used to describe the nations' trembling and shaking when God delivered Israel. But it is probably also a play on the description of the women's rejoicing led by Miriam

A PASSOVER HAGGADAH: GO FORTH AND LEARN

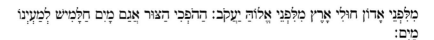

מִלְּפְנֵי אָדוֹן חוּלִי אָרֶץ מִלְּפְנֵי אֱלוֹהַ יַעֲקֹב: הַהֹפְכִי הַצּוּר אֲגַם מָיִם חַלָּמִישׁ לְמַעְיְנוֹ
מָיִם:

Before the Master, whirl, O earth, before the God of Jacob, who turns the rock to a pond of water, flint to a spring of water. (Ps. 114:7–8)

Here too, the Psalmist seems to adjust the biblical narrative: the description of God drawing water from a rock appears in the Torah several times and is intimately connected with the desert experience, but the Psalmist has transposed the theme to the moment of Exodus, when the actual event is still far ahead in the future.

In this respect, Psalm 114 mirrors the presentation of the main biblical narratives in the *Maggid* section. Of the four core texts of the Haggadah— Deuteronomy 6:21,23 (*Avadim hayinu*); Genesis 15:13–14 (God's covenant with Abraham); Joshua 24:2–4 (Israel's prehistory); and Deuteronomy 26:5– 8 (*Arami oved avi*)—not one is cited in full; rather, each passage is truncated. In their original contexts, all these passages refer to settling the Land of Israel, but the Haggadah ends its citation as soon as the Exodus from Egypt has been recounted.[138] By limiting the frame of the narrative, the Haggadah—and Psalm 114—succeed in heightening the drama of the moment at which the Israelites left Egypt.

Another unique feature of Psalm 114 is that verses 5–8 contain a four-part question and its response. Thus, the form of Psalm 114 also parallels the *Maggid*, which includes the *Mah Nishtanah* questions; the Four Children who inquire as to the seder's meaning; and the requirements of Rabban Gamliel, which the Haggadah also presents as a series of questions.[139] The four-part

---

that appears several verses after the song itself: "And Miriam the prophetess, Aaron's sister, took the timbrel in her hand, and all the women went out after her with timbrels and dances [*meholot*]" (Exod. 15:20). This textual wordplay that connects fear and rejoicing is reminiscent of the attitude the Talmud prescribes for prayer: *gilu be-re'adah* (exult in trembling) (Ps. 2:11); see B.T. Ber. 30b.

[138] The narrative from the book of Joshua is actually suspended before the people enter Egypt.

[139] In the Mishnah itself, Rabban Gamliel's requirements are presented as statements rather than questions; see M. Pes. 10:5. The Haggadah, however, distinctly presents these recitations in the form of questions: "The Passover sacrifice . . . for what reason?" See Joseph Tabory, *JPS Commentary on the Haggadah: Historical Introduction, Translation, and Commentary* (Philadelphia: The Jewish Publication Society, 2008), 99.

HALLEL AT THE SEDER: A SONG OF REDEMPTION

question of Psalm 114 is an ideal conclusion to this question-answer session, emphasizing that the acknowledgment of God's deliverance is part and parcel of the narrative and critical to telling the story.

After the Meal: Psalms 115–118

I n accordance with the position of *Beit Hillel*, Psalms 115–118 are recited after the seder meal. These four final psalms of *Hallel* appear from a structural standpoint to be an integrated unit, lending support to *Beit Hillel's* position that they be read together.

The opening psalm in the sequence, 115, appears to be linked with Psalms 117 and 118. It begins with an appeal to God to deliver us not for our own sake but rather for God's sake, lest our continued suffering cause the nations of the world to question the competence of Israel's God (Ps. 115:1–3). Psalm 117, only two verses long, suggests that the nations of the world should praise God because God is good to the People of Israel. This is a somewhat baffling argument; but it is more understandable if read in conjunction with the beginning of Psalm 115; and reading the two psalms together makes sense, given both the linguistic and substantive connections between them. The exact phrasing of Psalm 115 is עַל חַסְדְּךָ עַל אֲמִתֶּךָ /"for Your kindness and Your steadfast truth" (v. 1). Strikingly, in Psalm 117, the author turns to the nations of the world, who had previously rejected God, and insists that they now praise God, whose greatness is once again described in terms of kindness and truth: כִּי גָבַר עָלֵינוּ חַסְדּוֹ וֶאֱמֶת יהוה לְעוֹלָם /"For His kindness overwhelms us, and the Lord's steadfast truth is forever" (v. 2). Toward the end of Psalm 115, the poet turns to Israel and implores its people to trust in God, dividing them into three groups: Israel, the House of Aaron, and those who fear God:

יִשְׂרָאֵל בְּטַח בַּיהוה עֶזְרָם וּמָגִנָּם הוּא: בֵּית אַהֲרֹן בִּטְחוּ בַיהוה עֶזְרָם וּמָגִנָּם הוּא:
יִרְאֵי יהוה בִּטְחוּ בַיהוה עֶזְרָם וּמָגִנָּם הוּא:

O Israel, trust in the Lord, *their help and their shield is He. House of Aaron, O trust in the* Lord, *their help and their shield is He. You who fear the* Lord, *trust in the* Lord, *their help and their shield is He.* (Ps. 115:9–11)

A Passover Haggadah: Go Forth and Learn

These three groups are invoked again in the following verses when the poet beseeches God to bless the people (115:12–13). And the same division appears at the beginning of Psalm 118 where, enjoining the people to praise God, the poet specifies:

יֹאמַר נָא יִשְׂרָאֵל כִּי לְעוֹלָם חַסְדּוֹ: יֹאמְרוּ נָא בֵית אַהֲרֹן כִּי לְעוֹלָם חַסְדּוֹ: יֹאמְרוּ נָא יִרְאֵי יהוה כִּי לְעוֹלָם חַסְדּוֹ:

Let Israel now say: forever is His kindness. Let the house of Aaron now say: forever is His kindness. Let those who fear the LORD now say: forever is His kindness. (Ps. 118:2–4)

Thus, whereas the first half of Psalm 115 is echoed in Psalm 117, the second half of Psalm 115 is paralleled in Psalm 118.

A close reading of Psalm 116 demonstrates that it parallels the second section of Psalm 118, further emphasizing the structural integrity of Psalms 115–118. Significantly, both Psalm 116 and Psalm 118 feature an individual who has been saved from a near-death experience and wants to thank God publicly for his deliverance; but whereas in Psalm 116, this theme is explicit, its appearance in Psalm 118 becomes evident primarily through comparison with 116. In Psalm 116, the author describes the experience of salvation from death and questions how he will possibly be able to repay God for the kindnesses that have been bestowed upon him (116:3–10). The answer that the Psalmist proposes is to raise a cup and call out in the name of God, paying his vows in the sight of God's people (116:13–14). This theme is repeated a few verses later, when the Psalmist again pledges to pay his vows, this time by offering a thanksgiving sacrifice and calling out in the name of God (116:17–19). Psalm 118 records a similar cry to God, although it is from the depths of despair:

מִן הַמֵּצַר קָרָאתִי יָּהּ עָנָנִי בַמֶּרְחָב יָהּ:

From the straits I called to Yah. Yah answered me in a wide-open place. (Ps. 118:5)

As in Psalm 116, the poet of 118 goes on to praise God for salvation and to extol the benefits of placing one's faith in God (118:7–9). The poet's repeated use of the term *sevavuni* (surrounded me) in 118:10–11 is noteworthy because elsewhere in the Bible that word functions as a poetic parallel to *afafuni* (encircled me)—a term that appears in 116:3.[140] In yet another parallel to the themes of Psalm 116, the poet of 118 reiterates the experience of deliverance from a near-death experience (118:13–14).[141] And in 118:25 he utters a cry beseeching God for salvation and prosperity that closely echoes 116:4. The poet then imagines that the response to his cry is an invitation to God's own residence (118:26), much as in 116 the Psalmist concludes his soliloquy with an allusion to the courtyard of God's home. And finally, the sacrifices mentioned in 116 are referenced in 118 as well (118:27).

Thus, the four final psalms of *Hallel* can be read as a unit in which the first three sections parallel the next three sections, thereby lending support to *Beit Hillel's* argument that they should be recited together.

Psalm 118: An Exodus Paradigm

In addition to its function within the structural unit described, Psalm 118 contributes independently to the seder-night liturgy. This psalm is a poetic expression of personal redemption that draws heavily from motifs present in the Exodus narrative. As a description of the poet's own personal exodus from Egypt, it is an ode to God for deliverance from travails.

The Psalmist's suffering is expressed in a metaphor that depicts him trapped in a narrow space:

מִן הַמֵּצַר קָרָאתִי יָּהּ עָנָנִי בַמֶּרְחָב יָהּ׃

From the straits [metzar] *I called to Yah. Yah answered me in a wide-open place.* (Ps. 118:5)

The nuance of the Hebrew words (often lost in translation) evokes Israel's historical oppression in Egypt: the word *metzar*—narrow place—sounds like the Hebrew name for Egypt, *Mitzrayim*. Furthermore, both biblically and in

---

[140] See Ps. 18:5–6.

[141] The poet may not be referring to an actual deliverance but rather to an imagined one.

A Passover Haggadah: Go Forth and Learn

the Haggadah, the oppression in Egypt is described with the same spatial metaphor employed by Psalm 118: as confinement in a narrow space. As we recount in the Haggadah:

וַנִּצְעַק אֶל יהוה אֱלֹהֵי אֲבֹתֵינוּ וַיִּשְׁמַע יהוה אֶת קֹלֵנוּ וַיַּרְא אֶת עָנְיֵנוּ וְאֶת עֲמָלֵנוּ וְאֶת לַחֲצֵנוּ... וְאֶת לַחֲצֵנוּ — זֶה הדחק, כמו שנאמר: וְגַם רָאִיתִי אֶת הַלַּחַץ אֲשֶׁר מִצְרַיִם לֹחֲצִים אֹתָם.

And we cried out to the LORD *God of our fathers, and the* LORD *heard our voice and saw our abuse and our trouble and our oppression (Deut. 26:7)...Our oppression—this is the persecution [dehak], as it is said: "And I have also seen the oppression with which the Egyptians oppress them" (Exod. 3:9).*

The association of the term used here to describe Israel's slavery—*lahatz*—with confinement in a narrow space derives from its usage in Numbers. When Balaam sets out to curse Israel, a sword-wielding angel impedes him by blocking the narrow path he is traveling astride his donkey:

וַתֵּרֶא הָאָתוֹן אֶת מַלְאַךְ יהוה וַתִּלָּחֵץ אֶל הַקִּיר וַתִּלְחַץ אֶת רֶגֶל בִּלְעָם אֶל הַקִּיר וַיֹּסֶף לְהַכֹּתָהּ:

And the ass saw the LORD'S *messenger and was pressed [va-tilahetz] against the wall and pressed [va-tilhatz] Balaam's leg against the wall, and once more he struck her. (Num. 22:25)*

The path is described in the Torah as becoming narrower and narrower until the donkey finally reaches an impasse:

וַיּוֹסֶף מַלְאַךְ יהוה עֲבוֹר וַיַּעֲמֹד בְּמָקוֹם צָר אֲשֶׁר אֵין דֶּרֶךְ לִנְטוֹת יָמִין וּשְׂמֹאול:

And the LORD'S *messenger crossed over and stood in a narrow [tzar] place in which there was no way to swerve right or left. (Num. 22:26)*

In the Balaam story, then, as in Exodus, *lahatz* appears as the violence and pain borne of constriction in a confined space: in Numbers, a *makom tzar*, in Exodus, *Mitzrayim*. In describing Israel's slavery in Egypt as *lahatz*, the Torah extends the metaphor of *Mitzrayim* to the suffering of people trapped, or in the language of Psalm 118, people who are in "the straits."[142]

But the parallels between Psalm 118 and the Exodus narrative go even further. The author of the psalm augments the depiction of the narrow place from which he calls out to God with words that evoke the experience of being enclosed, encircled, and enveloped:

כָּל גּוֹיִם סְבָבוּנִי בְּשֵׁם יהוה כִּי אֲמִילַם: סַבּוּנִי גַם סְבָבוּנִי בְּשֵׁם יהוה כִּי אֲמִילַם:
סַבּוּנִי כִדְבוֹרִים דֹּעֲכוּ כְּאֵשׁ קוֹצִים בְּשֵׁם יהוה כִּי אֲמִילַם:

All the nations surrounded me [sivavuni]. With the LORD's name I cut them down. They swarmed round me [sabuni], oh they surrounded me [sivavuni]. With the LORD's name I cut them down. They swarmed round me [sabuni] like bees, burned out like a fire among thorns. With the LORD's name I cut them down. (Ps. 118:10–12)

The Psalmist describes his terrible straits as the condition of being surrounded on all sides, of sensing the enemies closing in. This image resembles the Israelites at the edge of the sea, surrounded by the raging waters before them and the Egyptian army closing in behind them. According to the Torah, this desperate situation was, in fact, engineered by God, who purposefully "turned the people round [*va-yasev*]" (Exod. 13:18), sending them on a circuitous route. There at the sea, with no place to go, the people experience miraculous redemption and are inspired to sing a song of thanksgiving. At the beginning of this song, they summarize their experience and their gratitude:

עָזִּי וְזִמְרָת יָהּ וַיְהִי לִי לִישׁוּעָה...

My strength and my power is Yah, and He became my deliverance . . . (Exod. 15:2)

To reinforce the association, the Psalmist later transposed this verse, word for word, into 118:14.

---

[142] Picking up on this theme, the Haggadah translates *lahatz* as *dehak*, a descriptive term that in the talmudic literature means "a narrow place." Both Targum Onkelos and Targum Jonathan translate the word *lahatz* in a similar vein when it appears in Exod. 3:9.

A PASSOVER HAGGADAH: GO FORTH AND LEARN

The relationship between the Song at the Sea and Psalm 118 is even more extensive. The Psalmist describes redemption as being delivered by God's right arm no less than three times:

קוֹל רִנָּה וִישׁוּעָה בְּאָהֳלֵי צַדִּיקִים יְמִין יהוה עֹשָׂה חָיִל: יְמִין יהוה רוֹמֵמָה יְמִין יהוה עֹשָׂה חָיִל:

A voice of glad song and rescue in the tents of the just: The Lord's right hand does valiantly. The Lord's right hand is raised, the Lord's right hand does valiantly. (Ps. 118:15–16)[143]

Not surprisingly, the phrase *yemin Ha-Shem* (God's right arm) appears exactly three times in the song as well:

יְמִינְךָ יהוה נֶאְדָּרִי בַּכֹּחַ יְמִינְךָ יהוה תִּרְעַץ אוֹיֵב . . . נָטִיתָ יְמִינְךָ תִּבְלָעֵמוֹ אָרֶץ:

Your right hand, O Lord, is mighty in power. Your right hand, O Lord, smashes the enemy . . . You stretched out Your hand—earth swallowed them up. (Exod. 15:6,12)

The poet of Psalm 118, intent on paying tribute to God by telling the story of his deliverance (*lo amut ki ehyeh va-asaper ma'aseh Yah*), understands from the Song at the Sea that this can only be achieved in the context of the national Temple.[144] So he sets out on a (metaphorical) journey to find God's dwelling,

---

[143] In the verses just cited, the poet of Psalm 118 uses an A–B–A structure to frame and highlight the middle clause. This specific cry that the poet hears in the tents of the just, "the Lord's right hand is raised" (*yemin Ha-Shem romemah*), is significant because it further echoes the Song at the Sea. The continuation of the verse that the poet has transposed from Exodus uses a different form of the same verb, with a slightly different meaning:

עָזִּי וְזִמְרָת יָהּ וַיְהִי לִי לִישׁוּעָה זֶה אֵלִי וְאַנְוֵהוּ אֱלֹהֵי אָבִי וַאֲרֹמְמֶנְהוּ:

My strength and my power is Yah, and He became my deliverance. This is my God—I extol Him, God of my fathers—I exalt Him. (Exod. 15:2)

[144] The word *ve-anvehu* (I extol Him) in Exod. 15:2 derives from the same root as the word *neveh* which appears later in the song (15:13) as an allusion to God's holy habitation, the Temple. Thus, "This is my God—I extol Him [*ve-anvehu*]" is the speaker's declaration of his intent to extol God *in a temple*. (This is, in fact, the way that both Onkelos and Ibn Ezra translate the phrase; see their respective commentaries to Exod. 15:2).

HALLEL AT THE SEDER: A SONG OF REDEMPTION

beginning with the "tents of the just" (*ohalei tzaddikim*), which are not sufficiently public, and ultimately arriving at God's house, where he hopes to
fulfill his mission:

פִּתְחוּ לִי שַׁעֲרֵי צֶדֶק אָבֹא בָם אוֹדֶה יָהּ: זֶה הַשַּׁעַר לַיהוה צַדִּיקִים יָבֹאוּ בוֹ:

*Open for me the gates of justice—I would enter them, I would ac-
claim Yah. This is the gate of the* Lord—*the just will enter it.* (Ps.
118:19–20)

Upon finally arriving at God's abode and being welcomed there (Ps. 118:26),
the poet indeed offers his praises and expressions of thanksgiving (118:21).
And in the language of the Song at the Sea that was echoed by the just
in verse 16 (*yemin Ha-Shem romemah*) he acknowledges the truth of what he
heard in their tents: that in God's Temple he is at last able to extol God fully
(*Elokei avi ve-aromemekha*) (118:28).

From this perspective, the Psalmist seems to be arguing that true praise of God
is not possible in private but only in a communal setting. This notion is expressed in Psalm 116 through phrases such as "in the sight of all His people"
(116:14,18) and "in the courts of the house of the Lord" (116:19); and it is
even more clearly a theme of Psalm 118, which asserts that an individual can
say "My strength and my might is Yah" (118:14), but "my God, and I exalt
You" (118:28) can be declaimed only in the communal context. This is a
lesson that the Psalmist learned from the Song at the Sea, which emphasizes
that the most appropriate way to praise God is to publicly tell the story of
one's deliverance.

Hallel at its core is the narrative of a person who feels compelled to seek out
others so that he can tell his story. The significance of telling others about
the wonders God has performed—indeed, the deep religious need to do so—is
the key to the seder ritual as well. In the deepest sense, the seder is about creating community so that we can share with others the story of our collective
redemption. Thus, Psalm 118 is the perfect liturgical note on which to conclude the night's festivities.

Hallel at the Passover Seder

The Mishnah connects *Hallel* with two holidays in the Jewish calendar: Pesach and Sukkot. It seems that the primary association is actually with Sukkot, a Temple-based holiday on which the full *Hallel* is recited every day.[145] In contrast, the complete *Hallel* is recited only on the first of the seven days of Pesach, in conjunction with the slaughtering and eating of the Passover sacrifice.[146] Nonetheless, as we have attempted to demonstrate, the connection between Pesach and *Hallel* runs deep.

The psalms of *Hallel* are closely related to the song that the Israelites sang at the Sea of Reeds, a prayer of thanksgiving that both describes the personal experience of redemption and promotes worship at a central site where the glory and kingship of God can be proclaimed in public. As noted, the Song at the Sea concludes with a reference to the Temple, which can be accessed only by an act of "crossing over" from wasteland to the Promised Land:

עַד יַעֲבֹר עַמְּךָ יהוה עַד יַעֲבֹר עַם זוּ קָנִיתָ: תְּבִאֵמוֹ וְתִטָּעֵמוֹ בְּהַר נַחֲלָתְךָ מָכוֹן
לְשִׁבְתְּךָ פָּעַלְתָּ יהוה מִקְּדָשׁ אֲדֹנָי כּוֹנְנוּ יָדֶיךָ: יהוה יִמְלֹךְ לְעֹלָם וָעֶד:

. . . Till Your people crossed over, O LORD, *till the people you made Yours crossed over. You'll bring them, You'll plant them, on the mount of Your estate, a firm place for Your dwelling You wrought, O* LORD, *the sanctum, O Sovereign, Your hands firmly founded. The* LORD *shall be king for all time!* (Exod. 15:16–18)

This is precisely the form of thanksgiving that is expressed in the six psalms that comprise *Hallel*, and especially in the last four. The division of the *Hallel* at the seder into one unit of two psalms recited with *Maggid*, and one unit of four recited later in the evening, is a division suggested inherently by the

---

[145] M. Suk. 4:8. *Hallel* is mentioned in conjunction with *simhah*, holiday rejoicing. Hanukkah, which is a sort of Rabbinic Sukkot, is the other holiday on which we recite the full *Hallel* for eight days. See Tosefta Suk. 3:2, which provides a comprehensive list of the days on which the complete *Hallel* is recited and includes: eight days of Sukkot, eight days of Hanukkah, the first day and the first night of Pesach, and one day of Shavuot.

[146] M. Pes. 5:7 and 9:3.

text. The first two psalms relate to the Exodus itself, whereas the next four reflect the experience of leaving Egypt and journeying toward a holy site, the *Mikdash*.

It is clear that the recitation of *Hallel* is appropriate for Sukkot, which is the quintessential Temple holiday, because the Temple theme is so central to these psalms. However, the precise narrative arc traced in the *Hallel* passages is actually more reflective of the Passover experience: *Hallel* highlights the movement from Egypt to the Temple, and the movement from human bondage to service of God is what the Passover story is all about. Indeed, in the Torah, the concept of constructing sacred space marks both the culmination of the Exodus story (in the context of the Song at the Sea) and the conclusion of the book of Exodus as a whole.

But the Rabbis chose to end the seder with *Hallel* for another reason as well. The *Hallel* we recite at the seder and in holiday prayers is called "the Egyptian *Hallel*" not only because of the explicit reference to Israel leaving Egypt in Psalm 114, but also because the historical Exodus story and the experience of personal redemption are predominant motifs throughout the passages.

In the biblical text itself, the Israelites do not pray to God in response to their suffering at the hands of the Egyptians. The Israelites "groan" when their labor is intensified and "cry out" when they cannot bear the oppression (Exod. 2:23), and God responds to these cries of pain (2:23–25); but they are not expressions of prayer. Lack of voice and personal agency is a fundamental feature of slavery that precludes prayer. Remarkably, by the end of the story, the People of Israel are able to sing—to tell of their experiences, to express their gratitude, to articulate their hopes—which is the ultimate mark of freedom.[147]

---

[147] Over the course of the first section of Exodus, Moses himself undergoes a similar transformation from being a man who is "heavy of mouth and of tongue" to being a leader of song. This is one of many ways in which Moses' personal life experiences serve as symbols for the experiences of the entire nation; for further examples, see essay 3.

A PASSOVER HAGGADAH: GO FORTH AND LEARN

In a sense, the entire seder is a celebration of this newfound freedom of expression. By instituting the study of Torah as a centerpiece of the Passover-night ritual, the Rabbis intended to commemorate the emancipation from slavery, insofar as the cognitive acts that are entailed—questioning, answering, conversing, studying—reflect the unique rights and experiences of a free person. Prayer and song play a similar role. The *Hallel* with which we complete the seder is the perfect reflection of a process of becoming free, of moving from a state in which we lacked the ability to articulate ourselves to a state in which we are in full possession of our distinctive voice and can express both our gratitude for the past and our hopes for the future.

Abbreviations

For biblical references:

Chron.	Chronicles
Deut.	Deuteronomy
Eccles.	Ecclesiastes
Exod.	Exodus
Ezek.	Ezekiel
Gen.	Genesis
Is.	Isaiah
Jer.	Jeremiah
Jon.	Jonah
Josh.	Joshua
Judg.	Judges
Lam.	Lamentations
Lev.	Leviticus
Num.	Numbers
Ps.	Psalms
Sam.	Samuel

For talmudic references:

M.	Mishnah
T.	Tosefta
B.T.	Babylonian Talmud
J.T.	Jerusalem Talmud
Ber.	Berakhot
Bik.	Bikurim
Hor.	Horayot
Men.	Menahot
Naz.	Nazir
Pes.	Pesahim
Sanh.	Sanhedrin
Sot.	Sotah
Suk.	Sukah
Ta'an.	Ta'anit
Yev.	Yevamot

For biblical and talmudic commentaries:

Hizkuni	R. Hezekiah b. Manoah (c. 1250–1310)
Ibn Ezra	R. Abraham b. Meir ibn Ezra (1089–1164)
Radak	R. David b. Joseph Kimhi (1160–1235)
Rambam	R. Moses Maimonides (1138–1204)
Ramban	R. Moses Nachmanides (1194–c. 1270)
Rashi	R. Solomon b. Isaac (c. 1040–1105)
Seforno	R. Obadiah Seforno (1476–1550)

A Passover Haggadah: Go Forth and Learn

Bibliography and Suggestions
for Further Reading

Arnow, David. "The Passover Haggadah: Moses and the Human Role in Redemption." *Judaism* 55 (2006): 4–28.

Bakon, Shimon. "Creation, Tabernacle, and Sabbath." *Jewish Bible Quarterly* 25, no. 2 (1997): 79–85.

Bin-Nun, Yoel. "*Hametz* and *Matzah* on the Festivals of Pesah, Shavuot, and in the Bread Offerings" (in Hebrew). *Megadim* 13 (Adar 5751): 25–45.

Bokser, Barukh. *The Origins of the Seder: The Passover Rite and Early Rabbinic Judaism.* Berkeley, CA: University of California Press, 1984.

Buber, Martin. *The Way of the Bible* (in Hebrew). Jerusalem: Bialik Institute, 1964.

Cassuto, Umberto. *A Commentary on the Book of Genesis.* Jerusalem: Magnes Press, 1961.

Erlich, Tzvi. "The Garden of Eden Story as Compared to the Encounter at Mount Sinai and the *Mishkan*" (in Hebrew). *Alon shevut le-bogrei Yeshivat Har Etzion* 11 (5758): 17–35.

Geoghegan, Jeffrey C. "The Abrahamic Passover." In *Le-David Maskil*, ed. R. E. Friedman and W. H. C. Propp, 47–62. Winona Lake, In.: Eisenbrauns, 2004.

Goldschmidt, E. D. *The Passover Haggadah: Its Sources and History* (in Hebrew). Jerusalem: Bialik Institute, 1960.

Gottlieb, Freema. "Three Mothers." *Judaism* 30/2 (Spring 1981): 194–203.

Greenberg, Moshe. *Understanding Exodus*. New York: Behrman House, 1969.

Henshke, David. "'The Lord Brought Us Forth From Egypt': On the Absence of Moses in the Passover Haggadah." *AJS Review* 31 (2007): 61–73.

———. "The Midrash of the Passover Haggadah" (in Hebrew). *Sidra* 4 (1988): 33–52.

Hepner, Gershon. "Lot's Exodus from Sodom Foreshadows That of the Israelites from Egypt and the Passover Laws." *Zeitschrift für Altorientalische und Biblische Rechtsgeschichte* 9 (2003): 129–64.

Jacob, Beno. *The Second Book of the Bible: Exodus*. Trans. Walter Jacob. Hoboken, NJ: Ktav Publishing House, 1992.

Kasher, Menachem. *Haggadah Shleimah* (in Hebrew). Jerusalem: Torah Shleimah Institute, 1955.

Klitsner, Judy. *Subversive Sequels in the Bible*. Philadelphia: The Jewish Publication Society, 2009.

Kulp, Joshua and David Golinkin. *The Schechter Haggadah: Art, History, and Commentary*. Jerusalem: Schechter Institute of Jewish Studies, 2009.

Leibowitz, Nehama. *Studies in Shemot*. Jerusalem: The World Zionist Organization, 1976.

Peyser, Caroline. "The Book of Exodus: A Search for Identity." In *Torah of the Mothers*, ed. Ora Wiskind Elper and Susan Handelman, 379–97. Jerusalem: Urim, 2000.

Rovner, Jay. "Two Early Witnesses to the Formation of the 'Miqra Bikkurim Midrash' and Their Implications for the Evolution of the Haggadah Text." *HUCA* 75 (2004): 75–120.

BIBLIOGRAPHY AND SUGGESTIONS FOR FURTHER READING

Safrai, Shmuel and Ze'ev Safrai. *Haggadah of the Sages* (in Hebrew). Jerusalem: Carta, 1998.

Sarna, Nahum M. *Exploring Exodus: The Heritage of Biblical Israel*. New York: Schocken Books, 1986.

Shemesh, Aharon. "*Pesah zeh 'al shum mah?*" (in Hebrew). *AJS Review* 21, no. 2 (1996): 1–17.

Soloveitchik, Joseph B. *Shiurim le-zekher abba mari* (in Hebrew). 2 vols. Jerusalem: Mosad Ha-Rav Kook, 2002.

Steiner, Richard. "The 'Aramean' of Deuteronomy 26:5: Peshat and Derash." In *Tehillah le-Moshe: Biblical and Judaic Studies in Honor of Moshe Greenberg*, ed. Mordechai Cogan et al. 127–38. Winona Lake, In: Eisenbrauns, 1997.

Steinmetz, Devora. *From Father to Son: Kinship, Conflict, and Continuity in Genesis*. Louisville, KY: Westminster/John Knox Press, 1991.

Tabory, Joseph. *JPS Commentary on the Haggadah: Historical Introduction, Translation, and Commentary*. Philadelphia: The Jewish Publication Society, 2008.

Weitman, Zeev. "My Firstborn Son Israel" (in Hebrew). *Megadim* 48 (Iyar 5768): 37–46.

Yuval, Israel Jacob. *Two Nations in Your Womb: Perceptions of Jews and Christians in Late Antiquity and the Middle Ages*. Berkeley: University of California Press, 2006.

Bible Text Permissions

All verses from the Torah and Psalms are translated according to *The Five Books of Moses: A Translation with Commentary* (New York: W.W. Norton, 2004) and *The Book of Psalms: A Translation with Commentary* (New York: W.W. Norton, 2007) by Robert Alter, with a few minor changes. All other biblical texts are translated according to the *NJPS Hebrew-English Tanakh* (Philadelphia: The Jewish Publication Society, 1993).

צא ולמד

A Passover Haggadah

Go Forth and Learn

The Seder

The Seder Plate
הַקְּעָרָה

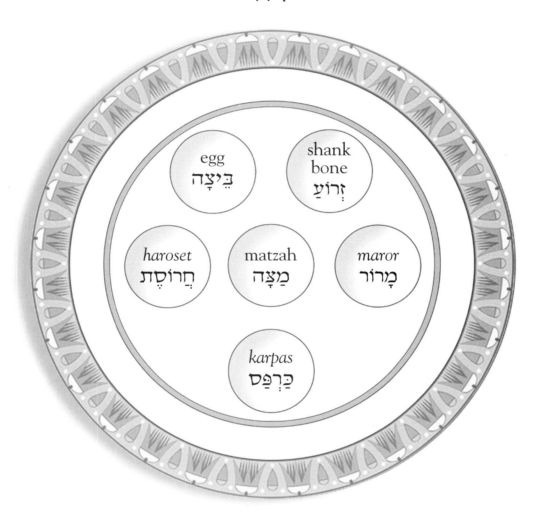

The symbolic foods are arranged on the seder plate according to custom.
This diagram reflects one common tradition.

The Seder Sections
סִימָנֵי הַסֵּדֶר

קַדֵּשׁ   Blessings over Wine

וּרְחַץ   First Hand-Washing

כַּרְפַּס   The Vegetables

יַחַץ   Breaking the Matzah

מַגִּיד   Telling the Story

רָחְצָה   Second Hand-Washing

מוֹצִיא   First Blessing on Matzah

מַצָּה   Second Blessing on Matzah

מָרוֹר   The Bitter Herbs

כּוֹרֵךְ   The Sandwich

שֻׁלְחָן עוֹרֵךְ   The Festive Meal

צָפוּן   The Hidden Matzah

בָּרֵךְ   Grace after Meals

הַלֵּל   Hymns of Praise

נִרְצָה   Concluding Songs

Kadesh
קַדֵשׁ

When Passover falls on Friday night, begin here.
On any other day, skip to the next paragraph.

(And it was evening and it was morning) the sixth day. Then the heavens and the earth were completed, and all their array. And God completed on the seventh day the task He had done, and He ceased on the seventh day from all the task He had done. And God blessed the seventh day and hallowed it, for on it He had ceased from all His task that He had created to do (Gen. 1:31–2:3).

(וַיְהִי עֶרֶב וַיְהִי בֹקֶר) יוֹם הַשִּׁשִּׁי: וַיְכֻלּוּ הַשָּׁמַיִם וְהָאָרֶץ וְכָל צְבָאָם: וַיְכַל אֱלֹהִים בַּיּוֹם הַשְּׁבִיעִי מְלַאכְתּוֹ אֲשֶׁר עָשָׂה וַיִּשְׁבֹּת בַּיּוֹם הַשְּׁבִיעִי מִכָּל מְלַאכְתּוֹ אֲשֶׁר עָשָׂה: וַיְבָרֶךְ אֱלֹהִים אֶת יוֹם הַשְּׁבִיעִי וַיְקַדֵּשׁ אֹתוֹ כִּי בוֹ שָׁבַת מִכָּל מְלַאכְתּוֹ אֲשֶׁר בָּרָא אֱלֹהִים לַעֲשׂוֹת: (בראשית א:לא-ב:ג)

Attention.

Blessed are You, Lord** our God, Creator of the fruit of the vine.**

סַבְרִי.

בָּרוּךְ אַתָּה יי אֱלֹהֵינוּ מֶלֶךְ הָעוֹלָם בּוֹרֵא פְּרִי הַגָּפֶן.

On the Sabbath, add the words in parentheses.

Blessed are You, Lord our God, King of the universe, who has chosen us from all the nations and has exalted us from all tongues and has sanctified us with His commandments. And You have given us, Lord our God, in love, (Sabbaths for rest and) appointed times for joy, festivals and times for rejoicing, (this day of Sabbath and) this day of the festival of matzot, the time of our freedom, (in love,) a holy convocation, a memorial of the Exodus from Egypt. For You have chosen us and sanctified us from among all nations and You have granted us (the

בָּרוּךְ אַתָּה יי אֱלֹהֵינוּ מֶלֶךְ הָעוֹלָם, אֲשֶׁר בָּחַר בָּנוּ מִכָּל עָם וְרוֹמְמָנוּ מִכָּל לָשׁוֹן וְקִדְּשָׁנוּ בְּמִצְוֹתָיו, וַתִּתֶּן לָנוּ יי אֱלֹהֵינוּ בְּאַהֲבָה (שַׁבָּתוֹת לִמְנוּחָה וּ)מוֹעֲדִים לְשִׂמְחָה, חַגִּים וּזְמַנִּים לְשָׂשׂוֹן, אֶת (יוֹם הַשַּׁבָּת הַזֶּה וְאֶת) יוֹם חַג הַמַּצּוֹת הַזֶּה, זְמַן חֵרוּתֵנוּ (בְּאַהֲבָה), מִקְרָא קֹדֶשׁ, זֵכֶר לִיצִיאַת מִצְרָיִם. כִּי בָנוּ בָחַרְתָּ וְאוֹתָנוּ קִדַּשְׁתָּ מִכָּל הָעַמִּים, (וְשַׁבָּת)

Sabbath and) Your holy appointed time (in love and in grace,) in joy and in gladness. Blessed are You, Lord, who sanctifies (the Sabbath and) Israel and the special times.

וּמוֹעֲדֵי קָדְשֶׁךָ (בְּאַהֲבָה וּבְרָצוֹן,) בְּשִׂמְחָה וּבְשָׂשׂוֹן הִנְחַלְתָּנוּ. בָּרוּךְ אַתָּה יי, מְקַדֵּשׁ (הַשַּׁבָּת וְ)יִשְׂרָאֵל וְהַזְּמַנִּים.

When Passover falls on Saturday night, the following two blessings are added.

Blessed are You, Lord our God, King of the universe, Creator of the lights of the fire.

בָּרוּךְ אַתָּה יי אֱלֹהֵינוּ מֶלֶךְ הָעוֹלָם, בּוֹרֵא מְאוֹרֵי הָאֵשׁ.

Blessed are You, Lord our God, King of the universe, who distinguishes between holy and profane, between light and darkness, between Israel and the nations, between the seventh day of the week and the six days of activity. You have distinguished between the sanctity of Sabbath and the sanctity of the festival, and You have sanctified the seventh day of the week over the six days of activity. You have distinguished Your people Israel and have sanctified them with Your sanctity. Blessed are You, Lord, who distinguishes between sanctity and sanctity.

בָּרוּךְ אַתָּה יי אֱלֹהֵינוּ מֶלֶךְ הָעוֹלָם הַמַּבְדִּיל בֵּין קֹדֶשׁ לְחֹל, בֵּין אוֹר לְחֹשֶׁךְ, בֵּין יִשְׂרָאֵל לָעַמִּים, בֵּין יוֹם הַשְּׁבִיעִי לְשֵׁשֶׁת יְמֵי הַמַּעֲשֶׂה, בֵּין קְדֻשַּׁת שַׁבָּת לִקְדֻשַּׁת יוֹם טוֹב הִבְדַּלְתָּ, וְאֶת יוֹם הַשְּׁבִיעִי מִשֵּׁשֶׁת יְמֵי הַמַּעֲשֶׂה קִדַּשְׁתָּ, הִבְדַּלְתָּ וְקִדַּשְׁתָּ אֶת עַמְּךָ יִשְׂרָאֵל בִּקְדֻשָּׁתֶךָ. בָּרוּךְ אַתָּה יי הַמַּבְדִּיל בֵּין קֹדֶשׁ לְקֹדֶשׁ.

On all days continue here.

Blessed are You, Lord our God, King of the universe, who has kept us alive, sustained us, and brought us to this time.

בָּרוּךְ אַתָּה יי אֱלֹהֵינוּ מֶלֶךְ הָעוֹלָם, שֶׁהֶחֱיָנוּ וְקִיְּמָנוּ וְהִגִּיעָנוּ לַזְּמַן הַזֶּה.

Drink while reclining to the left.

A Passover Haggadah: Go Forth and Learn

U-Rehatz

וּרְחַץ

Wash hands without reciting a blessing.

Karpas

כַּרְפַּס

Dip a vegetable in salt water and recite the following blessing.

Blessed are You, LORD our God, King of the universe, Creator of the fruit of the earth.

בָּרוּךְ אַתָּה יי אֱלֹהֵינוּ מֶלֶךְ הָעוֹלָם,
בּוֹרֵא פְּרִי הָאֲדָמָה.

Yahatz

יַחַץ

Break the middle matzah into two and put away
the larger part to eat later as the *afikoman*.

Maggid

מַגִּיד

It is customary to display the matzot while reciting the following.

¹**Behold, the bread of poverty** that our ancestors ate while in the land of Egypt. All who are hungry come and eat. ²All who are needy, come and participate in the Passover ritual. Today we are here; next year in the Land of Israel. Today we are slaves; next year we shall be free people.

¹ הָא לַחְמָא עַנְיָא דִּי אֲכָלוּ אַבְהָתָנָא בְּאַרְעָא דְמִצְרָיִם. כָּל דִּכְפִין יֵיתֵי וְיֵיכֻל. ² כָּל דִּצְרִיךְ יֵיתֵי וְיִפְסַח. הָשַׁתָּא הָכָא, לְשָׁנָה הַבָּאָה בְּאַרְעָא דְיִשְׂרָאֵל. הָשַׁתָּא עַבְדֵי, לְשָׁנָה הַבָּאָה בְּנֵי חוֹרִין.

---

1 Behold, the bread of poverty. *Ha lahma anya* is recited while raising the matzah for emphasis, to indicate that the matzah we use at the seder is the very bread our ancestors ate in Egypt. From the wording of this declaration, it sounds as though we are referring to bread they ate while still slaves; however, the Torah itself never explicitly refers to matzah as such. The Torah does instruct the Israelites to eat matzah together with the original Passover offering, during the Plague of the Firstborn (Exod. 12:8). But primarily it tells of the Israelites eating matzah on the way out of Egypt, the matzah they baked in haste as they rushed to leave (12:39). In fact, the very term *lahma anya*, which is an Aramaic translation of the Hebrew *lehem oni* (bread of poverty), derives from a verse that speaks of eating matzah on Passover to remember the hurriedness with which our ancestors left slavery:

לֹא תֹאכַל עָלָיו חָמֵץ שִׁבְעַת יָמִים תֹּאכַל עָלָיו מַצּוֹת לֶחֶם עֹנִי כִּי בְחִפָּזוֹן יָצָאתָ מֵאֶרֶץ מִצְרַיִם לְמַעַן תִּזְכֹּר אֶת יוֹם צֵאתְךָ מֵאֶרֶץ מִצְרַיִם כֹּל יְמֵי חַיֶּיךָ:

You shall not eat unleavened stuff with it. Seven days you shall eat it with flatcakes, poverty's bread [lehem oni], for in haste [be-hipazon] you did go out from the land of Egypt; so that you will remember the day of your going out from Egypt all the days of your life (Deut. 16:3).

The *lahma anya*, then, is not the bread of bondage but the bread of redemption. However, it is meant to remind us specifically of the unpreparedness that characterized our departure from Egypt, the swift and sudden way in which redemption occurred.

In biblical Hebrew, the word *hipazon*, which the Torah uses to describe the hasty redemption, typically carries a negative connotation. Jonathan's son Mephibosheth is crippled when he falls from the hands of his nurse, who flees in haste (*be-hofzah la-nus*) after hearing news of Jonathan's and Saul's deaths (2 Sam. 4:4). The Psalmist admits that he spoke rashly (*be-hofzi*) when he declared that all men are false (Ps. 116:11). Thus, in using this word, the Torah is suggesting that there is something negative about the hastiness with which the Israelites left Egypt and the lack of preparation that characterized the Exodus. If breaking bread in the Bible symbolizes understanding, loyalty, and

Remove the seder plate and fill the second cup of wine.

It is customary for the youngest child to ask the following questions.

[3] Why is [4] this night different from all other nights?

מַה נִּשְׁתַּנָּה [3] הַלַּיְלָה [4] הַזֶּה מִכָּל הַלֵּילוֹת?

---

covenantal relationship, eating matzah represents uncertainty, limited trust, and shaky relationships. (For further discussion, see essays 3 and 6.) The half-baked matzah signifies incompleteness and imperfection and implies that redemption did not occur in an ideal manner.

Yet the more common understanding is that the hastiness of the Exodus testifies to the Israelites' faith in God and trust in Moses. The fact that they were willing to leave Egypt immediately upon command, without planning or forethought, demonstrates their belief and their confidence. As the prophet Jeremiah declares, the devotion of youth and newlywed love with which the nation followed God into the wilderness is counted to their favor (Jer. 2:2). From this perspective, the matzah of haste is a most positive symbol.

It is this positive understanding of matzah that explains the paragraph's concluding lines. We recite, "Today we are here; next year in the Land of Israel. Today we are slaves; next year free people," and we hope that just as we left Egypt suddenly, in haste, so too may we leave our present exile quickly, at a moment's notice. We do not know how or when redemption will come; but we hope and pray that we will be redeemed soon, that even next year we will be free people in the Land of Israel.

2 All who are needy, come and participate in the Passover ritual. The Haggadah, which was composed primarily in Rabbinic Hebrew, begins in Aramaic with a last-minute invitation to the needy to join the seder. Traditionally, this call is understood as an invitation to participate in both the meal (*yeitei ve-yeikhol*, "come and eat") and in the sacrificial rite (*yeitei ve-yifsah*, "come and participate in the Passover ritual"). But this interpretation is problematic, because according to Jewish law participation in the Passover offering must be determined before the animal is slaughtered, and at this stage it would be too late to add "guests."

Alternatively, the term *va-yifsah* could be understood as an invitation to stay and linger at the seder. Most commentaries understand the word *pasah* to mean "pass over," as when God saw blood marking the Israelite homes during the Plague of the Firstborn (Exod. 12:13). But some claim that *pasah* means "lean" (Rav Saadiah Gaon) or "protect" (the Septuagint), implying that God did not skip over the Israelite homes but rather hovered above them in protection (see Ibn Ezra on Exod. 12:27). When we invite the needy to come and "make Pesach," we're not inviting them to eat and leave but rather to "hover" with us—that is, to join us for the duration of the ritual and to participate fully in the learning, the singing, and the celebration.

3 Why is this night different from all other nights? The four *Mah Nishtanah* questions that appear in our text are distinct from those found in earlier versions of the Haggadah.[1] The original *Mah*

---

[1] Tracing the provenance of our version of the *Mah Nishtanah* is complex and has been discussed extensively by other scholars: See Joseph Tabory, *JPS Commentary on the Haggadah: Historical Introduction, Translation, and*

On all other nights we may eat both leavened bread [5] and matzah; on this night we eat only matzah.

שֶׁבְּכָל הַלֵּילוֹת אָנוּ אוֹכְלִין חָמֵץ [5] וּמַצָּה — הַלַּיְלָה הַזֶּה כּוֹלוֹ מַצָּה.

Nishtanah (as reflected in reliable manuscripts of the Mishnah, including Kaufman and Parma) seems to have included only three questions:

שֶׁבְּכָל הַלֵּילוֹת אָנוּ מַטְבִּילִין פַּעַם אֶחָת, הַלַּיְלָה הַזֶּה שְׁתֵּי פְעָמִים.
שֶׁבְּכָל הַלֵּילוֹת אָנוּ אוֹכְלִין חָמֵץ וּמַצָּה, הַלַּיְלָה הַזֶּה כֻּלּוֹ מַצָּה.
שֶׁבְּכָל הַלֵּילוֹת אָנוּ אוֹכְלִין בָּשָׂר צָלִי שָׁלוּק וּמְבוּשָׁל, הַלַּיְלָה הַזֶּה כֻּלּוֹ צָלִי.

On all other nights we dip one time, on this night two times.
On all other nights we eat *hametz* and matzah, on this night only matzah.
On all other nights, we eat roasted, stewed, and boiled meat, on this night only roasted.

These three questions correspond to the three main foods eaten at the seder: *maror*, matzah, and the Passover offering. (The dipping question is primarily about the *maror*, although the bitter herbs are not explicitly mentioned.) In ancient texts, then, *Mah Nishtanah* paralleled Rabban Gamliel's statement (which is quoted at the end of *Maggid*) regarding the three items that must be mentioned at the seder: *Pesah*, matzah, and *maror*. The connection between *Mah Nishtanah* and Rabban Gamliel's teaching is further reflected in the Haggadah's response to these passages: the Haggadah answers the *Mah Nishtanah* questions by citing Deuteronomy 6:21 and follows Rabban Gamliel's statement with a quote from Deuteronomy 6:23. Thus the two passages, which frame the *Maggid* section both structurally and thematically, serve to highlight the core of the biblical Passover ritual: the *korban Pesah* and its accoutrements.

4 this night. The *Mah Nishtanah* and other liturgical portions of the Haggadah emphasize the centrality of nighttime to Passover ritual. The Exodus itself took place in the middle of the night (Exod. 12:29–32, Deut. 16:1) and consequently the night of 15 Nisan is considered an auspicious time, a *leil shimurim* (night of protection) (Exod. 12:42). In virtually all cultures, night is associated with danger and vulnerability; it is a fearful time, not a time one would normally choose to journey. Thus, conducting the seder at night highlights God's role as protector and savior of Israel and also underscores the unexpectedness that characterized the moment of redemption. The focus on nighttime, here and elsewhere in the Haggadah, reminds us that even at the darkest moment, salvation is possible.

5 and matzah. The etymology of the word "matzah" can be explained in two ways. "Matzah" is usually assumed to derive from the root מ-צ-ה, meaning "to drain" or "to squeeze." This appears to

----

Commentary (Philadelphia: The Jewish Publication Society), 28–31; and Joshua Kulp and David Golinkin, *The Schechter Haggadah: Art, History, and Commentary* (Jerusalem: Schechter Institute of Jewish Studies, 2009), 198–200.

A PASSOVER HAGGADAH: GO FORTH AND LEARN

On all other nights, we eat all kinds of vegetables; on this night we eat bitter herbs.

שֶׁבְּכָל הַלֵּילוֹת אָנוּ אוֹכְלִין שְׁאָר יְרָקוֹת — הַלַּיְלָה הַזֶּה מָרוֹר.

On all other nights we do not dip even once; on this night we dip twice.

שֶׁבְּכָל הַלֵּילוֹת אֵין אָנוּ מַטְבִּילִין אֲפִילוּ פַּעַם אֶחָת — הַלַּיְלָה הַזֶּה שְׁתֵּי פְעָמִים.

On all other nights we may eat either while sitting or leaning; on this night we all eat while leaning.

שֶׁבְּכָל הַלֵּילוֹת אָנוּ אוֹכְלִין בֵּין יוֹשְׁבִין וּבֵין מְסֻבִּין — הַלַּיְלָה הַזֶּה כֻּלָּנוּ מְסֻבִּין.

Return the seder plate to the table and uncover the matzot.

Slaves were we to Pharaoh in Egypt, and the LORD brought us out (Deut. 6:21) from there with a strong hand and an outstretched arm (Deut. 5:15). And if the Blessed Holy One had not taken our ancestors out of Egypt, we, our children, and our children's children would be enslaved to Pharaoh in Egypt.

עֲבָדִים הָיִינוּ לְפַרְעֹה בְּמִצְרַיִם, וַיּוֹצִיאֵנוּ יהוה (דברים ו:כא) אֱלֹהֵינוּ מִשָּׁם בְּיָד חֲזָקָה וּבִזְרוֹעַ נְטוּיָה (דברים ה:טו). וְאִלּוּ לֹא הוֹצִיא הַקָּדוֹשׁ בָּרוּךְ הוּא אֶת אֲבוֹתֵינוּ מִמִּצְרַיִם, הֲרֵי אָנוּ וּבָנֵינוּ וּבְנֵי בָנֵינוּ מְשֻׁעְבָּדִים הָיִינוּ לְפַרְעֹה בְּמִצְרַיִם.

---

be the understanding in Deuteronomy, which calls matzah *lehem oni* (16:3), "the bread of poverty," meaning the bread of hardship and affliction, the bread from which everything has been drained out. Alternatively, the word "matzah" may derive from the root נ-צ-ה, meaning "to struggle" or "to fight," suggesting that matzah is the bread of conflict and strife.

Variations on the root נ-צ-ה appear several times in the Bible to depict people engaged in conflict. At the beginning of the Exodus narrative, Moses attempts to separate two scuffling Hebrew slaves described as *nitzim* (Exod. 2:13). Later, in the desert, a fight breaks out (*va-yinatzu*) between an Israelite and the son of an Egyptian man, who blasphemes God's name (Lev. 24:10). The Torah rules that if two men are fighting (*yinatzu*) and one hits a pregnant woman, causing her to miscarry, he must pay damages (Exod. 21:22). Alternatively, if two men are fighting (*yinatzu*) and the wife of one attempts to save her husband by seizing the genitals of his attacker, she is punished (Deut. 25:11). In Samuel, a wise woman from Tekoa tells King David about two fatherless sons who were arguing in a field (*va-yinatzu*) with no one to intervene, when one arose and killed his brother (2 Sam. 14:6). In each of these instances, two people are engaged in a conflict that involves, or should involve, a third party. Perhaps, then, the word "matzah" represents God's intervention in the conflict between the Egyptians and the Israelites, without which redemption could not have come about. The Torah's command to observe, or to remember, the matzah (*u-shmartem et ha-matzot*) (Exod.12:17) requires us to consider that without God's intervention we might still be slaves in a place of conflict and affliction.

⁶And even if we were all wise, we were all understanding, we were all elders, we all knew the Torah, we would still be obligated to tell about the Exodus from Egypt. And the more one tells about the Exodus from Egypt, behold it is praiseworthy.

⁷**It happened** that R. Eliezer, R. Joshua, R. Eleazar b. Azaryah, R. Akiva, and R. Tarfon were reclining in Bnei Brak and were discussing the Exodus throughout the night,

⁶ וַאֲפִילוּ כֻּלָּנוּ חֲכָמִים, כֻּלָּנוּ נְבוֹנִים, כֻּלָּנוּ זְקֵנִים, כֻּלָּנוּ יוֹדְעִים אֶת הַתּוֹרָה, מִצְוָה עָלֵינוּ לְסַפֵּר בִּיצִיאַת מִצְרָיִם. וְכָל הַמַּרְבֶּה לְסַפֵּר בִּיצִיאַת מִצְרָיִם הֲרֵי זֶה מְשֻׁבָּח.

⁷ מַעֲשֶׂה בְּרַבִּי אֱלִיעֶזֶר וְרַבִּי יְהוֹשֻׁעַ וְרַבִּי אֶלְעָזָר בֶּן עֲזַרְיָה וְרַבִּי עֲקִיבָא וְרַבִּי טַרְפוֹן שֶׁהָיוּ מְסֻבִּין בִּבְנֵי בְרַק, וְהָיוּ מְסַפְּרִים בִּיצִיאַת מִצְרַיִם כָּל אוֹתוֹ

---

6 And even if we were all wise. The word *kulanu* (we all) repeats itself four times in this brief passage and echoes the last of the Four Questions, which asserts that on the seder night *kulanu mesubin* (we all recline). In its repeated use of this word, the Haggadah seems to be underscoring the importance of inclusiveness at the seder; but it also highlights another theme central to Passover. The repetition of the word *kulanu* conveys a sense of multitude and abundance, and indeed the seder is a ritual of exaggeration and excess. The Haggadah declares that everyone (*kol*) who lengthens the Exodus narration is worthy of praise, and in the narrative passage that follows we tell of the five scholars in Bnei Brak who stayed awake telling of the Exodus throughout the entire (*kol*) seder night. Rather than resolving a talmudic dispute concerning which passage should begin the Exodus narrative (B.T. Pes. 116a), we include both options. We dip vegetables not once but twice. We speak of ten plagues that become forty and then fifty. We don't end the ritual at the seder's natural conclusion but continue singing songs of praise. For as we say in the *Nishmat* prayer that is appended to the *Hallel* section of the seder, it is impossible to express sufficient gratitude for all the wonders God has performed or to praise God sufficiently for all the goodness God has bestowed upon us.

7 It happened that . . . were reclining in Bnei Brak. This anecdote about the rabbis gathered in Bnei Brak is presumably cited by the Haggadah to substantiate the two directives of the previous paragraph: that the Exodus story must be told at the seder even if all participants are learned; and that one should aim to prolong and extend the Exodus narration. This specific account does not appear in other Rabbinic texts, suggesting that it was composed expressly for the Haggadah. Several striking details bear examination, in particular the description of the rabbis "reclining in Bnei Brak" (a more precise translation than the usual "gathered in Bnei Brak") and the manner in which their students announce the dawning of a new day: "the time to recite the morning *Shema* has arrived." Assuming that the Haggadah's presentation is precise and intentional, these two details may offer a new perspective on one of the main ritual acts at the seder.

In Rabbinic sources, reclining (*hasavah*) is generally associated with eating. Our Haggadah's version of *Mah Nishtanah* asserts, "On all other nights we may eat either while sitting or leaning . . ." Mishnah *Pesahim* 10:1 teaches that "even the poorest person in Israel should not eat until he

A Passover Haggadah: Go Forth and Learn

| until their students came and said to them: "Our masters, the time to recite the morning *Shema* has arrived." | הַלַּיְלָה עַד שֶׁבָּאוּ תַלְמִידֵיהֶם וְאָמְרוּ לָהֶם: רַבּוֹתֵינוּ, הִגִּיעַ זְמַן קְרִיאַת שְׁמַע שֶׁל שַׁחֲרִית. |
| **8 R. Eleazar ben Azaryah said**: Behold, I am about seventy years old, and I had never | ⁸ אָמַר רַבִּי אֶלְעָזָר בֶּן עֲזַרְיָה: הֲרֵי אֲנִי כְּבֶן שִׁבְעִים שָׁנָה, וְלֹא זָכִיתִי שֶׁתֵּאָמֵר |

reclines." And later rulings require one to recline at the seder specifically when eating certain ritual foods. But the Bnei Brak anecdote suggests that reclining at the seder is not restricted to eating: the rabbis reclined all night long, throughout the hours they narrated the Exodus story! According to the Talmud, *hasavah* while eating is an expression of freedom (J.T. Pes. 10:1,37b); but *hasavah* while telling the Exodus story may assume an additional meaning. Here, the students' comment is key.

In Bnei Brak the students arrive to tell their teachers that it is morning and, therefore, time to conclude the seder. But their comment regarding the *Shema* seems out of context and unnecessarily complicated; the story's closest parallel in Tosefta *Pesahim* (10:12–13) represents the arrival of dawn simply as "cock's crow." The students' announcement that "the time to recite the morning *Shema* has arrived" suggests that they perceived this new obligation as conflicting with the rabbis' night-time activity. What the rabbis had been doing at night was reclining, or lying down. They had been engaged in telling the Exodus story, but the position they adopted is strikingly similar to the posture required by the School of Shammai for the recitation of the evening *Shema*. According to the School of Shammai, the evening *Shema* is recited while reclining to fulfill the Torah's command that it be said "when you lie down" (*be-shokhbekha*); and accordingly, the morning *Shema* is recited while standing up to fulfill the command that it be said "when you rise" (*be-kumekha*) (M. Ber. 1:6). The similar reclining posture mandated for both telling the Exodus story and reciting the *Shema*— a posture that recalls sleeping—highlights the depth of their association with the night. In announcing that it was time to recite the morning *Shema*, the students meant to say: nighttime is over; it is time to stand up and engage in other commandments!

The recitation of the *Shema* is additionally related to Passover-night storytelling insofar as both are declarations of faith in God and both mention the Exodus. (Indeed, framing the *Shema* in this manner may also explain the connection between the Bnei Brak story and the narrative that follows regarding Rabbi Eleazar ben Azaryah and "remembering" the Exodus.) But telling the Exodus story at the seder is a way of re-creating and re-experiencing the moment of redemption, whereas reciting the daily *Shema* is a means of ritualizing that moment and thereby keeping it alive throughout the year. Thus, the students' announcement about the morning *Shema* was also a way of saying to their teachers: now that the seder is over, it is time to consider how you will preserve the sacred moment of redemption on a daily basis.

8 R. Eleazar ben Azaryah said. The dispute recorded in this passage is taken from Mishnah *Berakhot* 1:5 and concerns the number of times one is obligated to mention the Exodus on a daily basis (in the context of the *Shema*). Ostensibly, this discussion is unrelated to the seder night: it is about the ongoing, daily mitzvah to remember the Exodus (*zekhirah*), rather than the one-time, annual

THE SEDER

convinced anyone that the Exodus should be mentioned at night until Ben Zoma expounded it from a verse, as it says: *so that you will remember the day of your going out from Egypt all the days of your life* (Deut. 16:3); *the days of your life*—daytimes; *all the days of your life*—nighttimes. But the Sages say: *the days of your life*—this world; *all the days of your life*—to include the world to come.

Blessed is the Omnipresent, blessed is He. Blessed is the One who gave the Torah to His people, Israel, blessed is He.

יְצִיאַת מִצְרַיִם בַּלֵּילוֹת עַד שֶׁדְּרָשָׁהּ בֶּן זוֹמָא: שֶׁנֶּאֱמַר, לְמַעַן תִּזְכֹּר אֶת יוֹם צֵאתְךָ מֵאֶרֶץ מִצְרַיִם כֹּל יְמֵי חַיֶּיךָ (דברים טז:ג). יְמֵי חַיֶּיךָ — הַיָּמִים, כָּל יְמֵי חַיֶּיךָ — הַלֵּילוֹת. וַחֲכָמִים אוֹמְרִים: יְמֵי חַיֶּיךָ — הָעוֹלָם הַזֶּה, כָּל יְמֵי חַיֶּיךָ — לְהָבִיא לִימוֹת הַמָּשִׁיחַ.

בָּרוּךְ הַמָּקוֹם, בָּרוּךְ הוּא. בָּרוּךְ שֶׁנָּתַן תּוֹרָה לְעַמּוֹ יִשְׂרָאֵל, בָּרוּךְ הוּא.

---

mitzvah to tell the story (*sippur*) of leaving Egypt. However, the verse at the heart of this debate is about eating the Passover offering together with matzah on the holiday of Pesach, and actually combines the two mitzvot:

לֹא תֹאכַל עָלָיו חָמֵץ שִׁבְעַת יָמִים תֹּאכַל עָלָיו מַצּוֹת לֶחֶם עֹנִי כִּי בְחִפָּזוֹן יָצָאתָ מֵאֶרֶץ מִצְרַיִם לְמַעַן תִּזְכֹּר אֶת יוֹם צֵאתְךָ מֵאֶרֶץ מִצְרַיִם כֹּל יְמֵי חַיֶּיךָ:

You shall not eat unleavened stuff with it [i.e. the Passover offering]. Seven days you shall eat it with flatcakes, poverty's bread [lehem oni], for in haste you did go out from the land of Egypt; so that you will remember the day of your going out from Egypt all the days of your life. (Deut. 16:2–3)

Strikingly, in this passage, the one-time Passover offering, which may not be eaten with *hametz*, generates both a seven-day observance marked by the eating of matzah and a lifelong obligation to remember the Exodus on a daily basis. Although the seder night is a unique opportunity to relive and retell the Exodus, the use of this verse from Deuteronomy in the Mishnah and its inclusion in the Haggadah emphasize that remembering and ritualizing the Exodus is an ongoing obligation.

(The citation of Deut. 16:2–3 at this point in the seder may also serve a structural function: As we noted earlier, this is the passage upon which the *Ha lahma anya* paragraph is based, the passage that opened the *Maggid* section. Citing it again at this point suggests that we are about to conclude the first unit of this section.)

The Torah refers to four children: one **wise**; one **wicked**; one **simple**; and one **who does not know how to ask a question**.

What does the **wise one** say? *What are the terms and the statutes and the laws with which the LORD our God has charged you?* (Deut. 6:20). [10] And so you should tell him as in the laws of Passover, "one may not partake of the *afikoman* after the Passover meal."

⁹ כְּנֶגֶד אַרְבָּעָה בָנִים דִּבְּרָה תוֹרָה. אֶחָד חָכָם, וְאֶחָד רָשָׁע, וְאֶחָד תָּם, וְאֶחָד שֶׁאֵינוֹ יוֹדֵעַ לִשְׁאוֹל.

חָכָם מָה הוּא אוֹמֵר? מָה הָעֵדוֹת וְהַחֻקִּים וְהַמִּשְׁפָּטִים אֲשֶׁר צִוָּה יהוה אֱלֹהֵינוּ אֶתְכֶם? (דברים ו:כ). ¹⁰ וְאַף אַתָּה אֱמֹר לוֹ כְּהִלְכוֹת הַפֶּסַח: אֵין מַפְטִירִין אַחַר הַפֶּסַח אֲפִיקוֹמָן.

---

9 The Torah refers to four children. The *baraita* of the Four Children presents four models of education, which derive from the four passages in the Torah that depict parent-child exchanges regarding the Exodus (Exod. 12:26–27; 13:8,14–15; and Deut. 6:20–25). The Haggadah draws on these four biblical passages in its rendering of the children's questions but cites only two of the verses in its presentation of the parents' responses. Notably, the Haggadah does not cite the response that corresponds to the wicked child's question in the Torah (Exod. 13:14). Instead, the response given to the wicked child is the same as that given to the child who does not know how to ask: "[And you shall tell your son (*ve-higadeta le-binkha*) on that day, saying,] 'For the sake of what the LORD did for me when I went out of Egypt'" (Exod. 13:8). In this manner, the Haggadah highlights a basic similarity between these two archetypes: neither asks a question. Although the wicked child presents his comment as an inquiry, the Haggadah understands it to be fundamentally a statement of rejection: the wicked child is not interested in an answer. Hence, neither the wicked child nor the child who does not know how to ask are answered; they are simply "told" (*ve-higadeta*). In this manner, the *baraita* of the Four Children touches upon a fundamental aspect of the seder-night obligation to tell the Exodus story. The mitzvah to tell—*le-saper*—requires answering questions, but it also necessitates engaging and involving those who seem uninterested.

10 And so you should tell him as in the laws of Passover. The parent's detailed response to the wise child is the only one of the four responses in this *baraita* that is not based on any biblical source, despite the fact that the Torah does provide such an answer, which appears elsewhere in the Haggadah as the answer to the *Mah Nishtanah* questions: "Slaves were we to Pharaoh in Egypt..." (6:21). Why does the Haggadah craft an original response to the wise child's query, rather than citing the Torah's answer?

In its biblical context, the question assigned the wise child is not particular to Passover: it is a general question about the meaning of the Torah. And the parent's answer is that our redemption from slavery in Egypt was the fulfillment of a divine promise that binds us covenantally to God and obligates us to fulfill divine commands. In replacing the Torah's response to this general question with a very specific answer, the Haggadah suggests that the laws of Pesach are essentially equivalent to all the other mitzvot. If you understand Passover, the Haggadah seems to be saying, you will understand the entire Torah.

13

THE SEDER

What does the **wicked one** say? *What is this service to you?* (Exod. 12:26). *To you* and not to him. And since he has excluded himself from the community, he has denied the fundamental principle. [11] So you should blunt his teeth and say to him: *For the sake of what the LORD did for me when I went out of Egypt* (Exod. 13:8). *For me* and not for him—if he had been there he would not have been redeemed.

What does the **simple one** say? *What is this?* (Exod. 13:14). And you shall say to him: *By strength of hand the LORD brought us out of Egypt, from the house of slaves* (Exod. 13:14).

And the **one who does not know how to ask a question**—you should begin for him, as it says: *And you shall tell your son on that day, saying, "For the sake of what the LORD did for me when I went out of Egypt"* (Exod. 13:8).

רָשָׁע מָה הוּא אוֹמֵר? מָה הָעֲבֹדָה הַזֹּאת לָכֶם? (שמות יב:כו). לָכֶם — וְלֹא לוֹ. וּלְפִי שֶׁהוֹצִיא אֶת עַצְמוֹ מִן הַכְּלָל כָּפַר בְּעִקָּר. [11] וְאַף אַתָּה הַקְהֵה אֶת שִׁנָּיו וְאֶמֹר לוֹ: בַּעֲבוּר זֶה עָשָׂה יהוה לִי בְּצֵאתִי מִמִּצְרָיִם (שמות יג:ח). לִי — וְלֹא לוֹ. אִלּוּ הָיָה שָׁם, לֹא הָיָה נִגְאָל.

תָּם מָה הוּא אוֹמֵר? מַה זֹּאת? (שמות יג:יד). וְאָמַרְתָּ אֵלָיו: בְּחֹזֶק יָד הוֹצִיאָנוּ יהוה מִמִּצְרַיִם, מִבֵּית עֲבָדִים (שמות יג:יד).

וְשֶׁאֵינוֹ יוֹדֵעַ לִשְׁאוֹל — אַתְּ פְּתַח לוֹ, שֶׁנֶּאֱמַר: וְהִגַּדְתָּ לְבִנְךָ בַּיּוֹם הַהוּא לֵאמֹר, בַּעֲבוּר זֶה עָשָׂה יהוה לִי בְּצֵאתִי מִמִּצְרָיִם (שמות יג:ח).

11 So you should blunt his teeth and say to him. The wicked child does not merit a genuine answer, only a harsh rebuke, because the Haggadah understands the wicked child to be scoffing and rejecting the tradition rather than inquiring sincerely. But the wicked child's question—"What is this service to you?"—is, in fact, the most basic of religious queries and the very question that the Haggadah as a whole is designed to answer: what is the relevance of the Exodus to our faith and our practice? The Haggadah's ultimate response to this question is twofold: the Exodus is relevant because the Israelites' subjugation in Egypt is an experience that repeats itself in every generation; and it is relevant because it is the basis for the Jewish people's covenantal relationship with God. To make this point, shortly after the *baraita* of the Four Children, the Haggadah cites God's promise to Abraham at the Covenant between the Pieces (Gen. 15) and declares, "And it is this promise that has sustained us, for not just once did somebody try to destroy us, rather in every generation they have tried to destroy us, but the Blessed Holy One saves us from them."

One could think that [the obligation to tell the story of the Exodus] begins on the first of the month; therefore it says *on that day* (Exod. 13:8). Based on this, I could think that it begins during the daytime; therefore it says *for the sake of [this]* (ibid.). I cannot say *for the sake of [this]* except when I have the matzah and *maror* before me.

יָכוֹל מֵרֹאשׁ חֹדֶשׁ, תַּלְמוּד לוֹמַר בַּיּוֹם הַהוּא (שמות יג:ח). אִי בַּיּוֹם הַהוּא, יָכוֹל מִבְּעוֹד יוֹם, תַּלְמוּד לוֹמַר בַּעֲבוּר זֶה (שם) — בַּעֲבוּר זֶה לֹא אָמַרְתִּי אֶלָּא בְּשָׁעָה שֶׁיֵּשׁ מַצָּה וּמָרוֹר מֻנָּחִים לְפָנֶיךָ.

¹²**In the beginning**, our ancestors were idol worshipers, and now the Omnipresent has drawn us to His worship. As it says: *Then Joshua said to all the people, "Thus said the* L*ORD, the God of Israel: In olden times, your forefathers—Terah, father of Abraham and father of Nahor—lived beyond the Euphrates and worshiped other gods. But I took your father Abraham from beyond the Euphrates and led him through the whole land of Canaan and multiplied his offspring. I gave him Isaac, and to Isaac I gave Jacob and Esau. I gave Esau the hill country of Seir as his possession, while Jacob and his children went down to Egypt"* (Josh. 24:2–4).

¹² מִתְּחִלָּה עוֹבְדֵי עֲבוֹדָה זָרָה הָיוּ אֲבוֹתֵינוּ, וְעַכְשָׁיו קֵרְבָנוּ הַמָּקוֹם לַעֲבֹדָתוֹ, שֶׁנֶּאֱמַר: וַיֹּאמֶר יְהוֹשֻׁעַ אֶל כָּל הָעָם, כֹּה אָמַר יהוה אֱלֹהֵי יִשְׂרָאֵל, בְּעֵבֶר הַנָּהָר יָשְׁבוּ אֲבוֹתֵיכֶם מֵעוֹלָם, תֶּרַח אֲבִי אַבְרָהָם וַאֲבִי נָחוֹר, וַיַּעַבְדוּ אֱלֹהִים אֲחֵרִים. וָאֶקַּח אֶת אֲבִיכֶם אֶת אַבְרָהָם מֵעֵבֶר הַנָּהָר, וָאוֹלֵךְ אוֹתוֹ בְּכָל אֶרֶץ כְּנָעַן, וָאַרְבֶּה אֶת זַרְעוֹ, וָאֶתֶּן לוֹ אֶת יִצְחָק. וָאֶתֵּן לְיִצְחָק אֶת יַעֲקֹב וְאֶת עֵשָׂו, וָאֶתֵּן לְעֵשָׂו אֶת הַר שֵׂעִיר לָרֶשֶׁת אוֹתוֹ, וְיַעֲקֹב וּבָנָיו יָרְדוּ מִצְרָיִם (יהושע כד:ב-ד).

---

12 In the beginning, our ancestors were idol worshipers. The Babylonian scholar Rav posited that in order to fulfill the Mishnah's requirement to begin the Exodus story with disgrace (*genut*) and conclude it with glory (*shevah*) (M. Pes. 10:4), we must recite a passage from the book of Joshua that tells of our idol-worshiping heritage (B.T. Pes. 116a and J.T. Pes. 10:5,37d). Thus we recite the beginning of Joshua's final speech to the People of Israel in Shechem, on the eve of his death. But as with the other historical narratives in the Haggadah, we cut short our recitation of Joshua's speech; although Joshua goes on to tell of the Ten Plagues, the Splitting of the Sea, the desert wanderings, the battle with the Amorites, and Balaam's attempt to curse the People of Israel, we conclude the narrative with Jacob's descent to Egypt. This truncation focuses our attention on the Israelites' prehistory, and particularly on the life of Abraham. Later, the Haggadah will present Jacob's experiences in the house of Laban as the ultimate parallel to the Exodus narrative. But here the Haggadah suggests that there is also a correspondence between Abraham's departure from his birthplace on "the other side of the river" and the Israelites' departure from slavery in Egypt.

THE SEDER

13 Blessed is He who keeps His promise to Israel, Blessed is He. For the Blessed Holy One calculated the end, to do as He had promised Abraham in the Covenant between the Pieces. As it says: *And He said to Abram, "Know well that your seed shall be strangers in a land not theirs and they shall be enslaved and afflicted four hundred years. But upon the nation*

בָּרוּךְ שׁוֹמֵר הַבְטָחָתוֹ לְיִשְׂרָאֵל, בָּרוּךְ ¹³ הוּא. שֶׁהַקָּדוֹשׁ בָּרוּךְ הוּא חִשַּׁב אֶת הַקֵּץ, לַעֲשׂוֹת כְּמַה שֶׁאָמַר לְאַבְרָהָם אָבִינוּ בִּבְרִית בֵּין הַבְּתָרִים, שֶׁנֶּאֱמַר: וַיֹּאמֶר לְאַבְרָם, יָדֹעַ תֵּדַע כִּי גֵר יִהְיֶה זַרְעֲךָ בְּאֶרֶץ לֹא לָהֶם, וַעֲבָדוּם וְעִנּוּ אֹתָם אַרְבַּע מֵאוֹת שָׁנָה. וְגַם אֶת הַגּוֹי אֲשֶׁר

Joshua's exhortation to the people in the continuation of chapter 24 (which we do not recite at the seder) makes this connection explicit:

וְעַתָּה יְראוּ אֶת יהוה וְעִבְדוּ אֹתוֹ בְּתָמִים וּבֶאֱמֶת וְהָסִירוּ אֶת אֱלֹהִים אֲשֶׁר עָבְדוּ אֲבוֹתֵיכֶם בְּעֵבֶר הַנָּהָר וּבְמִצְרַיִם וְעִבְדוּ אֶת יהוה:

Now, therefore, revere the LORD and serve Him with undivided loyalty; put away the gods that your forefathers served beyond the Euphrates and in Egypt, and serve the LORD (Josh. 24:14).

In contrast, the Torah never states clearly that the Israelites worshiped idols in Egypt. Although the ultimate goal of the Exodus was to enable the nation to serve God, the Torah suggests that Pharaoh was the impediment to doing so in Egypt, not foreign gods. Thus, it is through the prism of the book of Joshua that we are able to fully appreciate the parallel between Abraham's life story and the history of the nation.

But the section of Joshua's address that we do not recite at the seder actually contains an even stronger link to both Abraham's story and the Exodus experience. After an exchange in which Joshua affirms that the People of Israel are truly committed to abandoning their idols and serving God alone, the text reports that Joshua "made a covenant for the people" (*va-yikhrot . . . berit*) and "made a fixed rule for them" (*va-yasem lo hok u-mishpat*) (Josh. 24:25). The final step in the conquest of the Land was to reenter into a covenant with God. This *berit* evokes the covenant God forged with Abraham, which established for eternity the terms of his descendants' relationship with the Divine. Thus, in the next paragraph, the Haggadah asserts, "Blessed is He who keeps his promise to Israel . . . to do as He had promised Abraham in the Covenant between the Pieces." But the phrase *va-yasem lo hok u-mishpat* also calls to mind one of the nation's first experiences after the Exodus and the Splitting of the Sea: the incident at Marah, where, in response to the people's grumblings, God sweetened the drinking water and "made for them a fixed rule" (*sham sam lo hok u-mishpat*) (Exod. 15:25). In describing the people's reentry into the divine covenant, the book of Joshua borrows language from the Torah, thereby highlighting the conquest of the Land as the ultimate fulfillment of the Exodus promise.

13 Blessed is He who keeps His promise to Israel. The Haggadah prefaces the central text of *Maggid* with praises to God for planning out the redemption of the Israelites even prior to their captivity, striking a covenant with Abraham that serves as a blueprint for the Exodus. In the covenant,

for whom they slave I will bring judgment, and afterward they shall come forth with great substance" (Gen. 15:13–14).

יַעֲבֹדוּ דָּן אָנֹכִי וְאַחֲרֵי כֵן יֵצְאוּ בִּרְכֻשׁ גָּדוֹל (בראשית טו:יג-יד).

Cover the matzah and raise the cup of wine.

And it is this promise that has sustained our ancestors and us, for not just once did somebody try to destroy us, rather in every generation they try to destroy us, but the Blessed Holy One saves us from them.

וְהִיא שֶׁעָמְדָה לַאֲבוֹתֵינוּ וְלָנוּ, שֶׁלֹּא אֶחָד בִּלְבָד עָמַד עָלֵינוּ לְכַלּוֹתֵנוּ, אֶלָּא שֶׁבְּכָל דּוֹר וָדוֹר עוֹמְדִים עָלֵינוּ לְכַלּוֹתֵנוּ, וְהַקָּדוֹשׁ בָּרוּךְ הוּא מַצִּילֵנוּ מִיָּדָם.

Put down the cup of wine and uncover the matzah.

[14]**Go forth and learn** what Laban the Aramean tried to do to our forefather Jacob. For Pharaoh's decree was only against the males, while Laban tried to destroy everything. [15]As it is said: [16]***My father was an Aramean***

[14]**צֵא וּלְמַד** מַה בִּקֵּשׁ לָבָן הָאֲרַמִּי לַעֲשׂוֹת לְיַעֲקֹב אָבִינוּ. שֶׁפַּרְעֹה לֹא גָזַר אֶלָּא עַל הַזְּכָרִים וְלָבָן בִּקֵּשׁ לַעֲקוֹר אֶת הַכֹּל, [15]שֶׁנֶּאֱמַר: [16]**אֲרַמִּי אֹבֵד אָבִי**,

---

three forms of suffering are invoked—*gerut* (alienation), *avdut* (servitude), and *innuy* (affliction)— and God promises that once these have been endured, redemption will occur. This covenant echoes both in the story of Jacob and Laban and in the Exodus narrative. What is the significance of this recurring motif? For extensive analysis, see essay 2.

14 Go forth and learn what Laban the Aramean tried to do to our ancestor Jacob . . . With these words the Haggadah introduces its longest midrashic passage, an extended explication of Deuteronomy 26:5–8. The midrash begins by responding to the Haggadah's assertion that in every generation enemies have attempted to destroy us, demonstrating that Pharaoh's evil was a repeat of Laban's deviousness. But it also responds to the previously cited verses from Genesis 15, God's promise to Abraham at the Covenant between the Pieces that his descendants will be enslaved but ultimately redeemed. Genesis itself does not specify the identity of the descendants or the enslavers. With the help of the midrash on Deuteronomy 26, the Haggadah claims that God's promise to Abraham refers to both Jacob and Laban as well as to the Israelites and the Egyptians and perhaps to other victims and perpetrators at different stages of Jewish history. Thus the opening lines of the midrash can be understood as a proof for the significance of two main themes in the Haggadah: the cyclical nature of history and the covenantal relationship between God and the People of Israel.

15 As it is said: *My father was an Aramean about to perish . . .* Deuteronomy 26:5–8 is the only biblical text explicitly prescribed by the Mishnah for inclusion in the *Maggid* section of the seder. What does this passage contribute to the Haggadah, and what is its significance for the seder participant? For a full discussion, see essay 1.

THE SEDER

about to perish, and he went down to Egypt, and he sojourned there with a few people, and he became there a great and mighty and multitudinous nation (Deut. 26:5).

וַיֵּרֶד מִצְרַיְמָה וַיָּגָר שָׁם בִּמְתֵי מְעָט, וַיְהִי שָׁם לְגוֹי גָּדוֹל, עָצוּם וָרָב (דברים כו:ה).

The precise dating of the *Arami oved avi* midrash is difficult to determine. Some scholars believe it is among the earliest midrashic passages in existence, but others claim that it was not compiled until the medieval period. The latter group argues that the midrash presented in our Haggadah is an amalgamation of earlier passages that were expanded and elaborated significantly over generations. On the basis of this historical claim, these scholars reject the idea that *Arami oved avi* is an integrated midrash with a specific theological, social, or political message. But that is not necessarily so; indeed, the midrash as it appears in our Haggadah does have an overarching structure and theme.

The *Arami oved avi* midrash comprises twenty-one *drashot* (explications) on the words of four verses from Deuteronomy. Most of the explications interpret the words of Deuteronomy on the basis of texts from elsewhere in the Bible. (Two of the explications do not offer proofs for their interpretations.) The *drashot* on the second and third verses cite prooftexts drawn exclusively from Exodus 1–3, and several of the *drashot* on the first and fourth verses reference Exodus as well. The preponderance of prooftexts from these chapters makes sense, given that the midrash's explications presumably serve to clarify and add detail to Deuteronomy's version of the Exodus narrative.

But the *drashot* on the first and fourth verses reference texts from the prophetic writings as well. The use of prophetic verses as prooftexts is typical of liturgy, such as the *Musaf* prayer of Rosh Hashanah. (In fact, the *drashot* on the fourth verse include verses from the Torah, the Prophets, and the Writings, just as the Rosh Hashanah service does.) The liturgical nature of these sections of the *Arami oved avi* midrash underscores its unique character and further emphasizes the intent behind its composition.

Strikingly, the final prooftext in the midrash is from the prophet Joel's eschatological vision: "I will set portents in the sky and on earth: blood and fire and pillars of smoke" (Joel 3:3). The citation of this particular text connects the divine revelation that accompanied the Exodus with the messianic revelation that will occur at the End of Days. Given that the Deuteronomy passage begins with a reference to the distant past—Jacob's experiences in Laban's home—Joel's vision of the messianic future completes the framing of the Exodus narrative, suggesting that it was a historical event with universal, eternal implications. The idea that the Exodus was both a recasting of earlier events and a paradigm for the future is one of the central messages of the Haggadah, and the reflection of that message in both the content and the structure of the *Arami oved avi* midrash indicates that it is indeed an integrated piece.

16 My father was an Aramean about to perish . . . *Arami oved avi* is a difficult phrase to translate because it is not immediately apparent to whom the words *arami* (an Aramean) or *avi* (my father) refer. The word *oved* too is unclear. Is it a description of a person or of an action, and to whom is the reference? An ancient tradition, with which many modern scholars agree, takes both the words

¹⁷*and he went down to Egypt*—¹⁸forced to do so by the word of God. אָנוּס עַל פִּי ¹⁸ — וַיֵּרֶד מִצְרַיְמָה ¹⁷ הַדִּבּוּר.

---

arami and *avi* to refer to Jacob. Depending on how the word *oved* is understood, this generates either the translation "my father [Jacob] was a wandering Aramean" or "my father [Jacob] was an Aramean about to perish." The Haggadah, however, takes *arami* to refer not to Jacob but to his father-in-law Laban, possibly because the Bible refers to Laban as an Aramean on several occasions (Gen. 25:20; 28:5; 31:20,24). Understanding the word *oved* to mean "destroy," the Haggadah renders the complete phrase "An Aramean [Laban] attempted to destroy my father [Jacob]." This understanding of the verse from Deuteronomy supports the Haggadah's assertion that "in every generation they have tried to destroy us, but the Blessed Holy One saves us from them."

17 *and he went down to Egypt*. In Genesis, Jacob's sojourn in Laban's home and Jacob's relocation to Egypt are presented as two discrete and disconnected events. However, in Deuteronomy, juxtaposing these two episodes—"An Aramean [Laban] attempted to destroy my father [Jacob], and he [Jacob] went down to Egypt"—suggests a connection between them. (See essay 2 for a fuller discussion of the relationship between them.) The Haggadah seems to understand our passage from Deuteronomy as claiming that Jacob's relocation to Egypt was the direct result of leaving Laban's home: because Laban attempted to destroy him, Jacob ran away and ended up in Egypt, where his children initially flourished but later fell into Pharaoh's clutches. This reading underscores the symbolic relationship between Laban and Pharaoh: both represent the external enemy.

18 forced to do so by the word of God. The Haggadah asserts that Jacob did not relocate to Egypt of his own accord but only because he was compelled by the Divine word. At first reading, this claim seems to contradict Genesis, which tells of Jacob's autonomous decision to go and see Joseph before his death (Gen. 45:28). The Haggadah's insistence that Jacob was forced to go down to Egypt suggests that Jacob would never have decided to go there on his own. This makes sense if one assumes that Jacob had good reason to dread going down to Egypt, understanding as he did that his experiences in Egypt would replicate his experiences in the house of Laban and that once again he would be going into exile and experiencing affliction at the hands of others.

In fact, this is not a fanciful midrashic interpretation. A plain reading of the biblical text indicates that Jacob feels bound by Divine decree; and indeed the obviousness of this reading may explain why the Haggadah does not bring a prooftext for its claim that Jacob and his family went to Egypt "forced to do so by the word of God," as it does for most of its other interpretations of the verses in our passage. When Jacob departs for Egypt, God appears to him in Beersheba to assure him that he need not fear the journey (Gen. 46:3), suggesting that Jacob was indeed fearful. And Jacob responds to God's call with the expression *hineini* ("here I am") (Gen. 46:2), which throughout Genesis indicates acceptance of one's covenantal destiny. (See essay 2 for elaboration.) With this word, Jacob acknowledges that he is going to Egypt not because Joseph or Pharaoh has asked him to do so, but because God has ordained it.

¹⁹*and he sojourned there*—this teaches us that our forefather Jacob did not intend to settle in Egypt but just to live there temporarily. As it says: *We have come to sojourn in the land, for there is no pasture for your servants' flocks because the famine is grave in the land of Canaan. And so, let your servants, pray, dwell in the land of Goshen* (Gen. 47:4).

²⁰*with a few people*—as it is said: *With seventy persons did your fathers go down to Egypt, and now the* Lord *your God has set you like the stars of the heavens for multitude* (Deut. 10:22).

²¹*and he became there a nation*—this teaches us that the Israelites were distinguished there.

¹⁹ וַיָּגָר שָׁם — מְלַמֵּד שֶׁלֹּא יָרַד יַעֲקֹב אָבִינוּ לְהִשְׁתַּקֵּעַ בְּמִצְרַיִם אֶלָּא לָגוּר שָׁם, שֶׁנֶּאֱמַר: וַיֹּאמְרוּ אֶל פַּרְעֹה, לָגוּר בָּאָרֶץ בָּאנוּ, כִּי אֵין מִרְעֶה לַצֹּאן אֲשֶׁר לַעֲבָדֶיךָ, כִּי כָבֵד הָרָעָב בְּאֶרֶץ כְּנָעַן, וְעַתָּה יֵשְׁבוּ נָא עֲבָדֶיךָ בְּאֶרֶץ גֹּשֶׁן (בראשית מז:ד).

²⁰ בִּמְתֵי מְעָט — כְּמָה שֶׁנֶּאֱמַר: בְּשִׁבְעִים נֶפֶשׁ יָרְדוּ אֲבוֹתֶיךָ מִצְרַיְמָה, וְעַתָּה שָׂמְךָ יהוה אֱלֹהֶיךָ כְּכוֹכְבֵי הַשָּׁמַיִם לָרֹב (דברים י:כב).

²¹ וַיְהִי שָׁם לְגוֹי — מְלַמֵּד שֶׁהָיוּ יִשְׂרָאֵל מְצֻיָּנִים שָׁם.

---

19 and he sojourned there. Although Jacob knew he would live out the remainder of his life in Egypt—God had indicated as much when appearing to him in Beersheba (Gen. 46:3–4)—the Haggadah asserts that Jacob went to Egypt to sojourn and not to settle there. This claim is based on the use of the word *va-yagar* in our passage: Joseph's brothers use a form of the same word in Genesis 47:4, when explaining to Pharaoh that they are coming to Egypt on a temporary basis because of the famine in the land of Canaan. The word *va-yagar* (and he sojourned) is based on the same root as the word *ger* (alien), and the Haggadah's emphasis that Jacob came merely to sojourn is consonant with Jacob's enduring sense of alienation in Egypt, as reflected in his despondent response upon meeting Pharaoh (47:9) and his deathbed request to be buried in the land of Canaan (49:29–32). Jacob never considered Egypt his home, whereas his children seem to have adopted a different attitude: they "took holdings" in Goshen and were fruitful and multiplied there (47:27).

20 with a few people. Genesis and Exodus report that Jacob arrived in Egypt with a seventy-person clan—why, then, does Deuteronomy call them "a few people" (*me'tay me'at*)? The Haggadah's prooftext from Deuteronomy 10, which contrasts the seventy-member family that came to Egypt with the multitudinous nation that left, demonstrates that the term "few" is relative—a large family is still a small nation. But the prooftext also points to a distinction that is more than numerical. When Jacob and his children arrived in Egypt they were *me'tay*, which could also be translated as "mortals"; but by the time they left Egypt, they had attained the strength and prominence of the stars of the heavens, which were created to govern the day and night (Gen. 1:18).

21 and he became there a nation. The Haggadah seems perplexed by Deuteronomy's assertion that the people became a nation specifically "there," in Egypt. What about the experience of the

A Passover Haggadah: Go Forth and Learn

great, mighty—as it is said: *And the sons of Israel were fruitful and swarmed and multiplied and grew very vast, and the land was filled with them* (Exod. 1:7).

גָּדוֹל, עָצוּם — כְּמָה שֶׁנֶּאֱמַר: וּבְנֵי יִשְׂרָאֵל פָּרוּ וַיִּשְׁרְצוּ וַיִּרְבּוּ וַיַּעַצְמוּ בִּמְאֹד מְאֹד, וַתִּמָּלֵא הָאָרֶץ אֹתָם (שמות א:ז).

²² *and multitudinous*—as it is said: *I let you grow like the plants of the field; and you continued to grow up until you attained to womanhood, until your breasts became firm and your hair sprouted. You were still naked and bare* (Ezek. 16:7). *When I passed by you and saw you wallowing in your blood, I said to you: "Live in spite of your blood." Yea, I said to you: "Live in spite of your blood"* (Ezek. 16:6).

²² וָרָב — כְּמָה שֶׁנֶּאֱמַר: רְבָבָה כְּצֶמַח הַשָּׂדֶה נְתַתִּיךְ, וַתִּרְבִּי וַתִּגְדְּלִי וַתָּבֹאִי בַּעֲדִי עֲדָיִים, שָׁדַיִם נָכֹנוּ וּשְׂעָרֵךְ צִמֵּחַ, וְאַתְּ עֵרֹם וְעֶרְיָה (יחזקאל טז:ז). וָאֶעֱבֹר עָלַיִךְ וָאֶרְאֵךְ מִתְבּוֹסֶסֶת בְּדָמָיִךְ, וָאֹמַר לָךְ בְּדָמַיִךְ חֲיִי, וָאֹמַר לָךְ בְּדָמַיִךְ חֲיִי (יחזקאל טז:ו).

And the Egyptians did evil to us and abused us and set upon us hard labor (Deut. 26:6).

וַיָּרֵעוּ אֹתָנוּ הַמִּצְרִים וַיְעַנּוּנוּ, וַיִּתְּנוּ עָלֵינוּ עֲבֹדָה קָשָׁה (דברים כו:ו).

(continue on page 24)

Israelites in Egypt was so significant in shaping their identity as a nation? The Haggadah's explanation is that there in Egypt the Israelites were *metzuyanim*—which is usually translated as "outstanding" but actually connotes "standing out." The formation of Israel's national identity was the result of the Egyptian insistence on painting the Israelites as outsiders.

22 and multitudinous. The Torah is famously sparing with words. Once we know that the nation has become great (*gadol*) and mighty (*atzum*), why are we told that the nation is also multitudinous, or large (*rav*)? It is with this question in mind that the Haggadah interprets the word *rav* in light of the prooftext from Ezekiel. The prophet narrates the life cycle of a mythical woman who represents the People of Israel in the various phases of their relationship with God. *Rav* in this instance does not mean "large," but "mature." The woman in Ezekiel, who was taken in as a newborn foundling, and has now reached physical maturity but continues to run around naked like a young child, is a perfect metaphor for the People of Israel in Egypt. At the cusp of redemption, the people had already grown to a critical mass—they were physically the size of a nation—but they lacked national and spiritual maturity. Like an adolescent, they were only just beginning the formation of their identity, and they had not yet arrived at a mature understanding of their destiny as God's nation.

The second verse from Ezekiel is not part of the original midrash; it is a later addition that is absent from many versions of the Haggadah. In fact, the two verses are presented out of order. In the biblical text, the second precedes the first and describes an earlier stage of the mythical woman's life: whereas the first verse describes an adolescent, the second verse represents the moment of her birth. The addition of the second verse introduces a powerful image that conveys an

(continue on page 24)

וַיִּתְּנוּ עָלֵינוּ עֲבֹדָה קָשָׁה
And set upon us hard labor

Scholars claim that the biblical word *parekh* derives from the ancient Near Eastern concept *pirkhu*, the assigning of slave work to free people.[2] Similarly, the Midrash asserts that one of the principal characteristics of slavery in Egypt was the inappropriate allocation of tasks: women's work was given to men, and men's work was given to women.[3] This form of labor distribution points to a system that was not concerned with maximal output but rather with producing maximal frustration. Pharaoh's motivation for imposing backbreaking labor on the Israelite slaves was not to advance his building projects, but rather to break the people by humiliating and dehumanizing them until they abandoned hope. Indeed, were the completion of the projects his true goal, he would not have taken away the building materials, as the Torah reports, thereby decelerating the process (Exod. 5:6–19); instead, he would have provided more materials and demanded increased production. But the *avodat parekh* inflicted by the Egyptians was, by definition, perpetual, purposeless work.[4]

In this regard, the Israelites' labor in Egypt contrasts with the other major building project in Exodus, the construction of the *Mishkan* (Tabernacle).[5] Unlike the forced labor in Egypt, the work entailed in building the *Mishkan* was characterized by its voluntary nature: the word that is repeated throughout the chapters that detail the construction of the *Mishkan* is *le-nadev*, "to donate" or "to volunteer" (Exod. 25:2, 35:22, 36:3, and elsewhere). With the exception of the required half-shekel (30:11–16), the entire project was undertaken with voluntarily donated materials, time, and effort; in fact, so much was volunteered that Moses had to ask the people to stop (36:3–7). In contrast to the purposeless labor of Egypt, described as *avodah*, the dominant word used to describe the building of the *Mishkan* is *melakhah*, the very same word used at the beginning of the Torah to describe God's work of Creation. More specifically, work on the *Mishkan* is described as *melekhet mahshevet*, creative and purposeful work (35:33), which is precisely the opposite of the building projects undertaken at the beginning of Exodus. Although the chapters that detail the construction of the *Mishkan* are punctuated by God's instructions and commands, human involvement in this project was radically different than the slaves' mechanical and unthinking execution of Pharaoh's orders. The Torah repeatedly emphasizes the wisdom, understanding, and skill that characterized the artisans responsible for crafting the holy structure and its vessels (28:3; 35:30–35; 36:1–2,4,8). Work on the *Mishkan* was both the fulfillment of Divine will and an outlet for human creativity and artistic expression.

---

[2] See entry for פרך in *Encyclopaedia Biblica* (in Hebrew), vol. 6 (Jerusalem: Bialik Institute, 1971), 583–84.

[3] B.T. Sot. 11b and Tanhuma Va-Yeze 9. Lev. Rabbah 37:2 adds that the Egyptians imposed work suited to large people on small people and work for young people on old people.

[4] See Rambam, *Mishneh Torah*, Hilkhot Avadim 1:6, who cites Leviticus's prohibition to impose *avodat parekh* on a Hebrew servant (Lev. 25:43,46,53). Rambam defines *parekh* as work that has no endpoint or work that has no purpose other than to busy the slave and burden him. See Menahem Kasher's *Torah Shleimah* commentary on Exodus 1:13, note 137, for a discussion of the Rambam's sources.

[5] A midrash quoted in the commentary of Tosafot on B.T. Pes. 117b inverts the letters of the word פרך according to the rules of א״ת ב״ש (a classic alphabet game where the last letter of the alphabet is switched with the first, and so forth) to read ג״ל, which numerically equals 39, the precise number of creative labors (*melakhot*) that were used in building the *Mishkan* and are therefore forbidden on the Sabbath. Consequently, the midrash concludes that the People of Israel's "release" from the performance of 39 labors on the Sabbath was compensation for the 39 labors that they were forced to perform as slaves in Egypt.

To reinforce these contrasts, the Torah juxtaposes its instructions regarding the *Mishkan* to the laws of the Sabbath (Exod. 31:13–17 and 35:2–3). According to the Midrash, this juxtaposition reflects the Torah's demand for periodic cessation from labor, even holy labor,[6] as opposed to Pharaoh's refusal to allow the people the briefest respite. God, unlike Pharaoh, recognizes that occasional pauses allow for assessment and evaluation and ensure that the work does not become an end unto itself but is always for the sake of a greater goal or a higher purpose. The construction of the *Mishkan* is thus a fitting culmination to a book that begins with the *avodah* of slavery—work with no purpose, no choice, no end, and no value. At its core, the book of Exodus, as well as the Exodus itself, reflects the transition from *avodat parekh* to *melekhet mahshevet*.

Chronicles clearly draws upon this Exodus account in its depiction of the Temple's construction in the days of David and Solomon. As in Exodus, Chronicles refers to the building of the Temple as work (*melakhah*) that requires insight and skill (*hokhmah*) (1 Chron. 28:21, 29:1). Echoing Exodus, David challenges the people to volunteer (*mitnadev*) materials for the Lord's house; and the author of Chronicles asserts that the project was financed by freewill offerings and voluntary gifts that the people gave willingly (*hitnadvu*) and wholeheartedly (29:1–9). In Chronicles as in Exodus, the construction of God's dwelling place is portrayed as inspiring work that elicits human creativity and goodwill.

Surprisingly, though, the parallel account in Kings casts the construction of the Temple in a very different light. There, Solomon's building projects, including the Temple, are depicted using imagery and language that evokes the slave labor of Egypt! Solomon does not actually enslave his own people (1 Kings 9:22), but he imposes forced labor (*mas*) on thirty thousand men, as well as on seventy thousand porters, eighty thousand quarriers, and over three thousand supervisors (5:27–30). In addition to building the Temple, palaces, citadels, and fortifications for several cities, Solomon obliges these laborers to build garrison towns (*arei miskenot*), chariot towns (*arei ha-rekhev*), and cavalry towns (*arei ha-parashim*) throughout his territory (1 Kings 9:15–22), projects whose very names recall Pharaoh and the Egyptians (Exod. 1:11, 14:6–9). After Solomon's death, the people complain to Rehoboam that the harsh labor his father imposed (*avodat avikha ha-kashah*) had been a heavy yoke upon them (*ulo ha-kaved asher natan aleinu*) (1 Kings 12:4), further evoking Pharaoh's oppression of the Israelites at the beginning of Exodus.[7] It seems clear that the author of Kings—a book that is deeply concerned with questions of power and its abuse—wants to frame Solomon's kingship as a form of Pharaoh-like rule. In light of the Exodus paradigm, the disparity between Chronicles and Kings serves to emphasize that even the construction of God's house can be undertaken in a manner that is more akin to Pharaoh's labor than to the work of God.

---

[6] See *Mekhilta* on the beginning of Parashat Va-yakhel and Rashi's commentary on Exod. 31:13, *Akh et shabtotai tishmoru*.

[7] Furthermore, from the beginning of his reign, Solomon allies himself closely with the king of Egypt by marrying his daughter (1 Kings 3:1), who is later singled out as the first of the foreign wives to lead him astray (1 Kings 11:1).

²³ And the Egyptians did evil to us—as it is said: *Come, let us be shrewd with them lest they multiply and then, should war occur, they will actually join our enemies and fight against us and go up from the land* (Exod. 1:10).

²⁴ and abused us—as it is said: *And they set over them forced-labor foremen so as to abuse them with their burdens, and they built store cities for Pharaoh: Pithom and Ramases* (Exod. 1:11).

and set upon us hard labor—as it is said: *And the Egyptians put the Israelites to work at crushing labor* (Exod. 1:13).

²³ וַיָּרֵעוּ אֹתָנוּ הַמִּצְרִים — כְּמָה שֶׁנֶּאֱמַר: הָבָה נִתְחַכְּמָה לוֹ פֶּן יִרְבֶּה, וְהָיָה כִּי תִקְרֶאנָה מִלְחָמָה וְנוֹסַף גַּם הוּא עַל שׂנְאֵינוּ וְנִלְחַם בָּנוּ, וְעָלָה מִן הָאָרֶץ (שמות א:י).

²⁴ וַיְעַנּוּנוּ — כְּמָה שֶׁנֶּאֱמַר: וַיָּשִׂימוּ עָלָיו שָׂרֵי מִסִּים לְמַעַן עַנֹּתוֹ בְּסִבְלֹתָם, וַיִּבֶן עָרֵי מִסְכְּנוֹת לְפַרְעֹה, אֶת פִּתֹם וְאֶת רַעַמְסֵס (שמות א:יא).

וַיִּתְּנוּ עָלֵינוּ עֲבֹדָה קָשָׁה — כְּמָה שֶׁנֶּאֱמַר: וַיַּעֲבִדוּ מִצְרַיִם אֶת בְּנֵי יִשְׂרָאֵל בְּפָרֶךְ (שמות א:יג).

---

important message about God's salvation of God's people. The verse describes a discarded newborn infant, still wallowing in blood. The passerby takes in the helpless baby and cares for it, allowing it to grow to its promise and potential. Such was God's kindness to the People of Israel in Egypt: to recognize their potential despite their pathetic, embryonic state.

23 And the Egyptians did evil to us. According to the Haggadah, this phrase does not mean that the Egyptians harmed us but rather that they incriminated or falsely implicated us. The prooftext is an expression of Pharaoh's fear that the multiplying Israelites would rise up against the local population. There is no evidence that the Israelites were planning a revolt, but that is what Pharaoh claimed in order to justify their oppression (see Ramban's commentary on Exod. 1:10). The Torah presents the Israelites' enslavement as the product of Egyptian paranoia.

Why does the Haggadah interpret the phrase from Deuteronomy in this fashion? Generally, the verb *va-yare'u* (they did evil) is followed by an object with the prefix *le-* (to), as demonstrated by a parallel verse in Numbers. When Moses sends a message to the king of Edom requesting safe passage through his lands, he includes a brief version of the Exodus story; only here the phrase used is *va-yare'u lanu ha-Mitzrim* ("and the Egyptians did evil to us") (Num. 20:15). In contrast, the unusual combination of the verb *va-yare'u* with the object *otanu* in our passage suggests that the phrase in our verse means something different—not that the Egyptians did evil *to* us but rather that they *made us* evil, that they attributed evil intentions to us.

24 and abused us. The phrasing of the prooftext emphasizes that Pharaoh's primary goal in enslaving the Israelites was to torture them and make them suffer (*le-ma'an anoto*), not to benefit from their labor. It is not that they had to suffer in order to build Pharaoh's cities; rather, Pharoah had them build his cities in order to make them suffer.

A PASSOVER HAGGADAH: GO FORTH AND LEARN

And we cried out to the LORD God of our fathers, and the LORD heard our voice and saw our abuse and our trouble and our oppression (Deut. 26:7).

וַנִּצְעַק אֶל יהוה אֱלֹהֵי אֲבֹתֵינוּ, וַיִּשְׁמַע יהוה אֶת קֹלֵנוּ, וַיַּרְא אֶת עָנְיֵנוּ וְאֶת עֲמָלֵנוּ וְאֶת לַחֲצֵנוּ (דברים כו:ז).

[25] And we cried out to the LORD God of our fathers—as it is said: And it happened when a long time had passed that the king of Egypt died, and the Israelites groaned from the bondage and cried out, and their plea from the bondage went up to God (Exod. 2:23).

וַנִּצְעַק אֶל יהוה אֱלֹהֵי אֲבֹתֵינוּ — כְּמָה [25] שֶׁנֶּאֱמַר: וַיְהִי בַיָּמִים הָרַבִּים הָהֵם וַיָּמָת מֶלֶךְ מִצְרַיִם, וַיֵּאָנְחוּ בְנֵי יִשְׂרָאֵל מִן הָעֲבוֹדָה וַיִּזְעָקוּ, וַתַּעַל שַׁוְעָתָם אֶל הָאֱלֹהִים מִן הָעֲבֹדָה (שמות ב:כג).

The Torah asserts that afflicting the Israelites was Pharaoh's response to their remarkable fertility (Exod. 1:9–11). Fearful of the encroaching outsiders, Pharaoh was convinced that enslavement—and particularly *innuy* (abuse)—would stem the population boom. The word *innuy* often has a sexual connotation in the Bible, including both sexual abuse and deprivation of sexual relations,[8] and in using the word *innuy* to describe Pharaoh's abuse of the Israelites, the Bible indicates that the purpose of this abuse was to limit the growth of the people. Thus, when the abuse resulted in further growth (*ve-kha'asher ya'anu oto ken yirbeh ve-khen yifrotz*—"And as they abused them, so did they multiply and so did they spread"), the Egyptians were baffled and became even more apprehensive (1:12).

The Torah prefaces the Egyptian plan to enslave the Israelites (Exod. 1:9–11) with the report that "a new king arose over Egypt who did not know Joseph" (1:8). This suggests that Pharaoh's lack of familiarity with Joseph is key to understanding his inappropriate and ineffective use of *innuy* for the purposes of population reduction. Joseph named his child Ephraim, meaning, "God has made me fruitful in the land of my affliction" (*ki hifrani Elokim be-eretz onyii*) (Gen. 41:52). Joseph represents the ability of an oppressed individual to rise above his affliction. Pharaoh's "not knowing" Joseph indicates that he did not give credence to the possibility that an individual, or a nation, might overcome hardship to flourish and grow despite their harsh environs. In response, the Torah asserts that while Pharaoh abused the people *lest* they multiply (*pen yirbeh*), in fact the result of this abuse is that they *did* multiply (*ken yirbeh*).

25 And we cried out to the LORD God of our fathers . . . and the LORD heard our voice. The Haggadah is concerned with the seeming discrepancy between the verse in our passage and the prooftext from Exodus. According to our passage, the Israelites cried out to God. But in Exodus, the cries of the

---

[8] See, for example, Gen. 16:6,9,11; 31:50; 34:2; 41:52; and Deut. 22:24,29. Note also the use of *innuy* with reference to the manna in Deut. 8:3; here too the word connotes deprivation of a basic human need.

and the LORD heard our voice—as it is said: *And God heard their moaning, and God remembered His covenant with Abraham, with Isaac, and with Jacob* (Exod. 2:24).

²⁶and saw our abuse—this is the disruption of sexual relations, as it is said: *And God saw the Israelites, and God knew* (Exod. 2:25).

²⁷and our trouble—these are the children, as it is said: *Every boy that is born you shall fling*

וַיִּשְׁמַע יהוה אֶת קֹלֵנוּ — כְּמָה שֶׁנֶּאֱמַר: וַיִּשְׁמַע אֱלֹהִים אֶת נַאֲקָתָם, וַיִּזְכֹּר אֱלֹהִים אֶת בְּרִיתוֹ אֶת אַבְרָהָם, אֶת יִצְחָק וְאֶת יַעֲקֹב (שמות ב:כד).

²⁶ וַיַּרְא אֶת עָנְיֵנוּ — זוֹ פְּרִישׁוּת דֶּרֶךְ אֶרֶץ, כְּמָה שֶׁנֶּאֱמַר: וַיַּרְא אֱלֹהִים אֶת בְּנֵי יִשְׂרָאֵל וַיֵּדַע אֱלֹהִים (שמות ב:כה).

²⁷ וְאֶת עֲמָלֵנוּ — אֵלוּ הַבָּנִים. כְּמָה שֶׁנֶּאֱמַר: כָּל הַבֵּן הַיִּלּוֹד הַיְאֹרָה

Israelites are not explicitly directed toward God. In Exodus, the Israelites cry out or moan instinctively in response to their pain and suffering.⁹ Although their cries are not directed toward God, God responds to their cries. The Haggadah's juxtaposition of these two verses suggests that God chooses to interpret the people's cries of suffering as a form of prayer.

The Haggadah's prooftext for the phrase *va-yishma Ha-Shem et kolenu* ("and the LORD heard our voice") is the very next verse in Exodus, which emphasizes that it was not the people's own merit that led to their redemption, but rather God's commitment to the covenant with their forefathers. Because of God's covenantal relationship with Abraham, Isaac, and Jacob, God responds to their descendants' suffering as to a prayer.

26 and saw our abuse—this is the disruption of sexual relations. According to the Haggadah, the abuse (*onyenu*) that God saw refers to the separation of spouses from one another, which precluded the possibility of conceiving children. This interpretation derives from the last verse in Exodus 2, where God is also described as "seeing" the People of Israel and subsequently as "knowing," a word that often bears a sexual connotation. Consequently, the Haggadah suggests that divine intervention in Egypt was triggered by God's perception that the people were unable to reproduce. On a figurative level, *va-yeda Elokim* ("and God knew") implies that God's response to the Israelites' sexual oppression was to father children Himself.¹⁰ God becomes the spiritual father of this nation that is about to be born.

27 and our trouble—these are the children. After asserting that the term *onyenu* ("our abuse") refers to sexual oppression that precludes childbearing, the Haggadah reads the term *amaleinu* ("our

---

⁹Compare the crying out of the residents of Sodom and God's response in Gen. 18:20–21. For further elaboration, see essay 6.

¹⁰My thanks to David Goshen for this insight. In fact, the term ידע is used similarly in Genesis 15, where the barren Abraham questions how he can be sure that his descendants will succeed him, and God says: "Know well" (*yado'a teda*) (15:13). There too the implication is that God stepped in metaphorically to father Isaac; indeed the Torah never reports that Abraham impregnated Sarah, but only that God "singled out" or "remembered" (*pakad*) Sarah (21:1–2).

A PASSOVER HAGGADAH: GO FORTH AND LEARN

into the Nile, and every girl you shall let live (Exod. 1:22).

תַּשְׁלִיכֻהוּ וְכָל הַבַּת תְּחַיּוּן (שמות א:כב).

[28] **and our oppression**—this is the persecution, as it is said: *and I have also seen the oppression with which the Egyptians oppress them* (Exod. 3:9).

וְאֶת לַחֲצֵנוּ — זוֹ הַדְּחַק, כְּמָה שֶׁנֶּאֱמַר: וְגַם רָאִיתִי אֶת הַלַּחַץ אֲשֶׁר מִצְרַיִם לֹחֲצִים אֹתָם (שמות ג:ט).

(continue on page 30)

trouble") as a reference to the extraordinary efforts required to raise those children who were born under the oppressive conditions in Egypt. Literally, *amaleinu* means "our laboring," which the Haggadah understands to mean grueling work with no fulfillment. Birthing children and raising them only to be killed is perhaps the most extreme expression of *amal*.

Although the root ע-מ-ל does not appear in the prooftext, it is elsewhere associated with children and childbearing. In fact, the word appears together with the root ע-נ-י (abuse or affliction) in the context of the births of Joseph's sons. Joseph names one of his sons Manasseh, signifying that "God has released me from all the debt of my hardship" (*amali*) (Gen. 41:51), and the other Ephraim, signifying that "God has made me fruitful in the land of my affliction" (*onyii*) (41:52).[11]

The verse cited to demonstrate the near impossibility of childrearing in Egypt, given Pharaoh's command to throw all male Israelite babies into the Nile, is the last verse in Exodus 1. As such, it serves as a bridge between the story of the Hebrew midwives who defy Pharaoh's orders to kill Israelite babies and the story of Moses' mother and sister, who conspire to keep him alive. Both of these narratives highlight the heroism of Israelite women in birthing and raising children despite the harsh circumstances.

28 and our oppression—this is the persecution. This is unquestionably the most problematic of the Haggadah's various explications of the *Arami oved avi* passage. First, rather than offering an interpretation of the word in question (*lahatzenu*), the Haggadah simply offers an Aramaic equivalent (*dehak*) of the Hebrew.[12] Second, the prooftext does not seem to contribute anything at all to our understanding of the base text; it simply offers a verse from Exodus that uses the word *lahatz*, just as our verse from Deuteronomy does.

But in fact, the verse from Exodus does offer an important insight into the term in question. The critical word in the prooftext is the word *Mitzrayim* (Egypt/Egyptians), which seems to be superfluous: the verse could have stated, "and I have also seen the oppression with which they oppress them" (Exod. 3:9). It is the extraneous word *Mitzrayim*, the subject of the verb "oppress" in this

(continue on page 30)

---

[11] Compare the use of the word *amal* in Jonah, where God chides the prophet for his unwarranted pain over the withered *kikayon*, a plant whose creation and cultivation entailed no effort on his part (Jon. 4:10).
[12] This is, in fact, the Aramaic word that both *targumim* use to translate *lahatz* in Exod. 3:9: ואף גלי קדמי (Onkelos); and ולחוד גלי קדמי ית דוחקא דמצראי דחקין יתהון (Targum Yonatan). דוחקא דמצראי דחקין להון

THE SEDER

אף הן היו באותו הנס
They too were involved in the miracle

According to tractate *Pesahim*, women—normally exempt from positive, time-bound commandments—are nonetheless obligated to drink four cups of wine on Passover night, *she-af hen hayu be-oto ha-nes*, "for they too were involved in that miracle" (B.T. Pes. 108a–b). This statement has traditionally been interpreted in one of two ways: either that the women were oppressed in Egypt no less than the men and they too experienced the miracle of redemption,[13] or that women in particular were instrumental in bringing about the miraculous deliverance.[14]

Pharaoh's decree concerning the Israelite babies pointedly distinguishes between males and females: "When you deliver the Hebrew women and look on the birth-stool," he instructs the Hebrew midwives, "if it is a boy, you shall put him to death, and if it is a girl, she may live [*ve-hayah*]" (Exod. 1:16). When the midwives defy his orders, Pharaoh charges the entire Egyptian people: "Every boy that is born you shall fling into the Nile, and every girl you shall let live [*tehayun*]" (1:22). A plain reading of Pharaoh's decree suggests that females were spared persecution, though they surely experienced emotional torture when their fathers, brothers, husbands, and sons were oppressed; but that is not the only way to interpret these verses. *Kol ha-bat tehayun* could also be understood as a more proactive and sinister instruction. According to the Midrash, "every girl you shall keep alive" suggests that Pharaoh's motive in sparing the females was to press them into sexual servitude, "for the Egyptians were steeped in depravity."[15] According to this reading, Israelite women were the objects of a unique form of persecution in Egypt, and they surely experienced redemption keenly and directly. It is fitting, then, that women participate fully in seder-night rituals, to mark their personal gratitude for God's deliverance.

The alternate explanation of *af hen hayu be-oto ha-nes*—that women played an active role in the redemption process—is supported by the biblical text as well. Women feature prominently in the opening narratives of Exodus: in chapter 1, the Hebrew midwives Shiphrah and Puah defy Pharaoh's orders and allow all the Israelite babies to live, and in chapter 2, Moses' mother and sister conspire to keep him alive despite the decree and arrange for him to be nursed and nurtured by his natural mother, even after he is adopted by Pharaoh's daughter. The heroic actions of these women lay the groundwork for redemption, literally enabling the birth of the redeemer and ensuring that his Israelite identity remains intact.[16] In both cases, the women's actions—birthing and nursing—fit stereotypical women's roles, and their heroism follows a traditional model.

The conventional nature of the Exodus women's heroism is brought into sharp relief when contrasted with the heroism of women elsewhere in the Bible. Judges 4, which recounts the Israelite victory over the Canaanites during the rule of Deborah the Prophetess, is actually modeled on the Exodus narrative. God throws the Canaanite general Sisera's armies and chariots into a panic (*va-yaham*) in the face of the Israelite onslaught (Judg. 4:15) just as God caused panic among the Egyptian ranks (*va-yaham et mahane Mitzrayim*) as they pursued the Israelites into the sea (Exod. 14:24). Sisera's fleeing soldiers and abandoned chariots (Judg. 4:15–16) recall the Egyptians' decision to flee from the Israelites when the

---

[13] See Tosafot on B.T. Pes. 108b, *Hayu be-oto ha-nes*.

[14] See Rashi on B.T. Pes. 108b, *She-af hen hayu be-oto ha-nes*, as well as the parallel commentary of Rashbam.

[15] Exod. Rabbah 1:23. See also Ramban's commentary on Gen. 12:10, *Va-yehi ra'av ba-aretz*. Ramban, who notes the many parallels between Abraham and Sarah's journey to Egypt and the Exodus story, picks up on the strikingly similar language with which Abraham expresses his fear of what will transpire when he and Sarah arrive in Pharaoh's land: *ve-hargu oti ve-otakh yehayu* ("they will kill me and let you live") (12:12). There, the threat is clearly sexual: Abraham believes that the Egyptians will kill him so as to take his wife for themselves.

[16] The comparable actions of these two pairs of women and their similarly cooperative manner leads the Midrash to conclude that they are one and the same: Shiphrah and Puah are actually Jochebed and Miriam. See B.T. Sot. 11b, Sifre Beha'alotekha 78, and others.

wheels of their chariots became mired in the mud of the seafloor (Exod. 14:25). And the song that Deborah composes with Barak after the Canaanite armies are defeated evokes the Israelites' Song at the Sea. Notably, women bring about the deliverance in both stories. But in contrast to the women of Exodus who operate in traditional, expected roles, the Bible presents Deborah and the women of Judges pushing the boundaries of convention for their time.[17]

Deborah is the only unflawed leader in the book of Judges. She is the only female judge and, notably, the only one who actually functions in a judicial capacity. She is also a charismatic political leader, summoning Barak ben Abinoam and sending him to war against Yachin, king of Canaan, with assurances of success (Judg. 4:6–7). But heroic as she is, the text seems to cast Deborah as an "unnatural" actor forced to assume a role that someone else should have taken up. Although Deborah calls herself a "mother in Israel" (5:7), her activity is decidedly nondomestic and nontraditional, suggesting that the appellation carries a touch of sarcasm. When she agrees to accompany Barak to the battlefield, Deborah warns him that credit for his victory will go to a woman, as though to say: I am assuming this nonconventional role only in the absence of a suitable man (4:9). In an era of political divisiveness and religious neglect, Deborah's reluctant leadership highlights the shortcomings and incompetence of the men around her.

In the same story, Yael, credited with Sisera's defeat, is also cast in a role that is heroic and yet disturbing. The wife of Heber the Kenite invites Sisera into her tent as he flees Barak and kills him while he sleeps, violating not only the norms of modesty, but also her husband's political alliance with the king of Canaan (Judg. 4:17). Judges 4:19 indicates that she fatigues the general with warm milk; but Deborah's retelling of the story in 5:24–27 is more ambiguous, suggesting that she exhausted him sexually.[18] Significantly, both milk, which sustains life, and sexual intercourse, which generates life, highlight Yael's femininity. Her actual murder weapon is the tent peg and throughout the Bible, the tent too is a symbol of domesticity and interiority strongly associated with women.[19] Yael's heroism secures victory for the Israelite armies, but it is a distorted heroism that breaches the traditional codes of her own womanhood: rather than giving life, she takes life. By presenting her heroism in this manner, the Bible seems to suggest that like Deborah, Yael is forced into a role she should not have had to assume: Barak, the Israelite general, should have been able to easily overcome the weary and weakened Sisera. In this book about flawed leadership, even valiant behavior serves to draw attention to overwhelming inadequacy and failure.

The heroism of the women in Exodus is different: it celebrates traditional, nurturing roles and serves only to highlight Pharaoh's cruelty.[20] But here too, to demonstrate approval of the women's heroism in Egypt and to credit them with facilitating the miracle of redemption, the Torah grants them voice in an unstereotypical setting. Following the Song at the Sea, which marks the culmination of the Exodus narrative and the first half of the book of Exodus, Miriam and other women lead the entire people in song.

Af hen hayu be-oto ha-nes.

---

[17] For a more extensive analysis of the unconventional roles of the women in Judges, see Freema Gottlieb, "Three Mothers," *Judaism* 30, no. 2 (Spring 1981): 194–203.

[18] The verses describe Sisera and Yael's interaction somewhat cryptically: "At her feet he sank, lay outstretched, At her feet he sank, lay still; Where he sank, there he lay—destroyed" (Judg. 5:27). The Talmud reads these verses as a clear allusion to sexual intercourse; see B.T. Yev. 103a, Naz. 84b, Hor. 10b.

[19] In her song of victory, Deborah calls Yael "most blessed of women in tents" (Judg. 5:24), implicitly comparing her to Sarah, Rebecca, Rachel, and Leah, each of whom is associated with the domestic sphere of the tent; see B.T. Naz. 23a–b and B.T. Hor. 10b.

[20] Zipporah, wife of Moses, is the one woman in Exodus whose heroic actions serve to highlight a man's failure to act. When a dangerous force confronts Moses on his way to Egypt from Midian, Zipporah assesses the situation and quickly circumcises their son, thereby averting the danger to her husband (Exod. 4:24–26). In this enigmatic episode, Zipporah seemingly steps in to perform a ritual that Moses himself has neglected. The Torah does not explicitly critique Moses for this failure, but later, when Jethro comes to meet Moses and the Israelites following the Exodus, Zipporah and children in tow, the Torah presents them as *her* children and not Moses' (18:3).

THE SEDER

²⁹*And the* Lᴏʀᴅ *brought us out from Egypt with a strong hand and with an outstretched arm and with great terror and with signs and with portents* (Deut. 26:8).

²⁹ וַיּוֹצִאֵנוּ יהוה מִמִּצְרַיִם בְּיָד חֲזָקָה וּבִזְרֹעַ נְטוּיָה, וּבְמֹרָא גָּדֹל, וּבְאֹתוֹת וּבְמֹפְתִים (דברים כו:ח).

verse, that offers an explanation of the term *lahatzenu.* The Haggadah understands the word *Mitzrayim*—which contains the Hebrew word *tzar* (narrow)—to signify a narrow place. And it cites the Exodus verse that emphasizes the oppression that stems from *Mitzrayim* in order to support its interpretation of the word *lahatz* (oppression) as *dehak* (constriction).

The Haggadah is suggesting that *lahatz*—both in our passage and in Exodus—denotes narrowness or confinement, a characteristic that aptly describes the spiritual, if not the physical, qualities of the land of Egypt. Indeed, in the verse from Exodus 3 that immediately precedes the prooftext, Egypt is contrasted with the Land of Israel, a land that is described as spacious:

וָאֵרֵד לְהַצִּילוֹ מִיַּד מִצְרַיִם וּלְהַעֲלֹתוֹ מִן הָאָרֶץ הַהִוא אֶל אֶרֶץ טוֹבָה וּרְחָבָה אֶל אֶרֶץ זָבַת חָלָב וּדְבַשׁ אֶל מְקוֹם הַכְּנַעֲנִי וְהַחִתִּי וְהָאֱמֹרִי וְהַפְּרִזִּי וְהַחִוִּי וְהַיְבוּסִי:

I have come down to rescue them from the Egyptians and to bring them out of that land to a good and spacious land, a land flowing with milk and honey, the region of the Canaanites, the Hittites, and Amorites, the Perizzites, the Hivites, and the Jebusites (Exod. 3:8).

Clearly, then, the Torah sees Egypt, *Mitzrayim,* as a place that is not spacious, a place that is constricted.

The Torah deems Egypt a place of "narrowness" because it is a place that presents no choices and does not allow for movement in any direction. That was precisely the experience of Israel in *Mitzrayim:* a defining characteristic of the Israelites' enslavement was constriction of the self. (For further development of these ideas, see essay 8.)

29 And the Lᴏʀᴅ **brought us out from Egypt . . . with signs and with portents.** The Haggadah presents six explications of this final verse from Deuteronomy 26. The ordering of these *drashot* corresponds to the words of the verse, but the citation of specific prooftexts—which include passages from the Torah, the Prophets, and the Writings—suggests a deliberate structuring that was intended to convey a specific religious message. The first two prooftexts refer to the Ten Plagues that scourged Egypt and demonstrated God's power and rule. The final prooftext refers to God's display of might that will portend the End of Days. The third prooftext refers to the sword, or staff, of God's angel, whereas the fifth prooftext refers to the staff of God's messenger, Moses. All of these passages frame the fourth prooftext, a verse from Deuteronomy about the revelation of the Divine Presence. The chiastic structure implies that this verse is the critical one and that the collective experience of revelation was essential to the Exodus experience.

A Pᴀssᴏᴠᴇʀ Hᴀɢɢᴀᴅᴀʜ: Gᴏ Fᴏʀᴛʜ ᴀɴᴅ Lᴇᴀʀɴ

30 And the Lord brought us out from Egypt—not by an angel, not by a seraph, not by a messenger, but the Blessed Holy One Himself in His glory, as it says: *And I will cross through the land of Egypt on this night, and I will strike down every firstborn in the land of Egypt from man to beast, and from all the gods of Egypt I will exact retributions. I am the Lord* (Exod. 12:12).

And I will cross through the land of Egypt on this night—I—and not an angel.

and I will strike down every firstborn in the land of Egypt—I—and not a seraph.

and from all the gods of Egypt I will exact retributions—I—and not a messenger.

I am the Lord—I and none other.

with a strong hand—this is pestilence, as it says: *Look, the hand of the Lord is about to be against your livestock which is in the field, against the horses, against the donkeys, against the camels, against the cattle, and against the sheep—a very heavy pestilence* (Exod. 9:3).

30 וַיּוֹצִאֵנוּ יהוה מִמִּצְרַיִם — לֹא עַל יְדֵי מַלְאָךְ, וְלֹא עַל יְדֵי שָׂרָף, וְלֹא עַל יְדֵי שָׁלִיחַ, אֶלָּא הַקָּדוֹשׁ בָּרוּךְ הוּא בִּכְבוֹדוֹ וּבְעַצְמוֹ, שֶׁנֶּאֱמַר: וְעָבַרְתִּי בְאֶרֶץ מִצְרַיִם בַּלַּיְלָה הַזֶּה, וְהִכֵּיתִי כָל בְּכוֹר בְּאֶרֶץ מִצְרַיִם מֵאָדָם וְעַד בְּהֵמָה, וּבְכָל אֱלֹהֵי מִצְרַיִם אֶעֱשֶׂה שְׁפָטִים, אֲנִי יהוה (שמות יב:יב).

וְעָבַרְתִּי בְאֶרֶץ מִצְרַיִם בַּלַּיְלָה הַזֶּה — אֲנִי וְלֹא מַלְאָךְ

וְהִכֵּיתִי כָל בְּכוֹר בְּאֶרֶץ מִצְרַיִם — אֲנִי וְלֹא שָׂרָף

וּבְכָל אֱלֹהֵי מִצְרַיִם אֶעֱשֶׂה שְׁפָטִים — אֲנִי וְלֹא הַשָּׁלִיחַ.

אֲנִי יהוה — אֲנִי הוּא וְלֹא אַחֵר.

בְּיָד חֲזָקָה — זוֹ הַדֶּבֶר, כְּמָה שֶׁנֶּאֱמַר: הִנֵּה יַד יהוה הוֹיָה בְּמִקְנְךָ אֲשֶׁר בַּשָּׂדֶה, בַּסּוּסִים, בַּחֲמֹרִים, בַּגְּמַלִּים, בַּבָּקָר וּבַצֹּאן, דֶּבֶר כָּבֵד מְאֹד (שמות ט:ג).

---

30 And the Lord brought us out from Egypt. The Haggadah reads the *Arami oved avi* passage as unequivocal about God's single-handed execution of the Exodus and specifically the Plague of the Firstborn. But in fact, the prooftext from Exodus, which depicts God's solo performance, contrasts with a verse from Numbers that describes an angel or Divine messenger freeing the Israelites from Egypt (20:16). The Haggadah's forceful assertion that God was solely responsible for the unfolding of events suggests that the conflict between Exodus and Numbers motivates this particular explication.

31 *and with an outstretched arm*—this is the sword, as it says: *with a drawn sword in his hand, stretched over Jerusalem* (1 Chron. 21:16).

and with great terror—this is the revelation of the Divine Presence, as it says: *Or has God tried to come to take Him a nation from within a nation in trials and signs and portents and in battle and with a strong hand and an outstretched arm and with great terrors, like all that the LORD your God did for you in Egypt before your eyes?* (Deut. 4:34).

32 *and with signs*—this is the staff, as it says: *And this staff you shall take in your hand, with which you will do the signs* (Exod. 4:17).

³¹ **וּבִזְרֹעַ נְטוּיָה** — זוֹ הַחֶרֶב, כְּמָה שֶׁנֶּאֱמַר: וְחַרְבּוֹ שְׁלוּפָה בְּיָדוֹ, נְטוּיָה עַל יְרוּשָׁלָיִם (דברי הימים א כא:טז).

וּבְמֹרָא גָּדֹל — זוֹ גִּלּוּי שְׁכִינָה, כְּמָה שֶׁנֶּאֱמַר: אוֹ הֲנִסָּה אֱלֹהִים לָבֹא לָקַחַת לוֹ גוֹי מִקֶּרֶב גּוֹי בְּמַסֹּת בְּאֹתֹת וּבְמוֹפְתִים, וּבְמִלְחָמָה וּבְיָד חֲזָקָה וּבִזְרוֹעַ נְטוּיָה, וּבְמוֹרָאִים גְּדֹלִים, כְּכֹל אֲשֶׁר עָשָׂה לָכֶם יהוה אֱלֹהֵיכֶם בְּמִצְרַיִם לְעֵינֶיךָ (דברים ד:לד).

³² **וּבְאֹתוֹת** — זֶה הַמַּטֶּה, כְּמָה שֶׁנֶּאֱמַר: וְאֶת הַמַּטֶּה הַזֶּה תִּקַּח בְּיָדֶךָ, אֲשֶׁר תַּעֲשֶׂה בּוֹ אֶת הָאֹתֹת (שמות ד:יז).

---

31 *and with an outstretched arm*—this is the sword. To support its understanding of the phrase *zero'a netuyah* (an outstretched arm) as an allusion to God's sword, the Haggadah cites 1 Chronicles 21:16, where David is castigated for taking a census of the people. In this context, David sees an angel with a sword in hand, "stretched out" (*netuyah*) over Jerusalem. A close reading of the relevant chapter in Chronicles and its parallel account in 2 Samuel 24 demonstrates that the prophetic authors borrowed themes and motifs from the Exodus story and particularly from God's confrontation with Pharaoh during the plagues to depict David's sin and punishment. For further analysis, see essay 4.

32 *and with signs*—this is the staff. Moses' staff played a role in several of the Ten Plagues, yet here it is cited for its role in demonstrating God's power and efficacy to the Israelites themselves. Following the Exodus, Moses' staff became a symbol of his leadership in the desert as well, where it continued to represent God's power and Moses' unique connection to God. Thus, the Haggadah's reference to Moses' staff in its explication of this final verse from Deut. 26 implies that the Exodus was a unique event in Israel's history, but not a discrete or disconnected one.

A PASSOVER HAGGADAH: GO FORTH AND LEARN

It is customary to spill three drops of wine
when mentioning "blood, fire, and pillars of smoke."

³³ *and with portents*—this is the blood, as it says: ³⁴ *I will set portents in the sky and on earth: blood and fire and pillars of smoke* (Joel 3:3).

³³ וּבְמֹפְתִים — זֶה הַדָּם, כְּמָה שֶׁנֶּאֱמַר: ³⁴ וְנָתַתִּי מוֹפְתִים בַּשָּׁמַיִם וּבָאָרֶץ דָּם וָאֵשׁ וְתִימְרוֹת עָשָׁן (יואל ג:ג).

Another explanation:

דָּבָר אַחֵר:

with a strong hand—two;

בְּיָד חֲזָקָה — שְׁתַּיִם,

with an outstretched arm—two;

וּבִזְרֹעַ נְטוּיָה — שְׁתַּיִם,

and with great terror—two;

וּבְמֹרָא גָּדֹל — שְׁתַּיִם,

and with signs—two;

וּבְאֹתוֹת — שְׁתַּיִם,

and with portents—two.

וּבְמֹפְתִים — שְׁתַּיִם.

---

33 *and with portents*—this is the blood. Blood is the only sign that was designated to convince both the Israelites and the Egyptians of God's presence and power. It was one of the original signs that God gave Moses at the Burning Bush to use in winning over the Israelites; it was the first of the Ten Plagues that wreaked havoc upon Egypt; and it was the sign that the Israelites were instructed to put on their doorframes to save them from the Plague of the Firstborn. The Haggadah's allusion to blood in its final explication of Deuteronomy 26 highlights this theme and underscores the connection between the Exodus from Egypt and all future redemptions.

34 *I will set portents in the sky and on earth: blood and fire and pillars of smoke.* This final prooftext is from the book of Joel and represents an eschatological vision in which old and young, free and slave, will prophesy (Joel 3:1–2). Joel describes revelation as awesome yet potentially destructive; only those who invoke God's name in Zion and Jerusalem will be spared (3:4–5). The Haggadah's invocation of this vision suggests a parallel between the saving of the Israelites from God's fury through the blood of the Passover sacrifice and the saving of those who are in Zion and Jerusalem at the End of Days. This parallel highlights a critical aspect of the Passover story: by marking the entryway into their homes with sacrificial blood during the Plague of the Firstborn, the Israelites are, for the very first time, creating a sacred space in which they can experience God's protective presence. The Haggadah suggests that in this way, the Exodus story is a model for the ultimate redemption and revelation of the Divine.

³⁵ These are the Ten Plagues that the Blessed Holy One brought upon the Egyptians in Egypt. And they are:

³⁵ אֵלּוּ עֶשֶׂר מַכּוֹת שֶׁהֵבִיא הַקָּדוֹשׁ בָּרוּךְ הוּא עַל הַמִּצְרִים בְּמִצְרַיִם, וְאֵלּוּ הֵן:

It is customary to spill a drop of wine when reciting each of the Ten Plagues and a drop when reciting each of the three words of R. Judah's mnemonic device for the plagues.

Blood — דָּם
Frogs — צְפַרְדֵּעַ
Lice — כִּנִּים
Swarming creatures — עָרוֹב
Pestilence — דֶּבֶר
Boils — שְׁחִין
³⁶ Hail — ³⁶ בָּרָד
Locusts — אַרְבֶּה
Darkness — חֹשֶׁךְ
Death of the Firstborn — מַכַּת בְּכוֹרוֹת

R. Judah referred to them by a mnemonic: detzakh, adash, be-ahav.

רַבִּי יְהוּדָה הָיָה נוֹתֵן בָּהֶם סִמָּנִים: דְּצַ"ךְ עַדַ"שׁ בְּאַחַ"ב.

---

35 These are the Ten Plagues. The Haggadah employs a range of midrashic tools for creatively reading and interpreting the Ten Plagues, a central feature of the biblical Exodus story. For full consideration, see essay 4.

36 Hail. Seven is a significant number in the Bible, and in various ways the Torah marks the seventh plague as unique.[21] Hail (*barad*) merits the most extensive description of all the plagues (Exod. 9:13–35). In warning Pharaoh of the imminent destruction, Moses describes the hail (or the set of plagues beginning with hail) as the sum of all God's punishments (9:14). The hail that devastates the land of Egypt is miraculously accompanied by fire (9:23–24), and throughout Exodus, fire represents the presence of God: at the beginning of the book, God appears to Moses for the first time in the small fire at the Burning Bush (3:2); in the middle of the book, God descends in a great fire

---

[21] Interestingly, Nahum Sarna argues that Ps. 78 and 105 list seven (rather than ten) plagues, though counting the plagues in these psalms is not simple, given their impressionistic rendering. See Nahum M. Sarna, *Exploring Exodus: The Heritage of Biblical Israel* (New York: Schocken Books, 1986), and essay 4.

A PASSOVER HAGGADAH: GO FORTH AND LEARN

| **37** R. Yose ha-Gelili **says**: How do you know that [38] the Egyptians were smitten with ten | [37] רַבִּי יוֹסֵי הַגְּלִילִי אוֹמֵר: מִנַּיִן אַתָּה אוֹמֵר [38] שֶׁלָּקוּ הַמִּצְרִים בְּמִצְרַיִם עֶשֶׂר |

upon Mount Sinai (19:18); and at the end of the book, fire (in addition to the Cloud of Glory) indicates God's Presence in the *Mishkan* (40:38). Symbolically, then, the fire that flashes in the midst of the icy hail marks the seventh plague as a moment of revelation.

It is no coincidence that the manner in which the hail rains down upon Egypt is described as a torrent of *matar* (Exod. 9:18,23), a word that typically refers to precipitation, but more precisely, to that which God releases from the heavens. Although rain is a natural phenomenon, *matar* represents God's judgment. According to Deuteronomy, God provides *matar* in accordance with the people's observance of the commandments: if they obey the laws, there will be rain, but if they sin, there will not (11:13–17, 28:12). Throughout the Torah, *matar* functions as a barometer of God's relationship with the People of Israel: the Flood comes down as *matar* (Gen. 7:4); Sodom is destroyed with *matar* (19:24); and the manna, designed to test the extent of the Israelites' compliance with the word of God, is also delivered as *matar* (Exod. 16:4).[22] The hail that devastates Egypt is represented as *matar* for similar reasons: it is a way to test or judge the Egyptians' fear of God. Indeed, after Moses warns Pharaoh of the impending hail, those who fear God bring their slaves and livestock inside, to shelter them, and those who are indifferent to God's word leave their slaves and livestock exposed in the fields (9:20–21). Ultimately, Pharaoh fails this test as he has failed the others before. At Pharaoh's behest, Moses agrees to ask God to end the hail; but at the same time, he asserts that he is aware Pharaoh still does not fear God (9:30). And indeed, as soon as the hail subsides, Pharaoh again hardens his heart and refuses to let the people go.

37 R. Yose ha-Gelili says. Most scholars agree that the *baraita* of Rabbi Yose ha-Gelili was not originally composed for inclusion in the Haggadah. To corroborate their arguments, it is worth noting that this discussion digresses from the Haggadah's narrow focus on the Exodus itself. Although the Torah clearly treats the Splitting of the Sea as part of the Exodus narrative—the Song at the Sea (Exod. 15) marks the account's finale—surprisingly, the Haggadah seems to discount it as a core part of the story. Accordingly, the passage from Joshua 24 cited earlier in *Maggid* ("In olden times, your forefathers . . . worshiped other gods") is truncated, excluding the verses that describe the Israelites' experience at the sea (Josh. 24:5–7).

The Haggadah's restricted focus reflects a well-conceived educational strategy. By limiting the frame of the narrative, the Haggadah succeeds in heightening the drama of the moment at which the Israelites leave Egypt. This is more than good storytelling. The goal of the seder night is to get participants to re-experience history, to see themselves in Egypt, and to see themselves as though they had personally witnessed redemption. But the people who experienced the Exodus firsthand did not know the end of the story; they could not see beyond the moment of departure. If we, generations later, are to truly re-create the drama of that moment, we too need to limit our vision.

---

[22] According to Rashi on Exod. 16:4, *Ha-yelekh be-torati*, God wanted to check whether the people would obey the rules concerning the manna: not leaving it over until morning and refraining from collecting it on the Sabbath. For an additional description of the manna falling as *matar*, see Ps. 78:24.

plagues in Egypt and were smitten with fifty plagues at the sea? What does it say regarding Egypt? *And the soothsayers said to Pharaoh, "God's **finger** it is!"* (Exod. 8:15). And what does it say regarding the sea? *And Israel saw the great **hand** that the LORD had performed against Egypt, and the people feared the LORD, and they trusted in the LORD and in Moses His servant* (Exod. 14:31). How much were they smitten with a finger? Ten plagues! Say, therefore, that in Egypt [with God's finger] they were smitten with ten plagues and at the sea [with God's hand] they were smitten with fifty plagues.

R. Eliezer says: How do we know that each and every plague that the Blessed Holy One brought upon the Egyptians in Egypt was composed of four plagues? As it says: *He sent against them His smoldering fury, anger, indignation, and distress, a cohort of evil messengers* (Ps. 78:49); *anger*—one, *indignation*—two, *distress*—three, *a cohort of evil messengers*—four. Say, therefore, that in Egypt [with God's finger] they were smitten with forty plagues and at the sea [with God's hand] they were smitten with two hundred plagues.

R. Akiva says: How do we know that each and every plague that the Blessed Holy One

מַכּוֹת וְעַל הַיָּם לָקוּ חֲמִשִּׁים מַכּוֹת? בְּמִצְרַיִם מָה הוּא אוֹמֵר? וַיֹּאמְרוּ הַחַרְטֻמִּים אֶל פַּרְעֹה: אֶצְבַּע אֱלֹהִים הִוא (שמות ח:טו). וְעַל הַיָּם מה הוּא אוֹמֵר? וַיַּרְא יִשְׂרָאֵל אֶת הַיָּד הַגְּדֹלָה אֲשֶׁר עָשָׂה יהוה בְּמִצְרַיִם, וַיִּירְאוּ הָעָם אֶת יהוה, וַיַּאֲמִינוּ בַּיהוה וּבְמשֶׁה עַבְדּוֹ (שמות יד:לא). כַּמָּה לָקוּ בָאֶצְבַּע? עֶשֶׂר מַכּוֹת. אֱמוֹר מֵעַתָּה: בְּמִצְרַיִם לָקוּ עֶשֶׂר מַכּוֹת וְעַל הַיָּם לָקוּ חֲמִשִּׁים מַכּוֹת.

רַבִּי אֱלִיעֶזֶר אוֹמֵר: מִנַּיִן שֶׁכָּל מַכָּה וּמַכָּה שֶׁהֵבִיא הַקָּדוֹשׁ בָּרוּךְ הוּא עַל הַמִּצְרִים בְּמִצְרַיִם הָיְתָה שֶׁל אַרְבַּע מַכּוֹת? שֶׁנֶּאֱמַר: יְשַׁלַּח בָּם חֲרוֹן אַפּוֹ, עֶבְרָה וָזַעַם וְצָרָה, מִשְׁלַחַת מַלְאֲכֵי רָעִים (תהלים עח:מט). עֶבְרָה — אַחַת, וָזַעַם — שְׁתַּיִם, וְצָרָה — שָׁלשׁ, מִשְׁלַחַת מַלְאֲכֵי רָעִים — אַרְבַּע. אֱמוֹר מֵעַתָּה: בְּמִצְרַיִם לָקוּ אַרְבָּעִים מַכּוֹת וְעַל הַיָּם לָקוּ מָאתַיִם מַכּוֹת.

רַבִּי עֲקִיבָא אוֹמֵר: מִנַּיִן שֶׁכָּל מַכָּה וּמַכָּה שֶׁהֵבִיא הַקָּדוֹשׁ בָּרוּךְ הוּא עַל

---

38 the Egyptians were smitten with ten plagues in Egypt and were smitten with fifty plagues at the sea. The *baraita* of R. Yose ha-Gelili is cited here because it expands upon a theme introduced in the previous passage. In its explication of Deut. 26, the Haggadah asserted that the Ten Plagues were experienced as moments of revelation; this *baraita* highlights the revelatory nature of the experience at the sea.

A PASSOVER HAGGADAH: GO FORTH AND LEARN

brought upon the Egyptians in Egypt was composed of five plagues? As it says: *He sent against them His smoldering fury, anger, indignation, and distress, a cohort of evil messengers* (Ps. 78:49); *smoldering fury*—one, *anger*—two, *indignation*—three, *distress*—four, *a cohort of evil messengers*—five. Say, therefore, that in Egypt [with God's finger] they were smitten with fifty plagues and at the sea [with God's hand] they were smitten with two hundred and fifty plagues.

הַמִּצְרִים בְּמִצְרַיִם הָיְתָה שֶׁל חָמֵשׁ מַכּוֹת? שֶׁנֶּאֱמַר: יְשַׁלַּח בָּם חֲרוֹן אַפּוֹ, עֶבְרָה וָזַעַם וְצָרָה, מִשְׁלַחַת מַלְאֲכֵי רָעִים (תהלים עח:מט). חֲרוֹן אַפּוֹ — אַחַת, עֶבְרָה — שְׁתַּיִם, וָזַעַם — שָׁלוֹשׁ, וְצָרָה — אַרְבַּע, מִשְׁלַחַת מַלְאֲכֵי רָעִים — חָמֵשׁ. אֱמוֹר מֵעַתָּה: בְּמִצְרַיִם לָקוּ חֲמִשִּׁים מַכּוֹת וְעַל הַיָּם לָקוּ חֲמִשִּׁים וּמָאתַיִם מַכּוֹת.

39 For how many good deeds are we indebted to the Omnipresent!

כַּמָּה מַעֲלוֹת טוֹבוֹת לַמָּקוֹם עָלֵינוּ! 39

40 If He had taken us out of Egypt but had not exacted retributions upon them

it would have been sufficient.

If He had exacted retributions upon them but had not destroyed their gods

it would have been sufficient.

אִלּוּ הוֹצִיאָנוּ מִמִּצְרַיִם, וְלֹא עָשָׂה בָהֶם שְׁפָטִים 40

דַּיֵּנוּ.

אִלּוּ עָשָׂה בָהֶם שְׁפָטִים, וְלֹא עָשָׂה בֵאלֹהֵיהֶם

דַּיֵּנוּ.

---

39 For how many good deeds are we indebted to the Omnipresent! The provenance of the *Dayenu* passage and its dating is a matter of dispute among scholars. Some claim it is very old, perhaps even from the Second Temple period. These scholars point to the climax of the poem—"If He had brought us into the Land of Israel but had not built the Temple for us, it would have been sufficient" (*dayenu*)—and argue that after the Temple's destruction, this would not have been cited as the ultimate expression of God's benevolence.[23] Yet others observe that *Dayenu* is not documented prior to the tenth-century siddur of Rav Saadiah Gaon and assert that it was most likely composed post-antiquity in Babylonia.[24]

Regardless of the poem's origins, it is significant that this litany is composed of fifteen items. The list follows the opening exclamation, "*Kama ma'alot tovot la-Makom aleinu!*" which is usually translated "For how many good deeds are we indebted to the Omnipresent." But the word *ma'alot*

---

[23] E. D. Goldschmidt, *The Passover Haggadah: Its Sources and History* (in Hebrew) (Jerusalem: Bialik Institute, 1960), 49–51.

[24] Tabory, *JPS Commentary*, 45–46.

THE SEDER

English	Hebrew
If He had destroyed their gods but had not killed their firstborn	אִלּוּ עָשָׂה בֵאלֹהֵיהֶם, וְלֹא הָרַג אֶת בְּכוֹרֵיהֶם
it would have been sufficient.	דַּיֵּנוּ.
If He had killed their firstborn but had not given us their money	אִלּוּ הָרַג אֶת בְּכוֹרֵיהֶם, וְלֹא נָתַן לָנוּ אֶת מָמוֹנָם
it would have been sufficient.	דַּיֵּנוּ.
If He had given us their money but had not split the sea for us	אִלּוּ נָתַן לָנוּ אֶת מָמוֹנָם, וְלֹא קָרַע לָנוּ אֶת הַיָּם
it would have been sufficient.	דַּיֵּנוּ.
If He had split the sea for us but had not brought us through it on dry land	אִלּוּ קָרַע לָנוּ אֶת הַיָּם, וְלֹא הֶעֱבִירָנוּ בְּתוֹכוֹ בֶּחָרָבָה
it would have been sufficient.	דַּיֵּנוּ.
If He had brought us through it on dry land but had not drowned our enemies in it	אִלּוּ הֶעֱבִירָנוּ בְּתוֹכוֹ בֶּחָרָבָה, וְלֹא שִׁקַּע צָרֵינוּ בְּתוֹכוֹ
it would have been sufficient.	דַּיֵּנוּ.

literally means "stairs" and many have suggested that the fifteen items of *Dayenu* were meant to recall the fifteen stairs in the Temple courtyard and to parallel the fifteen Songs of Ascent (*Shirei ha-Ma'alot*) in Psalms. In fact, *Dayenu* is analogous to the Songs of Ascent in another way as well. In Psalms, these songs, which comprise chapters 120 to 134, function structurally as a bridge between the psalms of *Hallel ha-Mitzri* (the "Egyptian *Hallel*," chapters 113 to 118) and the psalms of *Hallel ha-Gadol* (the "Great *Hallel*," chapter 136). In the Haggadah, *Dayenu* precedes these two versions of *Hallel*, the first of which we begin to recite at the end of *Maggid*. And *Dayenu* itself evokes the *Hallel ha-Gadol* insofar as its poetry is followed by a prosaic repetition; Psalm 136 follows Psalm 135, which is a more poetic rendition of the same ideas.

40 If He had taken us out of Egypt ... it would have been sufficient. *Dayenu*'s fifteen lines affirm God's active role in the major events of Israel's history, from the Exodus to the building of the Temple. Despite the fact that *Dayenu* concludes with the nation's arrival in the Land of Israel, it is clear that the template for this poem is the book of Exodus itself. The narrative arc that the poem traces—from redemption to the construction of sacred space—corresponds to the biblical storyline. In this respect, *Dayenu* (like the *baraita* of Rabbi Yose ha-Gelili) digresses from the narrative focus of the Haggadah, which concentrates on the Exodus itself, to the point of curtailing biblical passages whose narration reaches beyond the departure from Egypt or the Splitting of the Sea.

Although *Dayenu* does not conclude *Maggid*, it does end the narrative portion of this section, functioning for the Haggadah much in the way that major songs function in the biblical text. Just as the Song of the Sea (*Shirat ha-Yam*) formally concludes the Exodus narrative and the Song of the Well (*Shirat ha-Be'er*) marks the end of the desert narrative (inasmuch as it precedes the battles against Sihon, king of the Amorites, and Og, king of Bashan, which represent the beginning of the conquest of the Land), so *Dayenu* officially concludes the Exodus story in the Haggadah.

A Passover Haggadah: Go Forth and Learn

If He had drowned our enemies in it but had not satisfied our needs in the desert for forty years **it would have been sufficient.**

If He had satisfied our needs in the desert for forty years but had not fed us the manna

it would have been sufficient.

If He had fed us the manna but had not given us the Sabbath

it would have been sufficient.

If He had given us the Sabbath but had not brought us before Mount Sinai

it would have been sufficient.

If He had brought us before Mount Sinai but had not given us the Torah

it would have been sufficient.

If He had given us the Torah but had not brought us into the Land of Israel

it would have been sufficient.

If He had brought us into the Land of Israel but had not built the Temple for us

it would have been sufficient.

How much more so is the great goodness that the Omnipresent has done for us! He took us out of Egypt, and exacted retributions upon them, and destroyed their gods, and killed their firstborn, and gave us their money, and split the sea for us, and brought us through it on dry land, and drowned our enemies in it, and satisfied our needs in the desert for forty years, and fed us the manna, and gave us the Sabbath, and brought us before Mount Sinai, and gave us the Torah, and brought us into the Land of Israel, and built the Temple for us to atone for all our sins.

אִלּוּ שִׁקַּע צָרֵינוּ בְּתוֹכוֹ, וְלֹא סִפֵּק צָרְכֵּנוּ בַּמִּדְבָּר אַרְבָּעִים שָׁנָה

דַּיֵּנוּ.

אִלּוּ סִפֵּק צָרְכֵּנוּ בַּמִּדְבָּר אַרְבָּעִים שָׁנָה, וְלֹא הֶאֱכִילָנוּ אֶת הַמָּן

דַּיֵּנוּ.

אִלּוּ הֶאֱכִילָנוּ אֶת הַמָּן, וְלֹא נָתַן לָנוּ אֶת הַשַּׁבָּת

דַּיֵּנוּ.

אִלּוּ נָתַן לָנוּ אֶת הַשַּׁבָּת, וְלֹא קֵרְבָנוּ לִפְנֵי הַר סִינַי

דַּיֵּנוּ.

אִלּוּ קֵרְבָנוּ לִפְנֵי הַר סִינַי, וְלֹא נָתַן לָנוּ אֶת הַתּוֹרָה

דַּיֵּנוּ.

אִלּוּ נָתַן לָנוּ אֶת הַתּוֹרָה וְלֹא הִכְנִיסָנוּ לְאֶרֶץ יִשְׂרָאֵל

דַּיֵּנוּ.

אִלּוּ הִכְנִיסָנוּ לְאֶרֶץ יִשְׂרָאֵל וְלֹא בָנָה לָנוּ אֶת בֵּית הַבְּחִירָה

דַּיֵּנוּ.

עַל אַחַת, כַּמָּה וְכַמָּה, טוֹבָה כְפוּלָה וּמְכֻפֶּלֶת לַמָּקוֹם עָלֵינוּ: שֶׁהוֹצִיאָנוּ מִמִּצְרַיִם, וְעָשָׂה בָהֶם שְׁפָטִים, וְעָשָׂה בֵאלֹהֵיהֶם, וְהָרַג אֶת בְּכוֹרֵיהֶם, וְנָתַן לָנוּ אֶת מָמוֹנָם, וְקָרַע לָנוּ אֶת הַיָּם, וְהֶעֱבִירָנוּ בְּתוֹכוֹ בֶּחָרָבָה, וְשִׁקַּע צָרֵינוּ בְּתוֹכוֹ, וְסִפֵּק צָרְכֵּנוּ בַּמִּדְבָּר אַרְבָּעִים שָׁנָה, וְהֶאֱכִילָנוּ אֶת הַמָּן, וְנָתַן לָנוּ אֶת הַשַּׁבָּת, וְקֵרְבָנוּ לִפְנֵי הַר סִינַי, וְנָתַן לָנוּ אֶת הַתּוֹרָה, וְהִכְנִיסָנוּ לְאֶרֶץ יִשְׂרָאֵל, וּבָנָה לָנוּ אֶת בֵּית הַבְּחִירָה לְכַפֵּר עַל כָּל עֲוֹנוֹתֵינוּ.

The Seder

It is customary to raise the matzah and the *maror*
while reciting their explanations.

41 Rabban Gamliel used to say: Whoever did not explain these three things on Passover has not fulfilled his obligation. They are: **Pesah**, **matzah** and **maror**.

The Passover sacrifice (*Pesah*) that our ancestors ate when the Temple still stood—for what reason? Because the Blessed Holy One passed over the homes of our ancestors in Egypt, as it says: ⁴²*You shall say, "A Passover sacrifice to the LORD, who passed over the houses of the Israelites in Egypt when He scourged Egypt and our households He rescued.' And the people bowed and did obeisance* (Exod. 12:27).

⁴¹ רַבָּן גַּמְלִיאֵל הָיָה אוֹמֵר: כָּל שֶׁלֹּא אָמַר שְׁלֹשָׁה דְבָרִים אֵלּוּ בַּפֶּסַח, לֹא יָצָא יְדֵי חוֹבָתוֹ, וְאֵלּוּ הֵן: פֶּסַח, מַצָּה, וּמָרוֹר.

פֶּסַח שֶׁהָיוּ אֲבוֹתֵינוּ אוֹכְלִים בִּזְמַן שֶׁבֵּית הַמִּקְדָּשׁ הָיָה קַיָּם, עַל שׁוּם מָה? עַל שׁוּם שֶׁפָּסַח הַקָּדוֹשׁ בָּרוּךְ הוּא עַל בָּתֵּי אֲבוֹתֵינוּ בְּמִצְרַיִם, שֶׁנֶּאֱמַר: ⁴² וַאֲמַרְתֶּם זֶבַח פֶּסַח הוּא לַיהוה, אֲשֶׁר פָּסַח עַל בָּתֵּי בְנֵי יִשְׂרָאֵל בְּמִצְרַיִם בְּנָגְפּוֹ אֶת מִצְרַיִם, וְאֶת בָּתֵּינוּ הִצִּיל, וַיִּקֹּד הָעָם וַיִּשְׁתַּחֲווּ (שמות יב:כז).

41 R. Gamliel used to say. The source for Rabban Gamliel's teaching that all three ritual foods must be mentioned explicitly at the seder is Exodus 12:27, "You shall **say**, 'A Passover sacrifice to the Lord, who passed over the houses of the Israelites in Egypt...'" Although the Haggadah cites this verse to explain the symbolic significance of the Passover offering in particular, Rabban Gamliel understands the phrase *zevah pesah* (Passover sacrifice) as a reference to the complete meal, which includes the matzah and the *maror*. Thus, the order in which Rabban Gamliel lists the foods—*pesah*, matzah, *maror*—reflects their relative significance to the Passover ritual rather than the chronological order of the experiences they symbolize.

The appropriate chronological ordering would seem to be just the opposite: *maror*, matzah, *pesah*. Accordingly, some explain the *maror* as a symbol of slavery, the matzah as a symbol of the transition from bondage to freedom, and the *pesah* as a symbol of redemption. But in fact the verses cited demonstrate that the more accurate chronological ordering of the symbols is: *maror*, *pesah*, matzah. The *maror* is indeed a symbol of the bitterness of slavery, of the Egyptian oppression and the Israelites' vulnerability before God intervenes to redeem them. The Passover offering represents the actual moment of God's intervention, emphasizing that the Exodus occurred only by virtue of God's direct involvement. And the matzah symbolizes the unpreparedness with which the Israelites left Egypt—they didn't even take food for the way—and the fact that, even after the Exodus, they were dependent on God's ongoing protection and care.

42 You shall say, "A Passover sacrifice to the LORD..." Bible translations and commentaries dispute the meaning of the final words in this verse, *va-yikod ha-am va-yishtahavu* ("And the people bowed and did obeisance"). Some understand them as an instruction to the people—they should

A PASSOVER HAGGADAH: GO FORTH AND LEARN

This **matzah** that we eat—for what reason? Because the dough of our ancestors had not had a chance to leaven before the King of Kings, the Blessed Holy One, appeared before them and redeemed them. As it says: *And they baked the dough that they had brought out of Egypt in rounds of flatbread, for it had not leavened, since they had been driven out of Egypt and could not tarry, and provisions, too, they could not make for themselves* (Exod. 12:39–40).

This **maror** that we eat—for what reason? Because the Egyptians embittered the lives of our ancestors in Egypt, as it says: *And they made their lives bitter with hard work, with mortar and bricks and every work in the field— all their crushing work that they performed* (Exod. 1:14).

מַצָּה זוֹ שֶׁאָנוּ אוֹכְלִים, עַל שׁוּם מָה? עַל שׁוּם שֶׁלֹּא הִסְפִּיק בְּצֵקָם שֶׁל אֲבוֹתֵינוּ לְהַחֲמִיץ עַד שֶׁנִּגְלָה עֲלֵיהֶם מֶלֶךְ מַלְכֵי הַמְּלָכִים, הַקָּדוֹשׁ בָּרוּךְ הוּא וּגְאָלָם, שֶׁנֶּאֱמַר: וַיֹּאפוּ אֶת הַבָּצֵק אֲשֶׁר הוֹצִיאוּ מִמִּצְרַיִם עֻגֹת מַצּוֹת, כִּי לֹא חָמֵץ, כִּי גֹרְשׁוּ מִמִּצְרַיִם וְלֹא יָכְלוּ לְהִתְמַהְמֵהַּ, וְגַם צֵדָה לֹא עָשׂוּ לָהֶם (שמות יב:לט).

מָרוֹר זֶה שֶׁאָנוּ אוֹכְלִים, עַל שׁוּם מָה? עַל שׁוּם שֶׁמֵּרְרוּ הַמִּצְרִים אֶת חַיֵּי אֲבוֹתֵינוּ בְּמִצְרַיִם, שֶׁנֶּאֱמַר: וַיְמָרְרוּ אֶת חַיֵּיהֶם בַּעֲבֹדָה קָשָׁה, בְּחֹמֶר וּבִלְבֵנִים וּבְכָל עֲבֹדָה בַּשָּׂדֶה אֵת כָּל עֲבֹדָתָם אֲשֶׁר עָבְדוּ בָהֶם בְּפָרֶךְ (שמות א:יד).

bow in homage—but others claim that they are a description of what actually happened—when Moses concluded his instructions regarding the first Passover sacrifice, the people bowed low. Presumably, their response was intended as an expression of gratitude to God for promising to protect them during the Plague of the Firstborn. The Passover sacrifice, then, might be viewed as a type of *korban todah* (thanksgiving offering).[25] However, there is one significant distinction between a typical thanksgiving offering and the Passover sacrifice: a thanksgiving offering is accompanied by both unleavened matzah cakes and by cakes that are *hametz* (leavened) (Lev. 7:12–13), whereas the Passover sacrifice must be *hametz*-free (Deut. 16:3–4). This distinction is not merely a technical one. As we have noted elsewhere (see essays 3 and 6), in the Bible leavened bread represents a covenantal relationship, while in contrast matzah symbolizes an incomplete or "half-baked" one. The Passover sacrifice may indeed be a type of thanksgiving offering, but it is a limited one: the physical Exodus is but the beginning of a long redemption process. Consequently, the Torah itself never refers to Pesach as a holiday of *simhah* (joy): that is a label reserved for days that mark the accomplishment of a goal and carry with them a sense of completion. Pesach is a holiday of gratitude and celebration but one that denotes promise and possibility rather than achievement and satisfaction.

[25] Technically, the Passover sacrifice is similar to a *korban todah* (thanksgiving offering) insofar as both must be eaten on the day they are offered (Exod. 12:10 and Lev. 7:15). This is in contrast to other sacrifices of well-being (*shelamim*), which may be eaten the following day as well (Lev. 7:16).

THE SEDER

⁴³ **In each and every generation** one is obligated to see oneself as if one had gone out of Egypt. As it says: *For the sake of what the* LORD *did for me when I went out of Egypt* (Exod. 13:8). ⁴⁴ Not our ancestors alone did the Blessed Holy One redeem, but He redeemed us also with them. As it says: *But us did He take out from there, so that He might bring us to give us the land that He swore to our fathers* (Deut. 6:23).

⁴³ בְּכָל דּוֹר וָדוֹר חַיָּב אָדָם לִרְאוֹת אֶת עַצְמוֹ כְּאִלּוּ הוּא יָצָא מִמִּצְרַיִם, שֶׁנֶּאֱמַר: וְהִגַּדְתָּ לְבִנְךָ בַּיּוֹם הַהוּא לֵאמֹר, בַּעֲבוּר זֶה עָשָׂה יהוה לִי בְּצֵאתִי מִמִּצְרַיִם (שמות יג:ח). ⁴⁴ לֹא אֶת אֲבוֹתֵינוּ בִּלְבָד גָּאַל הַקָּדוֹשׁ בָּרוּךְ הוּא, אֶלָּא אַף אוֹתָנוּ גָּאַל עִמָּהֶם, שֶׁנֶּאֱמַר: וְאוֹתָנוּ הוֹצִיא מִשָּׁם, לְמַעַן הָבִיא אֹתָנוּ לָתֶת לָנוּ אֶת הָאָרֶץ אֲשֶׁר נִשְׁבַּע לַאֲבֹתֵינוּ (דברים ו:כג).

---

43 In each and every generation one is obligated to see oneself as if one had gone out of Egypt. The prooftext cited here—"For the sake of what the LORD did for me [*li*] when I went out of Egypt" (Exod. 13:8)—is the same verse used in the *baraita* of the Four Children to respond to the question of the wicked child. Whereas there, the Haggadah's emphasis on the word *li* was intended to exclude the wicked one, here the Haggadah's emphasis on the word *li* is meant to include the seder participant in the Exodus experience. This transition from exclusion to inclusion reflects the goal of the seder, and particularly of the *Maggid* section: to get everyone engaged. Through storytelling and study we hope to touch both the interested and the skeptical.

44 Not our ancestors alone did the Blessed Holy One redeem. The verse cited here to demonstrate that God redeemed each one of us from Egypt along with our ancestors (Deut. 6:23) is the continuation of a passage that was cited at the beginning of the *Maggid* section: *Avadim hayinu* (6:21). For this reason, in some ancient versions of the Haggadah, the paragraph we recite at this point was instead appended to the opening section of *Maggid*. Nonetheless, we reserve this statement about having personally experienced the Exodus until the end of *Maggid* because after telling the Exodus story and engaging with the biblical depictions of redemption and revelation, we are better positioned to make such a claim. It is through study and explication that we re-create the Exodus experience each seder night and enable ourselves to declare wholeheartedly that we feel as though God has redeemed us personally. Rigorous study binds us to the ancient text that represents the connection to our ancestors and allows us to embrace our covenantal heritage.

Some ancient versions of the Haggadah also included the *She-asah Nisim* (Who performed miracles) blessing that we recite on Hanukkah and Purim, but our Haggadah does not. The blessing *Asher Ge'alanu ve-Ga'al et Avoteinu* (Who redeemed us and redeemed our ancestors) was deemed more appropriate to the seder-night experience. Whereas the blessing *She-asah Nisim* focuses on the miracles and wonders God performed for our ancestors, the *Asher Ge'alanu* blessing emphasizes that on Passover we too are the recipients of God's benevolence, a message that is central to the Haggadah and to seder ritual. (Indeed, the wording of the two blessings is strikingly similar, highlighting the critical distinction: in *She-asah Nisim* we recite, "Who performed miracles for our ancestors," whereas in the *Asher Ge'alanu* blessing we recite, "Who performed all these miracles for our ancestors and for us.") Furthermore, from the narrow perspective of our ancestors, namely, the generation that left Egypt, the Exodus was not a success. They all died in the desert and did not live

A PASSOVER HAGGADAH: GO FORTH AND LEARN

Some raise the cup of wine at this point;
others wait until the blessing following the recitation of Psalms 113 and 114.

Therefore we are obligated to thank, to ac-claim, to praise, to laud, to exalt, to extol, to bless, to elevate, and to applaud Him who performed all these miracles for our ancestors and for us: He took us from slavery to free-dom, from suffering to joy, from mourning to celebration, from darkness to great light, and from subjection to redemption. And we shall sing for Him a new song: Hallelujah.

לְפִיכָךְ אֲנַחְנוּ חַיָּבִים לְהוֹדוֹת, לְהַלֵּל, לְשַׁבֵּחַ, לְפָאֵר, לְרוֹמֵם, לְהַדֵּר, לְבָרֵךְ, לְעַלֵּה וּלְקַלֵּס לְמִי שֶׁעָשָׂה לַאֲבוֹתֵינוּ וְלָנוּ אֶת כָּל הַנִּסִּים הָאֵלּוּ: הוֹצִיאָנוּ מֵעַבְדוּת לְחֵרוּת, מִיָּגוֹן לְשִׂמְחָה, וּמֵאֵבֶל לְיוֹם טוֹב, וּמֵאֲפֵלָה לְאוֹר גָּדוֹל, וּמִשִּׁעְבּוּד לִגְאֻלָּה. וְנֹאמַר לְפָנָיו שִׁירָה חֲדָשָׁה: הַלְלוּיָהּ.

Psalm 113

[45] *Hallelujah.*

Praise, O servants of the Lord,

praise the Lord's *name.*

May the Lord's *name be blessed*

now and forevermore.

From the place the sun rises to where it sets,

praised be the name of the Lord.

High over all nations, the Lord,

over the heavens His glory.

Who is like the Lord *our God,*

who sits high above,

תהלים קיג

[45] הַלְלוּיָהּ

הַלְלוּ עַבְדֵי יהוה,

הַלְלוּ אֶת שֵׁם יהוה:

יְהִי שֵׁם יהוה מְבֹרָךְ

מֵעַתָּה וְעַד עוֹלָם:

מִמִּזְרַח שֶׁמֶשׁ עַד מְבוֹאוֹ

מְהֻלָּל שֵׁם יהוה:

רָם עַל כָּל גּוֹיִם יהוה,

עַל הַשָּׁמַיִם כְּבוֹדוֹ:

מִי כַּיהוה אֱלֹהֵינוּ

הַמַּגְבִּיהִי לָשָׁבֶת,

---

to see the promises of redemption fulfilled. The *Asher Geʾalanu* blessing underscores the linking of generations that is so critical to the Exodus narrative: although the generation that left Egypt experienced only a partial deliverance, their children made it to the Promised Land, and we, today, continue to benefit from the process of redemption they set into motion.

45 Hallelujah. Praise, O servants of the Lord. We conclude *Maggid* by beginning to recite *Hallel*, which we will complete after the seder meal. In Mishnah *Pesahim*, the School of Shammai (*Beit Shammai*) and the School of Hillel (*Beit Hillel*) debate the number of *Hallel* psalms that are to be recited at this stage: according to Shammai, only one; according to Hillel, two. We rule in accord-ance with Hillel and, accordingly, recite Psalms 113 and 114 at this juncture. For further analysis of the significance behind the dispute and for close readings of the *Hallel* passages, see essay 8.

who sees down below

in the heavens and on the earth?

He raises the poor from the dust,

from the dungheap lifts the needy,

to seat him among princes,

among the princes of his people.

He seats the barren woman in her home

a happy mother of sons.

Hallelujah.

Psalm 114

When Israel came out of Egypt,

the house of Jacob from a barbarous-tongued folk,

Judah became His sanctuary,

Israel His dominion.

The sea saw and fled,

Jordan turned back.

The mountains danced like rams,

hills like lambs of the flock.

What is wrong with you, sea, that you flee,

Jordan, that you turn back,

mountains, that you dance like rams,

hills like lambs of the flock?

Before the Master, whirl, O earth,

before the God of Jacob,

who turns the rock to a pond of water,

flint to a spring of water.

הַמַּשְׁפִּילִי לִרְאוֹת

בַּשָּׁמַיִם וּבָאָרֶץ:

מְקִימִי מֵעָפָר דָּל,

מֵאַשְׁפֹּת יָרִים אֶבְיוֹן:

לְהוֹשִׁיבִי עִם נְדִיבִים,

עִם נְדִיבֵי עַמּוֹ:

מוֹשִׁיבִי עֲקֶרֶת הַבַּיִת,

אֵם הַבָּנִים שְׂמֵחָה,

הַלְלוּיָהּ:

תהלים קיד

בְּצֵאת יִשְׂרָאֵל מִמִּצְרַיִם,

בֵּית יַעֲקֹב מֵעַם לֹעֵז:

הָיְתָה יְהוּדָה לְקָדְשׁוֹ,

יִשְׂרָאֵל מַמְשְׁלוֹתָיו:

הַיָּם רָאָה וַיָּנֹס,

הַיַּרְדֵּן יִסֹּב לְאָחוֹר:

הֶהָרִים רָקְדוּ כְאֵילִים,

גְּבָעוֹת כִּבְנֵי צֹאן:

מַה לְּךָ הַיָּם כִּי תָנוּס,

הַיַּרְדֵּן תִּסֹּב לְאָחוֹר:

הֶהָרִים תִּרְקְדוּ כְאֵילִים,

גְּבָעוֹת כִּבְנֵי צֹאן:

מִלִּפְנֵי אָדוֹן חוּלִי אָרֶץ,

מִלִּפְנֵי אֱלוֹהַּ יַעֲקֹב:

הַהֹפְכִי הַצּוּר אֲגַם מָיִם,

חַלָּמִישׁ לְמַעְיְנוֹ מָיִם:

Raise the cup of wine.

Blessed are You, Lord our God, King of the universe, who redeemed us and redeemed our ancestors from Egypt, and brought us to this night to eat matzah and *maror*. So may the Lord, our God and the God of our ancestors, bring us to other holidays and other pilgrimage festivals, which come peacefully

בָּרוּךְ אַתָּה יי אֱלֹהֵינוּ מֶלֶךְ הָעוֹלָם, אֲשֶׁר גְּאָלָנוּ וְגָאַל אֶת אֲבוֹתֵינוּ מִמִּצְרַיִם, וְהִגִּיעָנוּ הַלַּיְלָה הַזֶּה לֶאֱכָל בּוֹ מַצָּה וּמָרוֹר. כֵּן יי אֱלֹהֵינוּ וֵאלֹהֵי אֲבוֹתֵינוּ יַגִּיעֵנוּ לְמוֹעֲדִים וְלִרְגָלִים אֲחֵרִים הַבָּאִים לִקְרָאתֵנוּ לְשָׁלוֹם, שְׂמֵחִים

A Passover Haggadah: Go Forth and Learn

upon us, rejoicing in the building of Your city and delighting in Your worship. And we shall eat there from the offerings and the paschal sacrifices (**on Saturday night substitute**: from the paschal sacrifices and the offerings) whose blood will be sprinkled in acceptance on Your altar and we shall praise You with a new song on account of our redemption and the liberation of our souls. **Blessed are You, Lord, redeemer of Israel.**

בְּבִנְיַן עִירֶךָ וְשָׂשִׂים בַּעֲבוֹדָתֶךָ, וְנֹאכַל שָׁם מִן הַזְּבָחִים וּמִן הַפְּסָחִים (**בְּמוֹצָאֵי שַׁבָּת**: מִן הַפְּסָחִים וּמִן הַזְּבָחִים) אֲשֶׁר יַגִּיעַ דָּמָם עַל קִיר מִזְבַּחֲךָ לְרָצוֹן, וְנוֹדֶה לְךָ שִׁיר חָדָשׁ עַל גְּאֻלָּתֵנוּ וְעַל פְּדוּת נַפְשֵׁנוּ. **בָּרוּךְ אַתָּה יי גָּאַל יִשְׂרָאֵל.**

Blessed are You, Lord our God, King of the universe, Creator of the fruit of the vine.

בָּרוּךְ אַתָּה יי אֱלֹהֵינוּ מֶלֶךְ הָעוֹלָם בּוֹרֵא פְּרִי הַגָּפֶן.

Drink while reclining to the left.

Rahetzah
רָחְצָה

Wash hands and recite the following blessing.

Blessed are You, Lord our God, King of the universe, who has sanctified us with His commandments and commanded us concerning washing hands.

בָּרוּךְ אַתָּה יי אֱלֹהֵינוּ מֶלֶךְ הָעוֹלָם, אֲשֶׁר קִדְּשָׁנוּ בְּמִצְוֹתָיו וְצִוָּנוּ עַל נְטִילַת יָדָיִם.

Motzi
מוֹצִיא

Hold the three matzot, with the broken one in the middle,
and recite the following blessing.

Blessed are You, Lord our God, King of the universe, who brings forth bread from the earth.

בָּרוּךְ אַתָּה יי אֱלֹהֵינוּ מֶלֶךְ הָעוֹלָם הַמּוֹצִיא לֶחֶם מִן הָאָרֶץ.

Matzah

מַצָּה

Hold the broken matzah and recite the following blessing.

Blessed are You, LORD our God, King of the universe, who has sanctified us with His commandments and commanded us concerning eating matzah.

בָּרוּךְ אַתָּה יי אֱלֹהֵינוּ מֶלֶךְ הָעוֹלָם, אֲשֶׁר קִדְּשָׁנוּ בְּמִצְוֹתָיו וְצִוָּנוּ עַל אֲכִילַת מַצָּה.

Break the top matzah and the broken matzah and distribute to the participants.
Eat the matzah while reclining to the left.

Maror

מָרוֹר

Take the bitter herbs and dip them into the *haroset*.
Recite the following blessing.

Blessed are You, LORD our God, King of the universe, who has sanctified us with His commandments and commanded us concerning eating *maror*.

בָּרוּךְ אַתָּה יי אֱלֹהֵינוּ מֶלֶךְ הָעוֹלָם, אֲשֶׁר קִדְּשָׁנוּ בְּמִצְוֹתָיו וְצִוָּנוּ עַל אֲכִילַת מָרוֹר.

Eat the *maror* without reclining.

Korekh

כּוֹרֵךְ

Break the third matzah and distribute to the participants. Prepare a sandwich of
matzah and bitter herbs (with *haroset*) and recite the following.

In commemoration of the Temple, according to Hillel. Thus did Hillel when the Temple still stood: he would wrap matzah and *maror* together and eat them to fulfill what is said: *With flatcakes and bitter herbs they shall eat it* (Num. 9:11).

זֵכֶר לְמִקְדָּשׁ כְּהִלֵּל. כֵּן עָשָׂה הִלֵּל בִּזְמַן שֶׁבֵּית הַמִּקְדָּשׁ הָיָה קַיָּם: הָיָה כּוֹרֵךְ מַצָּה וּמָרוֹר וְאוֹכֵל בְּיַחַד, לְקַיֵּים מַה שֶׁנֶּאֱמַר: עַל מַצּוֹת וּמְרֹרִים יֹאכְלֻהוּ (במדבר ט:יא).

Eat the sandwich while reclining to the left.

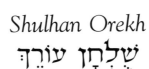

Shulhan Orekh
שֻׁלְחָן עוֹרֵךְ

Participants share a festive meal.

Some precede the meal with an egg dipped in salt water.

Tzafun
צָפוּן

Eat the *afikoman* while reclining to the left.

Barekh
בָּרֵךְ

Pour the third cup of wine.

Psalm 126

A song of ascents. When the LORD restores Zion's fortunes, we should be like dreamers. Then will our mouth fill with laughter and our tongue with glad song. Then will they say in the nations: "Great things has the LORD done with these." We shall rejoice. Restore, O LORD, our fortunes like freshets in the Negev. They who sow in tears in glad song will reap. He walks along and weeps, the bearer of the seed bag. He will surely come in with glad song bearing his sheaves.

תהלים קכו

שִׁיר הַמַּעֲלוֹת, בְּשׁוּב יהוה אֶת שִׁיבַת צִיּוֹן, הָיִינוּ כְּחֹלְמִים: אָז יִמָּלֵא שְׂחוֹק פִּינוּ וּלְשׁוֹנֵנוּ רִנָּה, אָז יֹאמְרוּ בַגּוֹיִם, הִגְדִּיל יהוה לַעֲשׂוֹת עִם אֵלֶּה: הִגְדִּיל יהוה לַעֲשׂוֹת עִמָּנוּ, הָיִינוּ שְׂמֵחִים: שׁוּבָה יהוה אֶת שְׁבִיתֵנוּ, כַּאֲפִיקִים בַּנֶּגֶב: הַזֹּרְעִים בְּדִמְעָה, בְּרִנָּה יִקְצֹרוּ: הָלוֹךְ יֵלֵךְ וּבָכֹה, נֹשֵׂא מֶשֶׁךְ הַזָּרַע, בֹּא יָבֹא בְרִנָּה, נֹשֵׂא אֲלֻמֹּתָיו:

THE SEDER

If three adults are present, recite the following lines responsively.
If ten adults are present, add the words in parentheses.

Leader: Come, let us bless.

Group: Blessed be the name of the LORD from now and forever.

Leader: Blessed be the Name of the LORD from now and forever! With the permission of the distinguished people present, let us bless (our God,) the one of whose bounty we have eaten.

Group: Blessed is (our God,) the one of whose bounty we have eaten and through whose goodness we live.

המברך: רַבּוֹתַי נְבָרֵךְ.

המסובים: יְהִי שֵׁם יי מְבֹרָךְ מֵעַתָּה וְעַד עוֹלָם.

המברך: בִּרְשׁוּת מָרָנָן וְרַבָּנָן וְרַבּוֹתַי נְבָרֵךְ (אֱלֹהֵינוּ) שֶׁאָכַלְנוּ מִשֶּׁלּוֹ.

המסובים: בָּרוּךְ (אֱלֹהֵינוּ) שֶׁאָכַלְנוּ מִשֶּׁלּוֹ וּבְטוּבוֹ חָיִינוּ: בָּרוּךְ הוּא וּבָרוּךְ שְׁמוֹ:

All continue here.

Blessed are You, LORD our God, King of the Universe, who nourishes the entire world in His goodness, with grace and kindness and mercy. He gives bread to all flesh, for His kindness is eternal. And in His great goodness we have never been in want; and we will never be in want of nourishment, for the sake of His great name, for He is a God who nourishes and supports all and is good to all, and He prepares food for all His creatures that He has created. Blessed are You, LORD, who nourishes all.

בָּרוּךְ אַתָּה יי אֱלֹהֵינוּ מֶלֶךְ הָעוֹלָם, הַזָּן אֶת הָעוֹלָם כֻּלּוֹ בְּטוּבוֹ, בְּחֵן, בְּחֶסֶד וּבְרַחֲמִים. הוּא נוֹתֵן לֶחֶם לְכָל בָּשָׂר כִּי לְעוֹלָם חַסְדּוֹ. וּבְטוּבוֹ הַגָּדוֹל תָּמִיד לֹא חָסַר לָנוּ, וְאַל יֶחְסַר לָנוּ מָזוֹן לְעוֹלָם וָעֶד, בַּעֲבוּר שְׁמוֹ הַגָּדוֹל, כִּי הוּא אֵל זָן וּמְפַרְנֵס לַכֹּל וּמֵטִיב לַכֹּל וּמֵכִין מָזוֹן לְכָל בְּרִיּוֹתָיו אֲשֶׁר בָּרָא. בָּרוּךְ אַתָּה יי הַזָּן אֶת הַכֹּל.

We thank You, LORD our God, for giving our ancestors a desirable, good and spacious land, and for bringing us out of Egypt, and for redeeming us from a house of slavery, and for the covenant that You have engraved in our flesh, and for Your Torah that You have taught us, and for Your laws that You have made known to us, and for the life, grace, and

נוֹדֶה לְּךָ יי אֱלֹהֵינוּ עַל שֶׁהִנְחַלְתָּ לַאֲבוֹתֵינוּ אֶרֶץ חֶמְדָּה טוֹבָה וּרְחָבָה, וְעַל שֶׁהוֹצֵאתָנוּ יי אֱלֹהֵינוּ מֵאֶרֶץ מִצְרַיִם, וּפְדִיתָנוּ מִבֵּית עֲבָדִים, וְעַל בְּרִיתְךָ שֶׁחָתַמְתָּ בִּבְשָׂרֵנוּ, וְעַל תּוֹרָתְךָ שֶׁלִּמַּדְתָּנוּ, וְעַל חֻקֶּיךָ שֶׁהוֹדַעְתָּנוּ, וְעַל חַיִּים, חֵן וָחֶסֶד שֶׁחוֹנַנְתָּנוּ, וְעַל אֲכִילַת

A PASSOVER HAGGADAH: GO FORTH AND LEARN

kindness that You have granted us, and for the eating of food by which You nourish and sustain us constantly, every day, every time and every moment.

And for all, Lord our God, we thank You and we bless You, may Your name be blessed by all life constantly and forever as it says: *And you will eat and be sated and bless the Lord your God on the goodly land that He has given you* (Deut. 8:10). Blessed are You, Lord, for the Land and the food.

Have mercy, Lord our God, on Your people Israel and on Your city, Jerusalem, and on Zion, the abode of Your glory, and on the kingdom of the house of David, Your anointed one, and on the great and holy house that is called by Your name. Our God, our Father, shepherd us, nourish us, support us, sustain us, and help us prosper, and relieve us, Lord our God, quickly from all our troubles. And please, Lord our God, do not put us in need of gifts from humans nor of their loans, but only of Your full, open hand, holy and vast, that we may never be shamed or embarassed.

מָזוֹן שָׁאַתָּה זָן וּמְפַרְנֵס אוֹתָנוּ תָּמִיד בְּכָל יוֹם וּבְכָל עֵת וּבְכָל שָׁעָה.

וְעַל הַכֹּל יי אֱלֹהֵינוּ, אֲנַחְנוּ מוֹדִים לָךְ וּמְבָרְכִים אוֹתָךְ, יִתְבָּרַךְ שִׁמְךָ בְּפִי כָּל חַי תָּמִיד לְעוֹלָם וָעֶד. כַּכָּתוּב, וְאָכַלְתָּ וְשָׂבָעְתָּ, וּבֵרַכְתָּ אֶת יהוה אֱלֹהֶיךָ עַל הָאָרֶץ הַטּוֹבָה אֲשֶׁר נָתַן לָךְ (דברים ח:י). בָּרוּךְ אַתָּה יי עַל הָאָרֶץ וְעַל הַמָּזוֹן.

רַחֵם נָא יי אֱלֹהֵינוּ עַל יִשְׂרָאֵל עַמֶּךָ, וְעַל יְרוּשָׁלַיִם עִירֶךָ, וְעַל צִיּוֹן מִשְׁכַּן כְּבוֹדֶךָ, וְעַל מַלְכוּת בֵּית דָּוִד מְשִׁיחֶךָ, וְעַל הַבַּיִת הַגָּדוֹל וְהַקָּדוֹשׁ שֶׁנִּקְרָא שִׁמְךָ עָלָיו. אֱלֹהֵינוּ אָבִינוּ, רְעֵנוּ, זוּנֵנוּ, פַּרְנְסֵנוּ, וְכַלְכְּלֵנוּ, וְהַרְוִיחֵנוּ, וְהַרְוַח לָנוּ יי אֱלֹהֵינוּ מְהֵרָה מִכָּל צָרוֹתֵינוּ, וְנָא אַל תַּצְרִיכֵנוּ יי אֱלֹהֵינוּ לֹא לִידֵי מַתְּנַת בָּשָׂר וָדָם וְלֹא לִידֵי הַלְוָאָתָם, כִּי אִם לְיָדְךָ הַמְּלֵאָה, הַפְּתוּחָה, הַקְּדוֹשָׁה וְהָרְחָבָה, שֶׁלֹּא נֵבוֹשׁ וְלֹא נִכָּלֵם לְעוֹלָם וָעֶד.

On the Sabbath add the following paragraph.

Accept and strengthen us, Lord our God, in Your commandments and in the command-ment of the seventh day, this great and holy Sabbath, for it is a great and holy day before You, to cease from work and to rest on it, in love, according to the commandment of Your will. And, in Your will, allow us, Lord our God, to have no distress or suffering or

רְצֵה וְהַחֲלִיצֵנוּ יי אֱלֹהֵינוּ בְּמִצְוֹתֶיךָ וּבְמִצְוַת יוֹם הַשְּׁבִיעִי, הַשַּׁבָּת הַגָּדוֹל וְהַקָּדוֹשׁ הַזֶּה, כִּי יוֹם זֶה גָּדוֹל וְקָדוֹשׁ הוּא לְפָנֶיךָ לִשְׁבָּת בּוֹ וְלָנוּחַ בּוֹ בְּאַהֲבָה כְּמִצְוַת רְצוֹנֶךָ, וּבִרְצוֹנְךָ הָנִיחַ לָנוּ יי אֱלֹהֵינוּ, שֶׁלֹּא תְהֵא צָרָה וְיָגוֹן וַאֲנָחָה בְּיוֹם מְנוּחָתֵנוּ, וְהַרְאֵנוּ יי אֱלֹהֵינוּ

THE SEDER

sighing on our day of rest. And show us, Lord our God, the comforting of Zion, Your city, and the building of Jerusalem, Your holy city, for You are the master of salvations and the master of consolations.

בְּנֶחָמַת צִיּוֹן עִירֶךְ, וּבְבִנְיַן יְרוּשָׁלַיִם עִיר קָדְשֶׁךָ, כִּי אַתָּה הוּא בַּעַל הַיְשׁוּעוֹת וּבַעַל הַנֶּחָמוֹת.

On all days continue here.

Our God and the God of our ancestors, may our memory and our recollection, and the memory of our ancestors, and the memory of the anointed son of Your servant David, and the memory of Jerusalem, Your holy city, and the memory of all of Your people, the house of Israel, arise and come and reach and be seen and be accepted and be heard and be recollected and remembered before You for salvation, for good and grace, for kindness and compassion, for life and peace, on this day of the festival of matzot. Remember us on it, Lord our God, for good and recollect us for blessing and save us for life. As for salvation and compassion, spare us, be graceful to us, be compassionate to us and save us, for our eyes are turned to You, for You are a graceful and compassionate God and King.

אֱלֹהֵינוּ וֵאלֹהֵי אֲבוֹתֵינוּ, יַעֲלֶה וְיָבֹא וְיַגִּיעַ וְיֵרָאֶה וְיֵרָצֶה וְיִשָּׁמַע וְיִפָּקֵד וְיִזָּכֵר זִכְרוֹנֵנוּ וּפִקְדוֹנֵנוּ, וְזִכְרוֹן אֲבוֹתֵינוּ, וְזִכְרוֹן מָשִׁיחַ בֶּן דָּוִד עַבְדֶּךָ, וְזִכְרוֹן יְרוּשָׁלַיִם עִיר קָדְשֶׁךָ, וְזִכְרוֹן כָּל עַמְּךָ בֵּית יִשְׂרָאֵל לְפָנֶיךָ, לִפְלֵיטָה, לְטוֹבָה, לְחֵן וּלְחֶסֶד וּלְרַחֲמִים, לְחַיִּים וּלְשָׁלוֹם, בְּיוֹם חַג הַמַּצוֹת הַזֶּה. זָכְרֵנוּ יי אֱלֹהֵינוּ בּוֹ לְטוֹבָה, וּפָקְדֵנוּ בוֹ לִבְרָכָה, וְהוֹשִׁיעֵנוּ בוֹ לְחַיִּים. וּבִדְבַר יְשׁוּעָה וְרַחֲמִים, חוּס וְחָנֵּנוּ, וְרַחֵם עָלֵינוּ וְהוֹשִׁיעֵנוּ, כִּי אֵלֶיךָ עֵינֵינוּ כִּי אֵל מֶלֶךְ חַנּוּן וְרַחוּם אָתָּה.

And build Jerusalem, the holy city, speedily in our own days. Blessed are You, Lord our God, builder of Jerusalem in His mercy. Amen.

וּבְנֵה יְרוּשָׁלַיִם עִיר הַקֹּדֶשׁ בִּמְהֵרָה בְיָמֵינוּ. בָּרוּךְ אַתָּה יי בּוֹנֵה בְרַחֲמָיו יְרוּשָׁלָיִם. אָמֵן.

Blessed are You, Lord our God, King of the universe, God, our Father, our King, our Powerful One, our Creator, our Redeemer, He who formed us, our Holy One, the Holy One of Jacob, our Shepherd, Shepherd of Israel, the King who is good and does good to

בָּרוּךְ אַתָּה יי אֱלֹהֵינוּ מֶלֶךְ הָעוֹלָם, הָאֵל אָבִינוּ מַלְכֵּנוּ אַדִּירֵנוּ בּוֹרְאֵנוּ גּוֹאֲלֵנוּ יוֹצְרֵנוּ קְדוֹשֵׁנוּ קְדוֹשׁ יַעֲקֹב, רוֹעֵנוּ רוֹעֵה יִשְׂרָאֵל, הַמֶּלֶךְ הַטּוֹב וְהַמֵּטִיב לַכֹּל, שֶׁבְּכָל יוֹם וָיוֹם הוּא הֵטִיב הוּא

A Passover Haggadah: Go Forth and Learn

all. For on every day He did good, He does good, and He will do good for us. He has granted us, he grants us, and he will grant us grace, kindness, compassion, prosperity, safety and success, blessing and salvation, comfort, support and sustenance, compassion and life and peace and all good things, and may He never deprive us of any good thing.

May the Compassionate One rule over us forever.

May the Compassionate One be blessed in heaven and earth.

May the Compassionate One be praised for all generations, and may He be glorified through us forever and ever, and may He be honored through us for all eternity.

May the Compassionate One sustain us in honor.

May the Compassionate One shatter the yoke from our necks, and may He lead us up-right into our Land.

May the Compassionate One send us much blessing to this house and upon the table at which we have eaten.

May the Compassionate One send us His prophet Elijah, of blessed memory, and an-nounce good news, salvation, and consolation.

May the Compassionate One bless
at one's own home: me (and my husband/wife) (and my children) and all that is mine

מֵטִיב הוּא יֵיטִיב לָנוּ, הוּא גְמָלָנוּ הוּא גוֹמְלֵנוּ הוּא יִגְמְלֵנוּ לָעַד, לְחֵן וּלְחֶסֶד וּלְרַחֲמִים וּלְרֶוַח, הַצָּלָה וְהַצְלָחָה, בְּרָכָה וִישׁוּעָה, נֶחָמָה, פַּרְנָסָה וְכַלְכָּלָה, וְרַחֲמִים וְחַיִּים וְשָׁלוֹם וְכָל טוֹב. וּמִכָּל טוּב לְעוֹלָם עַל יְחַסְּרֵנוּ.

הָרַחֲמָן הוּא יִמְלוֹךְ עָלֵינוּ לְעוֹלָם וָעֶד.

הָרַחֲמָן הוּא יִתְבָּרַךְ בַּשָּׁמַיִם וּבָאָרֶץ.

הָרַחֲמָן הוּא יִשְׁתַּבַּח לְדוֹר דּוֹרִים, וְיִתְפָּאַר בָּנוּ לָעַד וּלְנֶצַח נְצָחִים, וְיִתְהַדַּר בָּנוּ לָעַד וּלְעוֹלְמֵי עוֹלָמִים.

הָרַחֲמָן הוּא יְפַרְנְסֵנוּ בְּכָבוֹד.

הָרַחֲמָן הוּא יִשְׁבּוֹר עֻלֵּנוּ מֵעַל צַוָּארֵנוּ, וְהוּא יוֹלִיכֵנוּ קוֹמְמִיּוּת לְאַרְצֵנוּ.

הָרַחֲמָן הוּא יִשְׁלַח לָנוּ בְּרָכָה מְרֻבָּה בַּבַּיִת הַזֶּה, וְעַל שֻׁלְחָן זֶה שֶׁאָכַלְנוּ עָלָיו.

הָרַחֲמָן הוּא יִשְׁלַח לָנוּ אֶת אֵלִיָּהוּ הַנָּבִיא זָכוּר לַטּוֹב, וִיבַשֶּׂר לָנוּ בְּשׂוֹרוֹת טוֹבוֹת יְשׁוּעוֹת וְנֶחָמוֹת.

הָרַחֲמָן הוּא יְבָרֵךְ
בבית שלו/שלה: אוֹתִי (וְאֶת אִשְׁתִּי/ אִישִׁי) (וְאֶת זַרְעִי) וְאֶת כָּל אֲשֶׁר לִי

at one's parents' home: my father, my teacher, the master of this house/my mother, my teacher, the mistress of this house, together with their household, their children, and all that is theirs

at another's home: the master/mistress of this house, together with their household, (their children,) and all that is theirs

if guests are present add: and all who are gathered here

us and all that we have, as our forefathers, Abraham, Isaac, and Jacob were blessed, with all and with everything, so may He bless us all together with a complete blessing, and let us say: Amen.

May a plea be heard on high that presents them and us in a most favorable light that will bring us secure peace. May we receive blessing from the LORD and justice from our saving God, and may we find favor and grace in the eyes of God and of humanity.

בְּבֵית שֶׁל הוֹרָיו/הוֹרֶיהָ: אֶת אָבִי מוֹרִי בַּעַל הַבַּיִת הַזֶּה וְאֶת אִמִּי מוֹרָתִי בַּעֲלַת הַבַּיִת הַזֶּה, אוֹתָם וְאֶת בֵּיתָם וְאֶת זַרְעָם וְאֶת כָּל אֲשֶׁר לָהֶם

בְּבֵית שֶׁל אַחֵר: אֶת בַּעַל הַבַּיִת הַזֶּה וְאֶת בַּעֲלַת הַבַּיִת הַזֶּה, אוֹתָם וְאֶת בֵּיתָם וְאֶת זַרְעָם וְאֶת כָּל אֲשֶׁר לָהֶם כְּשֶׁיֵּשׁ אוֹרְחִים: וְאֶת כָּל הַמְסוּבִּים כָּאן

אוֹתָנוּ וְאֶת כָּל אֲשֶׁר לָנוּ, כְּמוֹ שֶׁנִּתְבָּרְכוּ אֲבוֹתֵינוּ אַבְרָהָם יִצְחָק וְיַעֲקֹב בַּכֹּל מִכֹּל כֹּל, כֵּן יְבָרֵךְ אוֹתָנוּ כֻּלָּנוּ יַחַד בִּבְרָכָה שְׁלֵמָה, וְנֹאמַר, אָמֵן.

בַּמָּרוֹם יְלַמְּדוּ עֲלֵיהֶם וְעָלֵינוּ זְכוּת שֶׁתְּהֵא לְמִשְׁמֶרֶת שָׁלוֹם. וְנִשָּׂא בְרָכָה מֵאֵת יי, וּצְדָקָה מֵאֱלֹהֵי יִשְׁעֵנוּ, וְנִמְצָא חֵן וְשֵׂכֶל טוֹב בְּעֵינֵי אֱלֹהִים וְאָדָם.

On the Sabbath add the following line.

May the Compassionate One grant us a day that will be wholly Sabbath and eternal rest.

הָרַחֲמָן הוּא יַנְחִילֵנוּ יוֹם שֶׁכֻּלּוֹ שַׁבָּת וּמְנוּחָה לְחַיֵּי הָעוֹלָמִים.

On all days continue here.

May the Compassionate One grant us a day that is totally good.

הָרַחֲמָן הוּא יַנְחִילֵנוּ יוֹם שֶׁכֻּלּוֹ טוֹב.

May the Compassionate One bless the State of Israel and protect it.

הָרַחֲמָן הוּא יְבָרֵךְ אֶת מְדִינַת יִשְׂרָאֵל וְיָגֵן עָלֶיהָ.

May the Compassionate One cause us to merit the Messianic Era and the life of the world to come.

הָרַחֲמָן הוּא יְזַכֵּנוּ לִימוֹת הַמָּשִׁיחַ וּלְחַיֵּי הָעוֹלָם הַבָּא.

A PASSOVER HAGGADAH: GO FORTH AND LEARN

Making great the rescues of His king, keeping faith with His anointed, for David and his seed forever (Ps. 18:51). He who imposes peace in His heights (Job 25:2), may He impose peace upon us and all of Israel and say: Amen.

Fear the Lord, O His holy ones, for those who fear Him know no want. Lions are wretched, and hunger, but the Lord's seekers lack no good (Ps. 34:10–11). Acclaim the Lord, for He is good, forever is His kindness (Ps. 118:1). Opening Your hand and sating to their pleasure all living things (Ps. 145:16). Blessed is he who trusts in the Lord, whose trust is the Lord alone (Jer. 17:7). A lad I was, and now I am old, and I have never seen a just man forsaken and his seed seeking bread (Ps. 37:25). May the Lord give strength to His people. May the Lord bless His people with peace (Ps. 29:11).

Blessed are You, Lord our God, King of the universe, Creator of the fruit of the vine.

מַגְדִּיל יְשׁוּעוֹת מַלְכּוֹ וְעֹשֶׂה חֶסֶד לִמְשִׁיחוֹ לְדָוִד וּלְזַרְעוֹ עַד עוֹלָם (תהלים יח:נא). עֹשֶׂה שָׁלוֹם בִּמְרוֹמָיו (איוב כה:ב), הוּא יַעֲשֶׂה שָׁלוֹם עָלֵינוּ וְעַל כָּל יִשְׂרָאֵל וְאִמְרוּ, אָמֵן.

יְראוּ אֶת יהוה קְדֹשָׁיו, כִּי אֵין מַחְסוֹר לִירֵאָיו. כְּפִירִים רָשׁוּ וְרָעֵבוּ, וְדֹרְשֵׁי יהוה לֹא יַחְסְרוּ כָל טוֹב (תהלים לד:י – יא). הוֹדוּ לַיהוה כִּי טוֹב, כִּי לְעוֹלָם חַסְדּוֹ (תהלים קיח:א). פּוֹתֵחַ אֶת יָדֶךָ, וּמַשְׂבִּיעַ לְכָל חַי רָצוֹן (תהלים קמה:טז). בָּרוּךְ הַגֶּבֶר אֲשֶׁר יִבְטַח בַּיהוה, וְהָיָה יהוה מִבְטַחוֹ (ירמיה יז:ז). נַעַר הָיִיתִי גַם זָקַנְתִּי, וְלֹא רָאִיתִי צַדִּיק נֶעֱזָב, וְזַרְעוֹ מְבַקֶּשׁ לָחֶם (תהלים לז:כה). יהוה עֹז לְעַמּוֹ יִתֵּן, יהוה יְבָרֵךְ אֶת עַמּוֹ בַשָּׁלוֹם (תהלים כט:יא).

בָּרוּךְ אַתָּה יי אֱלֹהֵינוּ מֶלֶךְ הָעוֹלָם בּוֹרֵא פְּרִי הַגָּפֶן.

Drink while reclining to the left.

THE SEDER

It is customary to fill the [46]Cup of Elijah
and open the door before reciting these verses.

[47]*Pour out Your wrath on the nations that did*
not know You and on the kingdoms that did not
call on Your name. For they have devoured Jacob
and his habitation laid waste (Ps. 79:6–7). *Pour*
out upon them Your wrath, and Your blazing
fury overtake them (Ps. 69:25). *Oh, pursue*
them in wrath and destroy them from under the
heavens of the Lord (Lam. 3:66).

[47] שְׁפֹךְ חֲמָתְךָ אֶל הַגּוֹיִם אֲשֶׁר לֹא יְדָעוּךָ וְעַל
מַמְלָכוֹת אֲשֶׁר בְּשִׁמְךָ לֹא קָרָאוּ. כִּי אָכַל אֶת
יַעֲקֹב וְאֶת נָוֵהוּ הֵשַׁמּוּ (תהלים עט:ו — ז).
שְׁפֹךְ עֲלֵיהֶם זַעְמֶךָ וַחֲרוֹן אַפְּךָ יַשִּׂיגֵם
(תהלים סט:כה). תִּרְדֹּף בְּאַף וְתַשְׁמִידֵם
מִתַּחַת שְׁמֵי יהוה (איכה ג:סו).

Pour the fourth cup of wine.

---

46 Cup of Elijah. The custom to pour an additional cup of wine at this point in the seder for the prophet Elijah probably dates to the 15th century. The Talmud records one opinion in favor of pouring and drinking a fifth cup (B.T. Pes. 118a), and early medieval authorities debated this practice; but until the early modern period, it was not associated with Elijah or with any other personality.[26]

For centuries, scholars have conjectured as to the origin of the Elijah association. The simplest explanation is that the Bible presents Elijah as the harbinger of redemption (Mal. 3:23) and the disputed fifth cup is also linked to deliverance. (According to the Midrash, the traditional four cups drunk at the seder reflect the four forms of salvation listed in Exodus 6:6–7—"I will take you out," "I will rescue you," "I will redeem you," "I will take you"—and later commentators connected the fifth cup with the final form of salvation mentioned in the following verse: "I will bring you.")

Regardless of why or how it began, the "Cup of Elijah" custom also recalls biblical connections between the figure of Elijah and the figure of Moses. Moses, a central character in the Passover story, is never explicitly mentioned in the Haggadah, so as not to detract from the unmediated nature of God's involvement in the Exodus. In Kings, Elijah is clearly modeled on the character of Moses; one striking parallel is 1 Kings 19, where Elijah fasts for 40 days and 40 nights as he journeys to Horev to speak with God, but there are many others. In the Talmud, Elijah, like Moses, is a wise and learned individual, an adjudicator of disputes. Malachi also connects the two figures, preceding the verse about Elijah with one about Moses:

---

[26] See Kulp and Golinkin, *The Schechter Haggadah*, 175–76 and 269–70.

A Passover Haggadah: Go Forth and Learn

זִכְרוּ תּוֹרַת מֹשֶׁה עַבְדִּי אֲשֶׁר צִוִּיתִי אוֹתוֹ בְחֹרֵב עַל כָּל יִשְׂרָאֵל חֻקִּים וּמִשְׁפָּטִים:
הִנֵּה אָנֹכִי שֹׁלֵחַ לָכֶם אֵת אֵלִיָּה הַנָּבִיא לִפְנֵי בּוֹא יוֹם יהוה הַגָּדוֹל וְהַנּוֹרָא:

Be mindful of the Teaching of My servant Moses, whom I charged at Horeb with laws and rules for all Israel. Lo, I will send the prophet Elijah to you before the coming of the awesome, fearful day of the LORD. (Mal. 3:22–23)

Thus, pouring a cup in honor of Elijah and the ultimate redemption may be a subtle way of remembering Moses and his role in the Passover redemption.

But it is also worth noting that the final verse in the Malachi passage that speaks of Elijah and the future deliverance contains an additional message of relevance to the seder. Malachi asserts that when Elijah arrives to augur the "Day of God," he will usher in an era of understanding and compassion between generations:

וְהֵשִׁיב לֵב אָבוֹת עַל בָּנִים וְלֵב בָּנִים עַל אֲבוֹתָם פֶּן אָבוֹא וְהִכֵּיתִי אֶת הָאָרֶץ חֵרֶם:

He shall reconcile parents with children and children with their parents, so that, when I come, I do not strike the whole land with utter destruction. (Mal. 3:24)

The relationship between parents and children and the dependency of the generations on one another is one of the central themes of both the book of Exodus and of the Haggadah. Pouring a cup for Elijah, who represents inter-generational understanding, is a way of indicating that by the end of the seder, we hope to have reached this goal.

47 *Pour out Your wrath.* The recitation of these verses from Psalms and Lamentations is a custom that seems to derive from the medieval period, as it is not mentioned in either the Talmud or the geonic literature, nor is it cited by most medieval scholars. Subsequently, this recitation was accepted almost universally, with slight variations. Some sources suggest that the custom of opening the door at this point in the seder is related to the recitation and is an expression of our confidence that God will protect us from those who intend evil on this *leil shimurim* (night of protection). But in fact it seems that the original practice of opening the door was not related to the *Shefokh hamatekha* verses at all: opening the door is mentioned by the *Geonim*, whereas the *Shefokh hamatekha* recitation started hundreds of years later!

Opening the door at this point, before *Hallel* commences, may instead be related to the figurative opening of our homes to guests at the start of the seder, via the recitation of the *Ha lahma anya* passage. At the beginning of *Maggid* we invite outsiders to join us for the telling of the Exodus story, as well as for the accompanying meal and ritual performances. So too, at the beginning of *Hallel*, we open the door to invite outsiders to join us for the singing of God's praises, which includes detailing the wonders and miracles that we have merited. Just as storytelling requires a listener, so does *le-sapper ma'asei Yah* (to recount the deeds of God) (Ps. 118:17), which is the goal of *Hallel* as well as of *Maggid*. So this time we actually open our doors to encourage those outside to join us for the concluding act of the seder.

THE SEDER

Hallel
הַלֵּל

Psalm 115

תהלים קטו

Not to us, O LORD, not to us

לֹא לָנוּ יהוה, לֹא לָנוּ,

but to Your name give glory

כִּי לְשִׁמְךָ תֵּן כָּבוֹד,

for Your kindness and Your steadfast truth.

עַל חַסְדְּךָ עַל אֲמִתֶּךָ:

Why should the nations say,

לָמָה יֹאמְרוּ הַגּוֹיִם,

"Where is their god?"

אַיֵּה נָא אֱלֹהֵיהֶם:

when our God is in the heavens—

וֵאלֹהֵינוּ בַשָּׁמָיִם,

all that He desired He has done.

כֹּל אֲשֶׁר חָפֵץ עָשָׂה:

Their idols are silver and gold,

עֲצַבֵּיהֶם כֶּסֶף וְזָהָב,

The handiwork of man.

מַעֲשֵׂה יְדֵי אָדָם:

A mouth they have but they do not speak,

פֶּה לָהֶם וְלֹא יְדַבֵּרוּ,

eyes they have but they do not see.

עֵינַיִם לָהֶם וְלֹא יִרְאוּ:

Ears they have but they do not hear,

אָזְנַיִם לָהֶם וְלֹא יִשְׁמָעוּ,

a nose they have but they do not smell.

אַף לָהֶם וְלֹא יְרִיחוּן:

Their hands—but they do not feel;

יְדֵיהֶם וְלֹא יְמִישׁוּן,

their feet—but they do not walk;

רַגְלֵיהֶם וְלֹא יְהַלֵּכוּ,

they make no sound with their throat.

לֹא יֶהְגּוּ בִּגְרוֹנָם:

Like them may be those who make them,

כְּמוֹהֶם יִהְיוּ עֹשֵׂיהֶם,

all who trust in them.

כֹּל אֲשֶׁר בֹּטֵחַ בָּהֶם:

O Israel, trust in the LORD,

יִשְׂרָאֵל בְּטַח בַּיהוה,

their help and their shield is He.

עֶזְרָם וּמָגִנָּם הוּא:

House of Aaron, O trust in the LORD,

בֵּית אַהֲרֹן בִּטְחוּ בַיהוה,

their help and their shield is He.

עֶזְרָם וּמָגִנָּם הוּא:

You who fear the LORD, trust in the LORD,

יִרְאֵי יהוה בִּטְחוּ בַיהוה,

their help and their shield is He.

עֶזְרָם וּמָגִנָּם הוּא:

The LORD recalls us, may He bless,

יהוה זְכָרָנוּ יְבָרֵךְ,

may He bless the house of Israel,

יְבָרֵךְ אֶת בֵּית יִשְׂרָאֵל,

may He bless the house of Aaron.

יְבָרֵךְ אֶת בֵּית אַהֲרֹן:

May He bless those who fear the LORD,

יְבָרֵךְ יִרְאֵי יהוה,

the lesser with the great.

הַקְּטַנִּים עִם הַגְּדֹלִים:

May the LORD grant you increase,

יֹסֵף יהוה עֲלֵיכֶם,

both you and your children.

עֲלֵיכֶם וְעַל בְּנֵיכֶם:

Blessed are you by the Lord,
maker of heaven and earth.
The heavens are heavens for the Lord,
and the earth He has given to humankind.
The dead do not praise the Lord,
nor all who go down into silence.
But we will bless Yah
now and forevermore.
Hallelujah.

בְּרוּכִים אַתֶּם לַיהוה,
עֹשֵׂה שָׁמַיִם וָאָרֶץ:
הַשָּׁמַיִם שָׁמַיִם לַיהוה,
וְהָאָרֶץ נָתַן לִבְנֵי אָדָם:
לֹא הַמֵּתִים יְהַלְלוּ יָהּ
וְלֹא כָּל יֹרְדֵי דוּמָה:
וַאֲנַחְנוּ נְבָרֵךְ יָהּ,
מֵעַתָּה וְעַד עוֹלָם,
הַלְלוּיָהּ:

Psalm 116

I love the Lord, for He has heard
my voice, my supplications.
For He has inclined His ear to me
when in my days I called.
The cords of death encircled me—
and the straits of Sheol found me—
distress and sorrow did I find.
And in the name of the Lord I called.
"Lord, pray, save my life."
Gracious the Lord and just,
and our God shows mercy.
The Lord protects the simple.
I plunged down, but me He did rescue.
Return, my being, to your calm,
for the Lord has requited you.
For You freed me from death,
my eyes from tears,
my foot from slipping.
I shall walk before the Lord
in the lands of the living.
I trusted, though I did speak—
Oh, I was sorely afflicted—
I in my rashness said,
"All humankind is false."

תהלים קטז
אָהַבְתִּי כִּי יִשְׁמַע יהוה,
אֶת קוֹלִי תַּחֲנוּנָי:
כִּי הִטָּה אָזְנוֹ לִי,
וּבְיָמַי אֶקְרָא:
אֲפָפוּנִי חֶבְלֵי מָוֶת
וּמְצָרֵי שְׁאוֹל מְצָאוּנִי,
צָרָה וְיָגוֹן אֶמְצָא:
וּבְשֵׁם יהוה אֶקְרָא,
אָנָּא יהוה מַלְּטָה נַפְשִׁי:
חַנּוּן יהוה וְצַדִּיק,
וֵאלֹהֵינוּ מְרַחֵם:
שֹׁמֵר פְּתָאִים יהוה,
דַּלּוֹתִי וְלִי יְהוֹשִׁיעַ:
שׁוּבִי נַפְשִׁי לִמְנוּחָיְכִי,
כִּי יהוה גָּמַל עָלָיְכִי:
כִּי חִלַּצְתָּ נַפְשִׁי מִמָּוֶת,
אֶת עֵינִי מִן דִּמְעָה,
אֶת רַגְלִי מִדֶּחִי:
אֶתְהַלֵּךְ לִפְנֵי יהוה,
בְּאַרְצוֹת הַחַיִּים:
הֶאֱמַנְתִּי כִּי אֲדַבֵּר,
אֲנִי עָנִיתִי מְאֹד:
אֲנִי אָמַרְתִּי בְחָפְזִי,
כָּל הָאָדָם כֹּזֵב:

What can I give back to the Lord	מָה אָשִׁיב לַיהוה,
for all He requited to me?	כֹּל תַּגְמוּלוֹהִי עָלָי:
The cup of rescue I lift	כּוֹס יְשׁוּעוֹת אֶשָּׂא,
and in the name of the Lord I call.	וּבְשֵׁם יהוה אֶקְרָא:
My vows to the Lord I shall pay	נְדָרַי לַיהוה אֲשַׁלֵּם,
in the sight of all His people.	נֶגְדָה נָּא לְכָל עַמּוֹ:
Precious in the eyes of the Lord	יָקָר בְּעֵינֵי יהוה,
is the death of His faithful ones.	הַמָּוְתָה לַחֲסִידָיו:
I beseech you, Lord,	אָנָּא יהוה כִּי אֲנִי עַבְדֶּךָ,
for I am Your servant.	אֲנִי עַבְדְּךָ
I am Your servant, Your handmaiden's son.	בֶּן אֲמָתֶךָ,
You have loosed my bonds.	פִּתַּחְתָּ לְמוֹסֵרָי:
To You I shall offer a thanksgiving sacrifice	לְךָ אֶזְבַּח זֶבַח תּוֹדָה,
and in the name of the Lord I shall call.	וּבְשֵׁם יהוה אֶקְרָא:
My vows to the Lord I shall pay	נְדָרַי לַיהוה אֲשַׁלֵּם,
in the sight of all His people,	נֶגְדָה נָּא לְכָל עַמּוֹ:
in the courts of the house of the Lord,	בְּחַצְרוֹת בֵּית יהוה,
in the midst of Jerusalem.	בְּתוֹכֵכִי יְרוּשָׁלָיִם,
Hallelujah.	הַלְלוּיָהּ:

Psalm 117   תהלים קיז

Praise the Lord, all nations;	הַלְלוּ אֶת יהוה כָּל גּוֹיִם,
extol him, all peoples.	שַׁבְּחוּהוּ כָּל הָאֻמִּים:
For His kindness overwhelms us,	כִּי גָבַר עָלֵינוּ חַסְדּוֹ,
and the Lord's steadfast truth is forever.	וֶאֱמֶת יהוה לְעוֹלָם,
Hallelujah.	הַלְלוּיָהּ:

Psalm 118   תהלים קיח

Acclaim the Lord, for He is good,	הוֹדוּ לַיהוה כִּי טוֹב
forever is His kindness.	כִּי לְעוֹלָם חַסְדּוֹ.
Let Israel now say:	יֹאמַר נָא יִשְׂרָאֵל
forever is His kindness.	כִּי לְעוֹלָם חַסְדּוֹ.
Let the house of Aaron now say:	יֹאמְרוּ נָא בֵית אַהֲרֹן
forever is His kindness.	כִּי לְעוֹלָם חַסְדּוֹ.
Let those who fear the Lord now say:	יֹאמְרוּ נָא יִרְאֵי יהוה
forever is His kindness.	כִּי לְעוֹלָם חַסְדּוֹ.

From the straits I called to Yah.	מִן הַמֵּצַר קָרָאתִי יָּה,
Yah answered me in a wide-open place.	עֲנָנִי בַמֶּרְחַב יָהּ:
The Lord is for me, I shall not fear.	יהוה לִי, לֹא אִירָא,
What can humankind do to me?	מַה יַּעֲשֶׂה לִי אָדָם:
The Lord is for me among my helpers,	יהוה לִי בְּעֹזְרָי,
and I shall see the defeat of my foes.	וַאֲנִי אֶרְאֶה בְשֹׂנְאָי:
Better to shelter in the Lord	טוֹב לַחֲסוֹת בַּיהוה,
than to trust in humankind.	מִבְּטֹחַ בָּאָדָם:
Better to shelter in the Lord	טוֹב לַחֲסוֹת בַּיהוה,
than to trust in princes.	מִבְּטֹחַ בִּנְדִיבִים:
All the nations surrounded me.	כָּל גּוֹיִם סְבָבוּנִי,
With the Lord's name I cut them down.	בְּשֵׁם יהוה כִּי אֲמִילַם:
They swarmed round me, oh they surrounded me.	סַבּוּנִי גַם סְבָבוּנִי,
With the Lord's name I cut them down.	בְּשֵׁם יהוה כִּי אֲמִילַם:
They swarmed round me like bees,	סַבּוּנִי כִדְבֹרִים,
burned out like a fire among thorns.	דֹּעֲכוּ כְּאֵשׁ קוֹצִים,
With the Lord's name I cut them down.	בְּשֵׁם יהוה כִּי אֲמִילַם:
You pushed me hard to knock me down,	דָּחֹה דְחִיתַנִי לִנְפֹּל,
but the Lord helped me.	וַיהוה עֲזָרָנִי:
My strength and my might is Yah,	עָזִּי וְזִמְרָת יָהּ,
And He has become my rescue.	וַיְהִי לִי לִישׁוּעָה:
A voice of glad song and rescue	קוֹל רִנָּה וִישׁוּעָה
in the tents of the just:	בְּאָהֳלֵי צַדִּיקִים,
The Lord's right hand does valiantly.	יְמִין יהוה עֹשָׂה חָיִל:
The Lord's right hand is raised,	יְמִין יהוה רוֹמֵמָה,
the Lord's right hand does valiantly.	יְמִין יהוה עֹשָׂה חָיִל:
I shall not die but live	לֹא אָמוּת כִּי אֶחְיֶה,
and recount the deeds of Yah.	וַאֲסַפֵּר מַעֲשֵׂי יָהּ:
Yah harshly chastised me	יַסֹּר יִסְּרַנִּי יָּהּ,
but to death did not deliver me.	וְלַמָּוֶת לֹא נְתָנָנִי:
Open for me the gates of justice—	פִּתְחוּ לִי שַׁעֲרֵי צֶדֶק,
I would enter them, I would acclaim Yah.	אָבֹא בָם אוֹדֶה יָהּ:
This is the gate of the Lord—	זֶה הַשַּׁעַר לַיהוה,
the just will enter it.	צַדִּיקִים יָבֹאוּ בוֹ:

THE SEDER

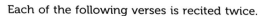

Each of the following verses is recited twice.

I acclaim You for You have answered me,	אוֹדְךָ כִּי עֲנִיתָנִי,
and You have become my rescue.	וַתְּהִי לִי לִישׁוּעָה:
The stone that the builders rejected	אֶבֶן מָאֲסוּ הַבּוֹנִים,
has become the chief cornerstone.	הָיְתָה לְרֹאשׁ פִּנָּה:
From the LORD did this come about—	מֵאֵת יהוה הָיְתָה זֹּאת,
it is wondrous in our eyes.	הִיא נִפְלָאת בְּעֵינֵינוּ:
This is the day the LORD has wrought.	זֶה הַיּוֹם עָשָׂה יהוה,
Let us exult and rejoice in it.	נָגִילָה וְנִשְׂמְחָה בוֹ:
We beseech You, LORD, pray, rescue.	אָנָּא יהוה, הוֹשִׁיעָה נָּא.
We beseech You, LORD, make us prosper.	אָנָּא יהוה, הַצְלִיחָה נָּא:
Blessed who comes in the name of the LORD.	בָּרוּךְ הַבָּא בְּשֵׁם יהוה,
We bless you from the house of the LORD.	בֵּרַכְנוּכֶם מִבֵּית יהוה:
The LORD *is God* and He shines upon us.	אֵל יהוה וַיָּאֶר לָנוּ,
Bind the festive offering with ropes	אִסְרוּ חַג בַּעֲבֹתִים
all the way to the horns of the altar.	עַד קַרְנוֹת הַמִּזְבֵּחַ:
You are my God, and I acclaim You,	אֵלִי אַתָּה וְאוֹדֶךָּ,
my God, and I exalt You.	אֱלֹהַי אֲרוֹמְמֶךָּ:
Acclaim the LORD, for He is good,	הוֹדוּ לַיהוה כִּי טוֹב,
forever is His kindness.	כִּי לְעוֹלָם חַסְדּוֹ:

The following blessing is usually recited after *Hallel.*
Many recite it at this point on the seder night
omitting the sentence in parentheses; some recite it at the end of the
Hallel section of the seder, including the sentence in parentheses.

All Your creations will praise You, LORD our God, and Your pious ones, righteous ones who do Your will, and all Your people, the house of Israel, with song will acknowledge and bless, praise and glorify, exalt and revere, sanctify and enthrone Your name, our King, for it is good to praise You and it is fit to sing to Your name, for You are God forever and ever. (Blessed are You, LORD, King who is extolled with praises.)

יְהַלְלוּךָ יי אֱלֹהֵינוּ כָּל מַעֲשֶׂיךָ, וַחֲסִידֶיךָ צַדִּיקִים עוֹשֵׂי רְצוֹנֶךָ, וְכָל עַמְּךָ בֵּית יִשְׂרָאֵל, בְּרִנָּה יוֹדוּ וִיבָרְכוּ וִישַׁבְּחוּ וִיפָאֲרוּ וִירוֹמְמוּ וְיַעֲרִיצוּ וְיַקְדִּישׁוּ וְיַמְלִיכוּ אֶת שִׁמְךָ, מַלְכֵּנוּ, כִּי לְךָ טוֹב לְהוֹדוֹת וּלְשִׁמְךָ נָאֶה לְזַמֵּר, כִּי מֵעוֹלָם וְעַד עוֹלָם אַתָּה אֵל. (בָּרוּךְ אַתָּה יי מֶלֶךְ מְהֻלָּל בַּתִּשְׁבָּחוֹת.)

A PASSOVER HAGGADAH: GO FORTH AND LEARN

Psalm 136

⁴⁸*Acclaim the* LORD, *for He is good,*

for His kindness is forever.

Acclaim the greatest God,

for His kindness is forever.

Acclaim the greatest Master,

for His kindness is forever.

Who alone performs great wonders,

for His kindness is forever.

Who makes the heavens in wisdom,

for His kindness is forever.

Who stamps firm the earth on the waters,

for His kindness is forever.

Who makes the great lights,

for His kindness is forever.

The sun for dominion of day,

for His kindness is forever.

The moon and stars for dominion of night,

for His kindness is forever.

Who strikes Egypt in its firstborn,

for His kindness is forever.

And brings out Israel from their midst,

for His kindness is forever.

תהלים קלו

⁴⁸ הוֹדוּ לַיהוה כִּי טוֹב

כִּי לְעוֹלָם חַסְדּוֹ.

הוֹדוּ לֵאלֹהֵי הָאֱלֹהִים

כִּי לְעוֹלָם חַסְדּוֹ.

הוֹדוּ לַאֲדֹנֵי הָאֲדֹנִים

כִּי לְעוֹלָם חַסְדּוֹ.

לְעֹשֵׂה נִפְלָאוֹת גְּדֹלוֹת לְבַדּוֹ

כִּי לְעוֹלָם חַסְדּוֹ.

לְעֹשֵׂה הַשָּׁמַיִם בִּתְבוּנָה

כִּי לְעוֹלָם חַסְדּוֹ.

לְרוֹקַע הָאָרֶץ עַל הַמָּיִם

כִּי לְעוֹלָם חַסְדּוֹ.

לְעֹשֵׂה אוֹרִים גְּדֹלִים

כִּי לְעוֹלָם חַסְדּוֹ.

אֶת הַשֶּׁמֶשׁ לְמֶמְשֶׁלֶת בַּיּוֹם

כִּי לְעוֹלָם חַסְדּוֹ.

אֶת הַיָּרֵחַ וְכוֹכָבִים לְמֶמְשְׁלוֹת בַּלָּיְלָה

כִּי לְעוֹלָם חַסְדּוֹ.

לְמַכֵּה מִצְרַיִם בִּבְכוֹרֵיהֶם

כִּי לְעוֹלָם חַסְדּוֹ.

וַיּוֹצֵא יִשְׂרָאֵל מִתּוֹכָם

כִּי לְעוֹלָם חַסְדּוֹ.

---

48 Acclaim the LORD, **for He is good.** In Rabbinic texts, the six-psalm *Hallel* recited at the seder is occasionally called *Hallel ha-Mitzri,* the Egyptian *Hallel* (B.T. Ber. 56a and Rashi, *Hallela mitzra'a*) to distinguish it from Psalm 136, known as *Hallel ha-Gadol,* the Great *Hallel* (B.T. Pes. 118a). The two *Hallels* are, in fact, companion pieces: *Hallel ha-Mitzri* (Ps. 113–18) expresses the yearnings of one who longs for the Temple, whereas *Hallel ha-Gadol* reflects the praises of one who has already reached the Temple. (Psalm 135, the prelude to *Hallel ha-Gadol,* begins: "Praise the name of the LORD . . . you servants of the LORD, who stand in the house of the LORD.") Additionally, the opening line of Psalm 136—"Acclaim the LORD, for He is good, for His kindness is forever"—echoes the opening line of Psalm 118.

With a strong hand and an outstretched arm,	בְּיָד חֲזָקָה וּבִזְרוֹעַ נְטוּיָה
for His kindness is forever.	כִּי לְעוֹלָם חַסְדּוֹ.
Who split the Reed Sea into parts,	לְגֹזֵר יַם סוּף לִגְזָרִים
for His kindness is forever.	כִּי לְעוֹלָם חַסְדּוֹ.
And made Israel pass through its midst,	וְהֶעֱבִיר יִשְׂרָאֵל בְּתוֹכוֹ
for His kindness is forever.	כִּי לְעוֹלָם חַסְדּוֹ.
And shook Pharaoh and his force into the Reed Sea,	וְנִעֵר פַּרְעֹה וְחֵילוֹ בְיַם סוּף
for His kindness is forever.	כִּי לְעוֹלָם חַסְדּוֹ.
Who led His people in the wilderness,	לְמוֹלִיךְ עַמּוֹ בַּמִּדְבָּר
for His kindness is forever.	כִּי לְעוֹלָם חַסְדּוֹ.
Who struck down great kings,	לְמַכֵּה מְלָכִים גְּדֹלִים
for His kindness is forever.	כִּי לְעוֹלָם חַסְדּוֹ.
And killed mighty kings,	וַיַּהֲרֹג מְלָכִים אַדִּירִים
for His kindness is forever.	כִּי לְעוֹלָם חַסְדּוֹ.
Sihon, king of the Amorites,	לְסִיחוֹן מֶלֶךְ הָאֱמֹרִי
for His kindness is forever.	כִּי לְעוֹלָם חַסְדּוֹ.
And Og, king of the Bashan,	וּלְעוֹג מֶלֶךְ הַבָּשָׁן
for His kindness is forever.	כִּי לְעוֹלָם חַסְדּוֹ.
And gave their land as an estate,	וְנָתַן אַרְצָם לְנַחֲלָה
for His kindness is forever.	כִּי לְעוֹלָם חַסְדּוֹ.
An estate for Israel His servant,	נַחֲלָה לְיִשְׂרָאֵל עַבְדּוֹ
for His kindness is forever.	כִּי לְעוֹלָם חַסְדּוֹ.
Who recalled us when we were low,	שֶׁבְּשִׁפְלֵנוּ זָכַר לָנוּ
for His kindness is forever.	כִּי לְעוֹלָם חַסְדּוֹ.
And delivered us from our foes,	וַיִּפְרְקֵנוּ מִצָּרֵינוּ
for His kindness is forever.	כִּי לְעוֹלָם חַסְדּוֹ.
Who gives bread to all flesh,	נֹתֵן לֶחֶם לְכָל בָּשָׂר
for His kindness is forever.	כִּי לְעוֹלָם חַסְדּוֹ.
Acclaim the God of the heavens	הוֹדוּ לְאֵל הַשָּׁמַיִם
for His kindness is forever.	כִּי לְעוֹלָם חַסְדּוֹ.

⁴⁹**The soul of every living thing** will bless Your name, Lord our God, and the spirit of all flesh will glorify Your fame, our King, constantly. Eternally You are God, and other than You we have no king who redeems and saves, sustains and shows compassion in all times of trouble and distress. We have no King but You, God of the first and the last, God of all creatures, God of all generations, praised with a multitude of praises, who guides His world with mercy and His creatures with compassion. And the Lord will neither sleep nor slumber. The one who awakens sleepers and arouses slumberers, who gives speech to the dumb and frees the fettered and supports the fallen and straightens the bowed, to You only we give thanks. Were our mouths filled with song as the sea, and our tongues with joy as the endless waves, and our lips with praise as the expanse of the firmament, and were our eyes shining like the sun and the moon, and our hands outstretched like those of the eagles of the

⁴⁹נִשְׁמַת כָּל חַי תְּבָרֵךְ אֶת שִׁמְךָ, יי אֱלֹהֵינוּ, וְרוּחַ כָּל בָּשָׂר תְּפָאֵר וּתְרוֹמֵם זִכְרְךָ, מַלְכֵּנוּ, תָּמִיד מִן הָעוֹלָם וְעַד הָעוֹלָם אַתָּה אֵל, וּמִבַּלְעָדֶיךָ אֵין לָנוּ מֶלֶךְ גּוֹאֵל וּמוֹשִׁיעַ, פּוֹדֶה וּמַצִּיל וּמְפַרְנֵס וּמְרַחֵם בְּכָל עֵת צָרָה וְצוּקָה. אֵין לָנוּ מֶלֶךְ אֶלָּא אַתָּה. אֱלֹהֵי הָרִאשׁוֹנִים וְהָאַחֲרוֹנִים, אֱלוֹהַּ כָּל בְּרִיּוֹת, אֲדוֹן כָּל תּוֹלָדוֹת, הַמְהֻלָּל בְּרֹב הַתִּשְׁבָּחוֹת, הַמְנַהֵג עוֹלָמוֹ בְּחֶסֶד וּבְרִיּוֹתָיו בְּרַחֲמִים, וַיי לֹא יָנוּם וְלֹא יִישָׁן. הַמְעוֹרֵר יְשֵׁנִים וְהַמֵּקִיץ נִרְדָּמִים, וְהַמֵּשִׂיחַ אִלְּמִים וְהַמַּתִּיר אֲסוּרִים, וְהַסּוֹמֵךְ נוֹפְלִים וְהַזּוֹקֵף כְּפוּפִים, לְךָ לְבַדְּךָ אֲנַחְנוּ מוֹדִים. אִלּוּ פִינוּ מָלֵא שִׁירָה כַּיָּם וּלְשׁוֹנֵנוּ רִנָּה כַּהֲמוֹן גַּלָּיו, וְשִׂפְתוֹתֵינוּ שֶׁבַח כְּמֶרְחֲבֵי רָקִיעַ, וְעֵינֵינוּ מְאִירוֹת כַּשֶּׁמֶשׁ וְכַיָּרֵחַ, וְיָדֵינוּ פְרוּשׂוֹת

---

49 The soul of every living thing. The *Nishmat* prayer begins with a series of universal praises, extolling the "God of all creatures," the "God of all generations," the God "who guides His world with mercy and His creatures with compassion." The first detail mentioned in this prayer is God's role in the Exodus: in addition to praising God for sustaining the entire world, we praise God for redeeming us from slavery in Egypt. Even the subsequent details, which appear to be more generic— "You nourished us in times of famine and You sustained us in times of prosperity, You saved us from the sword, and You rescued us from plague"—are, in fact, references to Egypt. Famine (*ra'av*) and prosperity (*sova*) are terms that evoke the Joseph story, and the word pair sword (*herev*) and plague (*dever*) appears, both in the Haggadah and in the Torah itself, as a shorthand reference to the Ten Plagues. The *Nishmat* prayer highlights the Exodus as an emblematic event that represents both God's interaction with the world and our obligation to praise God endlessly. By casting the Exodus as representative of humanity's collective indebtedness to God, the *Nishmat* prayer attempts to universalize the seder experience.

The Seder

heavens, and our legs nimble as antelope, we would not be capable of thanking You, LORD our God and the God of our fathers, or to bless Your name for one of the many, many thousands and myriads of good things that You did for our ancestors and for us. You redeemed us from Egypt, LORD our God, and You saved us from the house of slavery, You nourished us in times of famine and You sustained us in times of prosperity, You saved us from the sword and You rescued us from plague, and You delivered us from all evil and serious diseases. Until now, Your compassion has succored us and Your mercy has not abandoned us; may You never abandon us, LORD our God, for eternity! Therefore, all the limbs that You have created in us, the spirit and the soul that You have breathed into us and the tongue that You have put in our mouth—they will acknowledge, bless, praise and extol, exalt and revere, sanctify and enthrone Your name, our King. For every mouth will thank You, and every tongue will swear by You, every knee will kneel to You, all who stand erect shall bow, all hearts shall revere You, and all our innermost self will sing praise of Your name, as it is written: *All my bones say, "LORD, who is like You? Saving the poor from one stronger than he and the poor and the needy from his despoiler"* (Ps. 35:10). Who can compare to You, who can equal You, who can match You, God, great, mighty and awesome, supreme God, Creator of heaven and earth. We shall praise You, we shall extol You, we shall glorify You, and we shall bless Your holy

כְּנִשְׁרֵי שָׁמַיִם, וְרַגְלֵינוּ קַלּוֹת כָּאַיָּלוֹת, אֵין אֲנַחְנוּ מַסְפִּיקִים לְהוֹדוֹת לְךָ, יי אֱלֹהֵינוּ וֵאלֹהֵי אֲבוֹתֵינוּ, וּלְבָרֵךְ אֶת שְׁמֶךָ עַל אַחַת מֵאֶלֶף אַלְפֵי אֲלָפִים וְרִבֵּי רְבָבוֹת פְּעָמִים הַטּוֹבוֹת, שֶׁעָשִׂיתָ עִם אֲבוֹתֵינוּ וְעִמָּנוּ. מִמִּצְרַיִם גְּאַלְתָּנוּ, יי אֱלֹהֵינוּ, וּמִבֵּית עֲבָדִים פְּדִיתָנוּ, בְּרָעָב זַנְתָּנוּ, וּבְשָׂבָע כִּלְכַּלְתָּנוּ, מֵחֶרֶב הִצַּלְתָּנוּ וּמִדֶּבֶר מִלַּטְתָּנוּ, וּמֵחֳלָיִם רָעִים וְנֶאֱמָנִים דִּלִּיתָנוּ. עַד הֵנָּה עֲזָרוּנוּ רַחֲמֶיךָ, וְלֹא עֲזָבוּנוּ חֲסָדֶיךָ, וְאַל תִּטְּשֵׁנוּ יי אֱלֹהֵינוּ לָנֶצַח. עַל כֵּן אֵבָרִים שֶׁפִּלַּגְתָּ בָּנוּ, וְרוּחַ וּנְשָׁמָה שֶׁנָּפַחְתָּ בְּאַפֵּינוּ, וְלָשׁוֹן אֲשֶׁר שַׂמְתָּ בְּפִינוּ, הֵן הֵם יוֹדוּ וִיבָרְכוּ וִישַׁבְּחוּ וִיפָאֲרוּ וִירוֹמְמוּ וְיַעֲרִיצוּ וְיַקְדִּישׁוּ וְיַמְלִיכוּ אֶת שִׁמְךָ מַלְכֵּנוּ. כִּי כָל פֶּה לְךָ יוֹדֶה, וְכָל לָשׁוֹן לְךָ תִשָּׁבַע, וְכָל בֶּרֶךְ לְךָ תִכְרַע, וְכָל קוֹמָה לְפָנֶיךָ תִשְׁתַּחֲוֶה, וְכָל לְבָבוֹת יִירָאוּךָ, וְכָל קֶרֶב וּכְלָיוֹת יְזַמְּרוּ לִשְׁמֶךָ, כַּדָּבָר שֶׁכָּתוּב, כָּל עַצְמֹתַי תֹּאמַרְנָה: יהוה, מִי כָמוֹךָ, מַצִּיל עָנִי מֵחָזָק מִמֶּנּוּ וְעָנִי וְאֶבְיוֹן מִגֹּזְלוֹ (תהלים לה:י). מִי יִדְמֶה לָּךְ וּמִי יִשְׁוֶה לָּךְ וּמִי יַעֲרָךְ לָךְ, הָאֵל הַגָּדוֹל הַגִּבּוֹר וְהַנּוֹרָא, אֵל עֶלְיוֹן קֹנֵה שָׁמַיִם וָאָרֶץ. נְהַלֶּלְךָ וּנְשַׁבֵּחֲךָ

name, as it says: *For David. Bless, O my being, the LORD, and everything in me, His holy name* (Ps. 103:1).

God—in the might of Your power; great—in the glory of Your name; mighty—forever; and awesome—in Your awe-inspiring acts; the King who sits on a high and exalted throne.

He who abides forever, exalted and holy is His name. And it says: *Sing gladly, O righteous, of the LORD, for the upright, praise is befitting* (Ps. 33:1).

In the mouths of the upright—You shall be praised;

In the words of the righteous—You shall be blessed;

In the tongue of the pious—You shall be exalted;

Among the holy—You shall be sanctified.

In the choirs of the myriads of Your people, the house of Israel, Your name will be glorified in song, our King, in every generation. For it is the obligation of all creatures before You, our God and God of our ancestors, to thank, to acclaim, to praise, to laud, to exalt, to extol, to bless, to elevate, and to applaud beyond all the songs and praises of David son of Jesse, Your servant, Your anointed.

Some say "All Your creations will praise You" (see above, before Psalm 136) at this point, instead of the following blessing.

May Your name be praised forever, our King, God, the great and holy King in heaven and earth, because for You are fitting, our God

וּנְפָאֶרְךָ וּנְבָרֵךְ אֶת שֵׁם קָדְשֶׁךָ, כָּאָמוּר: לְדָוִד, בָּרְכִי נַפְשִׁי אֶת יהוה, וְכָל קְרָבַי אֶת שֵׁם קָדְשׁוֹ (תהלים קג:א).

הָאֵל בְּתַעֲצֻמוֹת עֻזֶּךָ, הַגָּדוֹל בִּכְבוֹד שְׁמֶךָ, הַגִּבּוֹר לָנֶצַח וְהַנּוֹרָא בְּנוֹרְאוֹתֶיךָ, הַמֶּלֶךְ הַיּוֹשֵׁב עַל כִּסֵּא רָם וְנִשָּׂא.

שׁוֹכֵן עַד מָרוֹם וְקָדוֹשׁ שְׁמוֹ. וְכָתוּב: רַנְּנוּ צַדִּיקִים בַּיהוה, לַיְשָׁרִים נָאוָה תְהִלָּה (תהלים לג:א).

בְּפִי יְשָׁרִים תִּתְהַלָּל,

וּבְדִבְרֵי צַדִּיקִים תִּתְבָּרַךְ,

וּבִלְשׁוֹן חֲסִידִים תִּתְרוֹמָם,

וּבְקֶרֶב קְדוֹשִׁים תִּתְקַדָּשׁ.

וּבְמַקְהֲלוֹת רִבְבוֹת עַמְּךָ בֵּית יִשְׂרָאֵל בְּרִנָּה יִתְפָּאֵר שִׁמְךָ מַלְכֵּנוּ בְּכָל דּוֹר וָדוֹר. שֶׁכֵּן חוֹבַת כָּל הַיְצוּרִים, לְפָנֶיךָ יי אֱלֹהֵינוּ וֵאלֹהֵי אֲבוֹתֵינוּ, לְהוֹדוֹת לְהַלֵּל לְשַׁבֵּחַ, לְפָאֵר לְרוֹמֵם לְהַדֵּר, לְבָרֵךְ לְעַלֵּה וּלְקַלֵּס, עַל כָּל דִּבְרֵי שִׁירוֹת וְתִשְׁבְּחוֹת דָּוִד בֶּן יִשַׁי עַבְדְּךָ מְשִׁיחֶךָ.

יִשְׁתַּבַּח שִׁמְךָ לָעַד מַלְכֵּנוּ, הָאֵל הַמֶּלֶךְ הַגָּדוֹל וְהַקָּדוֹשׁ, בַּשָּׁמַיִם וּבָאָרֶץ. כִּי לְךָ נָאֶה, יי, אֱלֹהֵינוּ וֵאלֹהֵי אֲבוֹתֵינוּ, שִׁיר

and the God of our ancestors: song and praise, psalm and melody, might and government, eternity, greatness and power, fame and glory, holiness and kingdom, blessings and thanks forever and ever. Blessed are You, Lord, God, King great in praise, God of thanks, Master of wonders, who chooses melodious song, King God, life of the universe.

Blessed are You, Lord our God, King of the universe, Creator of the fruit of the vine.

וּשְׁבָחָה, הַלֵּל וְזִמְרָה, עֹז וּמֶמְשָׁלָה, נֶצַח, גְּדֻלָּה וּגְבוּרָה, תְּהִלָּה וְתִפְאֶרֶת, קְדֻשָּׁה וּמַלְכוּת, בְּרָכוֹת וְהוֹדָאוֹת מֵעַתָּה וְעַד עוֹלָם. בָּרוּךְ אַתָּה יי, אֵל מֶלֶךְ גָּדוֹל בַּתִּשְׁבָּחוֹת, אֵל הַהוֹדָאוֹת, אֲדוֹן הַנִּפְלָאוֹת, הַבּוֹחֵר בְּשִׁירֵי זִמְרָה, מֶלֶךְ אֵל חֵי הָעוֹלָמִים.

בָּרוּךְ אַתָּה יי אֱלֹהֵינוּ מֶלֶךְ הָעוֹלָם בּוֹרֵא פְּרִי הַגָּפֶן.

Drink while reclining to the left. After drinking, recite the following blessing.

Blessed are You, Lord our God, King of the universe, for the vine and the fruit of the vine, for the produce of the field and for the desirable, good, and spacious land that You have desired and granted to our ancestors, to eat of its fruits and to be satisfied through its bounty. Please have mercy, Lord our God, on Your people Israel, on Your city, Jerusalem, on Zion, the abode of Your glory, on Your altar and Your palaces. And build Jerusalem, the holy city, speedily in our days, and bring us there and make us rejoice in its building, and we shall eat of its fruit and be satisfied with its bounty, and we shall bless You for it in sanctity and purity, (**on the Sabbath add**: and favor us and strengthen us on this Sabbath day,) and cause us to rejoice on the day of the festival of matzot, for You are Lord, good and beneficent to all, and we thank You for the land and the fruit of the vine. Blessed are You, Lord, for the vine and the fruit of the vine.

בָּרוּךְ אַתָּה יי אֱלֹהֵינוּ מֶלֶךְ הָעוֹלָם, עַל הַגֶּפֶן וְעַל פְּרִי הַגֶּפֶן, וְעַל תְּנוּבַת הַשָּׂדֶה, וְעַל אֶרֶץ חֶמְדָּה טוֹבָה וּרְחָבָה, שֶׁרָצִיתָ וְהִנְחַלְתָּ לַאֲבוֹתֵינוּ, לֶאֱכֹל מִפִּרְיָהּ וְלִשְׂבֹּעַ מִטּוּבָהּ. רַחֶם נָא יי אֱלֹהֵינוּ עַל יִשְׂרָאֵל עַמֶּךָ, וְעַל יְרוּשָׁלַיִם עִירֶךָ, וְעַל צִיּוֹן מִשְׁכַּן כְּבוֹדֶךָ, וְעַל מִזְבְּחֶךָ וְעַל הֵיכָלֶךָ. וּבְנֵה יְרוּשָׁלַיִם עִיר הַקֹּדֶשׁ בִּמְהֵרָה בְיָמֵינוּ, וְהַעֲלֵנוּ לְתוֹכָהּ וְשַׂמְּחֵנוּ בְּבִנְיָנָהּ וְנֹאכַל מִפִּרְיָהּ וְנִשְׂבַּע מִטּוּבָהּ, וּנְבָרֶכְךָ עָלֶיהָ בִּקְדֻשָּׁה וּבְטָהֳרָה. (**בשבת מוסיפים**: וּרְצֵה וְהַחֲלִיצֵנוּ בְּיוֹם הַשַּׁבָּת הַזֶּה,) וְשַׂמְּחֵנוּ בְּיוֹם חַג הַמַּצּוֹת הַזֶּה. כִּי אַתָּה יי טוֹב וּמֵטִיב לַכֹּל, וְנוֹדֶה לְּךָ עַל הָאָרֶץ וְעַל פְּרִי הַגָּפֶן. בָּרוּךְ אַתָּה יי עַל הָאָרֶץ וְעַל פְּרִי הַגָּפֶן.

A Passover Haggadah: Go Forth and Learn

Nirtzah
נִרְצָה

50 חֲסַל סִדּוּר פֶּסַח כְּהִלְכָתוֹ, כְּכָל מִשְׁפָּטוֹ וְחֻקָתוֹ.

כַּאֲשֶׁר זָכִינוּ לְסַדֵּר אוֹתוֹ, כֵּן נִזְכֶּה לַעֲשׂוֹתוֹ.

זָךְ שׁוֹכֵן מְעוֹנָה, קוֹמֵם קְהַל עֲדַת מִי מָנָה.

בְּקָרוֹב נַהֵל נִטְעֵי כַנָּה, פְּדוּיִם לְצִיּוֹן בְּרִנָּה.

50 The order of the Passover ritual has been completed according to law, in accordance with all its rules and regulations.

As we have been privileged to arrange it, so may we be privileged to perform it.

Pure One, who dwells on high, restore the community too numerous to count.

Soon, lead the firm saplings, redeemed to Zion in song.

Next year in Jerusalem rebuilt!

לְשָׁנָה הַבָּאָה בִּירוּשָׁלַיִם הַבְּנוּיָה!

....

50 The order of the Passover ritual has been completed. The opening song of *Nirtzah* is part of a longer poem by R. Yosef Tov Elem that was originally intended for *Shabbat ha-Gadol*, the Sabbath preceding Passover. At the seder we recite only the final stanza of this poem, which refers to the Passover offering and its attendant rituals. As the seder reaches its conclusion, we express our hope that we have conducted the service as the law requires and our wish that in the future we may be able not only to "arrange" a symbolic Passover offering but to actually "perform" the rite in the rebuilt Temple.

The song refers to the regulations governing the Passover offering as *mishpato* (its rules) and *hukato* (its regulations), two terms that the Torah itself uses in conjunction with this sacrifice (Num. 9:3).[27] At the beginning of the *Maggid* section, these terms also appear in the wise child's question—"What are the terms and the statutes [*hukim*] and the laws [*mishpatim*] with which the LORD our God has charged you?"—to which the parent responds by teaching the laws of Passover, particularly those rules that pertain to the Passover offering. As we noted earlier, in its original biblical context, the child's question is not about the laws of Passover but about the requirement to observe mitzvot in general—and indeed, the terms *hukim* and *mishpatim* are essentially generic. Thus, in co-opting those terms for the Passover ritual, both in *Maggid* and here in *Nirtzah*, the Haggadah suggests that the Passover regulations are equivalent to the rest of the Torah and that one who has observed the laws of Passover and internalized their significance has, in essence, understood the entire Torah.

---

[27] Later, the poet beseeches God to "restore the community [*kehal adat*] too numerous to count." The word *edah* (community) is also borrowed from the Torah's description of the Passover offering: Exodus 12 begins with an exhortation to Moses and Aaron to speak to the "entire community [*kol adat*] of Israel" (v. 3).

THE SEDER

Blessed are You, LORD our God, King of the universe, who has sanctified us with His commandments and has commanded us concerning counting the Omer.

בָּרוּךְ אַתָּה יי אֱלֹהֵינוּ מֶלֶךְ הָעוֹלָם, אֲשֶׁר קִדְּשָׁנוּ בְּמִצְוֹתָיו וְצִוָּנוּ עַל סְפִירַת הָעוֹמֶר.

Today is the first day of the Omer.

הַיּוֹם יוֹם אֶחָד בָּעוֹמֶר.

On the first night of Passover, the following poem is recited.

[51] *And it happened at midnight*	[51] וּבְכֵן וַיְהִי בַּחֲצִי הַלַּיְלָה
(Exod. 12:29)	(שמות יב:כט)

Then You performed many miracles		
	at night;	**בַּלַּיְלָה,**
At the beginning of the watch **of the night**;		אָז רוֹב נִסִּים הִפְלֵאתָ
	הַלַּיְלָה,	בְּרֹאשׁ אַשְׁמוֹרֶת זֶה
A righteous convert You caused to be victorious when he divided his men		גֵּר צֶדֶק נִצַּחְתּוֹ כְּנֶחֱלַק לוֹ
	at night;	**לַיְלָה,**
And it happened at midnight.		וַיְהִי בַּחֲצִי הַלַּיְלָה.

You judged the king of Gerar in a dream		
	at night;	**הַלַּיְלָה,**
		דַּנְתָּ מֶלֶךְ גְּרָר בַּחֲלוֹם
You frightened the Aramean	**at night**;	**לַיְלָה,**
		הִפְחַדְתָּ אֲרַמִּי בְּאֶמֶשׁ
Israel struggled with the angel and he defeated him		וַיָּשַׂר יִשְׂרָאֵל לְמַלְאָךְ וַיּוּכַל לוֹ
	at night;	**לַיְלָה,**
And it happened at midnight.		וַיְהִי בַּחֲצִי הַלַּיְלָה.

---

51 *And it happened at midnight.* The Talmud records a dispute between R. Akiva and R. Eleazar b. Azaryah as to whether the mitzvah to tell the Exodus story and the mitzvah to eat matzah must be performed before midnight or may continue throughout the night (B.T. Pes. 120b). It is possible that the custom to recite both this poem, which emphasizes the significance of the midnight hour, and the following poem, which refers to the events of Passover more generally, is a means of symbolically resolving the dispute by giving voice to both sides of the debate.

The seed of the firstborn of Pathros You crushed **at midnight;**
They did not find their forces when they rose **in the night;**
The flight of the prince of Haroshet You crushed with the stars **of night;**
And it happened at midnight.

The blasphemer threatened to stretch his hand over the desired place, and You caused his army to wither **at night;**
Bel and his founder collapsed **at night;**
To the beloved man was revealed the secret of the vision **at night;**
And it happened at midnight.

The one who got drunk from the holy vessels was killed **at night;**
The one who was saved from the lion's den interpreted the terrifying visions **of night;**
The Agagite bided his hatred and wrote letters **at night;**
And it happened at midnight.

You aroused Your victory over him by disturbing the sleep **of night;**
You will trod the vintage for the watchman who calls, "What **of the night?"**
He called like the watchman and said, "Day has come and **also night!"**
And it happened at midnight.

זֶרַע בְּכוֹרֵי פַתְרוֹס מָחַצְתָּ בַּחֲצִי **הַלַּיְלָה,**

חֵילָם לֹא מָצְאוּ בְּקוּמָם **בַּלַּיְלָה,**

טִיסַת נְגִיד חֲרֹשֶׁת סִלִּיתָ בְּכוֹכְבֵי **לַיְלָה,**

וַיְהִי בַּחֲצִי הַלַּיְלָה.

יָעַץ מְחָרֵף לְנוֹפֵף אִוּוּי, הוֹבַשְׁתָּ פְגָרָיו **בַּלַּיְלָה,**

כָּרַע בֵּל וּמַצָּבוֹ בְּאִישׁוֹן **לַיְלָה,**

לְאִישׁ חֲמוּדוֹת נִגְלָה רָז חֲזוֹת **לַיְלָה,**

וַיְהִי בַּחֲצִי הַלַּיְלָה.

מִשְׁתַּכֵּר בִּכְלֵי קֹדֶשׁ נֶהֱרַג בּוֹ **בַּלַּיְלָה,**

נוֹשַׁע מִבּוֹר אֲרָיוֹת פּוֹתֵר בְּעִתּוּתֵי **לַיְלָה,**

שִׂנְאָה נָטַר אֲגָגִי וְכָתַב סְפָרִים **בַּלַּיְלָה,**

וַיְהִי בַּחֲצִי הַלַּיְלָה.

עוֹרַרְתָּ נִצְחֲךָ עָלָיו בְּנֶדֶד שְׁנַת **לַיְלָה,**

פּוּרָה תִדְרוֹךְ לְשׁוֹמֵר מַה **מִלַּיְלָה,**

צָרַח כַּשּׁוֹמֵר וְשָׂח אָתָא בֹקֶר וְגַם **לַיְלָה,**

וַיְהִי בַּחֲצִי הַלַּיְלָה.

The day is coming that will be neither day **nor night;**

O High One, proclaim that Yours are day and **also night!**

Appoint watchmen over Your city all day and **all night!**

Brighten as the light of the day the darkness **of night!**

And it happened at midnight.

קָרֵב יוֹם אֲשֶׁר הוּא לֹא יוֹם וְלֹא **לַיְלָה,**

רָם הוֹדַע כִּי לְךָ הַיּוֹם אַף לְךָ **הַלַּיְלָה,**

שׁוֹמְרִים הַפְקֵד לְעִירְךָ כָּל הַיּוֹם וְכָל **הַלַּיְלָה,**

תָּאִיר כְּאוֹר יוֹם חֶשְׁכַּת **לַיְלָה,**

וַיְהִי בַּחֲצִי הַלַּיְלָה.

In the Land of Israel, the following poem is recited on the first night of Passover; outside of the Land of Israel, it is recited on the second night of Passover.

You shall say, "A Passover sacrifice!"
(Exod. 12:27)

וּבְכֵן וַאֲמַרְתֶּם זֶבַח פֶּסַח
(שמות יב:כז)

Your wondrous might You showed **on Passover;**

First of all festivals You celebrated **the Passover;**

You disclosed to the one from the East at midnight **on Passover;**

You shall say, "A Passover sacrifice!"

אֹמֶץ גְּבוּרוֹתֶיךָ הִפְלֵאתָ **בַּפֶּסַח,**

בְּרֹאשׁ כָּל מוֹעֲדוֹת נִשֵּׂאתָ **פֶּסַח,**

גִּלִּיתָ לְאֶזְרָחִי חֲצוֹת לֵיל **פֶּסַח,**

וַאֲמַרְתֶּם זֶבַח פֶּסַח.

You knocked at his door, at the heat of the day **on Passover;**

He fed the shining ones matzah cakes **on Passover;**

He ran to the cattle, to commemorate the ox of the ritual **of Passover;**

You shall say, "A Passover sacrifice!"

דְּלָתָיו דָּפַקְתָּ כְּחֹם הַיּוֹם **בַּפֶּסַח,**

הִסְעִיד נוֹצְצִים עֲגוֹת מַצּוֹת **בַּפֶּסַח,**

וְאֶל הַבָּקָר רָץ זֵכֶר לְשׁוֹר עֵרֶךְ **פֶּסַח,**

וַאֲמַרְתֶּם זֶבַח פֶּסַח.

A PASSOVER HAGGADAH: GO FORTH AND LEARN

The Sodomites were angry and burned in fire
on Passover;

Lot was saved from them and he baked matzah at the time **of Passover;**

You swept away the land of Moph and Noph when You passed by **on Passover;**

You shall say, "A Passover sacrifice!"

LORD, the first seed You crushed on the night of watching **of Passover;**

Mighty One, You passed over the firstborn son because of the blood **of Passover;**

To prevent the destroyer from entering my doors **on Passover;**

You shall say, "A Passover sacrifice!"

The besieged one fell at the time **of Passover;**

Midian was destroyed through a dream of *omer* barley **on Passover;**

The fattened ones of Pul and Lud were burned in the burning of the fire **on Passover;**

You shall say, "A Passover sacrifice!"

This same day at Nob he shall stand until he expires **at Passover;**

A hand wrote to destroy Babylon **on Passover;**

Watchman, watch! Set the table! **on Passover;**

You shall say, "A Passover sacrifice!"

זוֹעֲמוּ סְדוֹמִים וְלוֹהֲטוּ בָּאֵשׁ **בְּפֶסַח,**

חֻלַּץ לוֹט מֵהֶם וּמַצּוֹת אָפָה בְּקֵץ **פֶּסַח,**

טִאטֵאתָ אַדְמַת מֹף וְנֹף בְּעָבְרְךָ **בְּפֶסַח,**

וַאֲמַרְתֶּם זֶבַח פֶּסַח.

יָהּ רֹאשׁ כָּל אוֹן מָחַצְתָּ בְּלֵיל שִׁמּוּר **פֶּסַח,**

כַּבִּיר, עַל בֵּן בְּכוֹר פָּסַחְתָּ בְּדַם **פֶּסַח,**

לְבִלְתִּי תֵּת מַשְׁחִית לָבֹא בִּפְתָחַי **בְּפֶסַח,**

וַאֲמַרְתֶּם זֶבַח פֶּסַח.

מְסֻגֶּרֶת סֻגְּרָה בְּעִתּוֹתֵי **פֶּסַח,**

נִשְׁמְדָה מִדְיָן בִּצְלִיל שְׂעוֹרֵי עֹמֶר **פֶּסַח,**

שֹׂרְפוּ מִשְׁמַנֵּי פּוּל וְלוּד בִּיקַד יְקוֹד **פֶּסַח,**

וַאֲמַרְתֶּם זֶבַח פֶּסַח.

עוֹד הַיּוֹם בְּנֹב לַעֲמוֹד עַד גָּעָה עוֹנַת **פֶּסַח,**

פַּס יַד כָּתְבָה לְקַעֲקֵעַ צוּל **בְּפֶסַח,**

צָפֹה הַצָּפִית עָרוֹךְ הַשֻּׁלְחָן **בְּפֶסַח,**

וַאֲמַרְתֶּם זֶבַח פֶּסַח.

Hadassah gathered the community for a three-day fast **on Passover;**
The head of the evil house You destroyed by a fifty-cubit tree **on Passover;**
These two things You shall suddenly bring upon Utzit **on Passover;**
Strengthen Your hand, raise Your right arm as on the night of the hallowing of the festival **of Passover;**
You shall say, "A Passover sacrifice!"

קָהָל כִּנְּסָה הֲדַסָּה לְשַׁלֵּשׁ צוֹם **בַּפֶּסַח,**
רֹאשׁ מִבֵּית רָשָׁע מָחַצְתָּ בְּעֵץ חֲמִשִּׁים **בַּפֶּסַח,**
שְׁתֵּי אֵלֶּה רֶגַע תָּבִיא לְעוּצִית **בַּפֶּסַח,**
תָּעֹז יָדְךָ וְתָרוּם יְמִינְךָ כְּלֵיל הִתְקַדֶּשׁ חַג **פֶּסַח,**
וַאֲמַרְתֶּם זֶבַח פֶּסַח.

[52] **For to Him it is fitting,
for to Him it is suitable.**

[52] **כִּי לוֹ נָאֶה,
כִּי לוֹ יָאֶה.**

Powerful in kingship, properly chosen, His legions say to Him:
To You and to You, to You just to You, to You even to You, to You, Lord, is the kingdom.
For to Him it is fitting, for to Him it is suitable.

אַדִּיר בִּמְלוּכָה, בָּחוּר כַּהֲלָכָה, גְּדוּדָיו יֹאמְרוּ לוֹ:
לְךָ וּלְךָ, לְךָ כִּי לְךָ, לְךָ אַף לְךָ, לְךָ יי הַמַּמְלָכָה,
כִּי לוֹ נָאֶה, כִּי לוֹ יָאֶה.

....

52 For to Him it is fitting, for to Him it is suitable. Scholars have demonstrated that this song and the one that follows, *Adir Hu* ("He Is Powerful!"), were not originally composed for the seder. The theme of both songs is universal: each offers an alphabetized litany of praises to God with no particular connection to Passover or the Exodus. Nonetheless, the inclusion of these songs in the Haggadah is hardly coincidental; in fact, they highlight one of the seder's core messages: the limitless nature of our gratitude to God. In the *Nishmat* passage, which is included in the *Hallel* section of the Haggadah, we assert that we will never succeed in sufficiently thanking God for all the wonders and gifts we have received. And in the continuation of that prayer we list 15 forms of appropriate thanksgiving: "for You are fitting (*Ki lekha na'eh*), our God and the God of our ancestors: song and praise, psalm and melody, might and government, eternity, greatness and power, fame and glory, holiness and kingdom, blessings and thanks forever and ever." The song *Ki Lo Na'eh* ("For to Him It Is Fitting"), which echoes the words of the earlier passage, continues the list of praises to God, demonstrating that we will never completely satisfy our debt of gratitude.

A Passover Haggadah: Go Forth and Learn

Exalted in kingship, properly glorified, His faithful say to Him:

To You and to You, to You just to You, to You even to You, to You, LORD, is the kingdom.

For to Him it is fitting, for to Him it is suitable.

דָּגוּל בִּמְלוּכָה, הָדוּר כַּהֲלָכָה, וָתִיקָיו יֹאמְרוּ לוֹ:

לְךָ וּלְךָ, לְךָ כִּי לְךָ, לְךָ אַף לְךָ, לְךָ יי הַמַּמְלָכָה,

כִּי לוֹ נָאֶה, כִּי לוֹ יָאֶה.

Pure in kingship, properly faithful, His angels say to Him:

To You and to You, to You just to You, to You even to You, to You, LORD, is the kingdom.

For to Him it is fitting, for to Him it is suitable.

זַכַּאי בִּמְלוּכָה, חָסִין כַּהֲלָכָה, טַפְסְרָיו יֹאמְרוּ לוֹ:

לְךָ וּלְךָ, לְךָ כִּי לְךָ, לְךָ אַף לְךָ, לְךָ יי הַמַּמְלָכָה,

כִּי לוֹ נָאֶה, כִּי לוֹ יָאֶה.

Unique in kingship, properly mighty, His disciples say to Him:

To You and to You, to You just to You, to You even to You, to You, LORD, is the kingdom.

For to Him it is fitting, for to Him it is suitable.

יָחִיד בִּמְלוּכָה, כַּבִּיר כַּהֲלָכָה, לִמּוּדָיו יֹאמְרוּ לוֹ:

לְךָ וּלְךָ, לְךָ כִּי לְךָ, לְךָ אַף לְךָ, לְךָ יי הַמַּמְלָכָה,

כִּי לוֹ נָאֶה, כִּי לוֹ יָאֶה.

Lofty in kingship, properly awesome, those around Him say to Him:

To You and to You, to You just to You, to You even to You, to You, LORD, is the kingdom.

For to Him it is fitting, for to Him it is suitable.

מוֹשֵׁל בִּמְלוּכָה, נוֹרָא כַּהֲלָכָה, סְבִיבָיו יֹאמְרוּ לוֹ:

לְךָ וּלְךָ, לְךָ כִּי לְךָ, לְךָ אַף לְךָ, לְךָ יי הַמַּמְלָכָה,

כִּי לוֹ נָאֶה, כִּי לוֹ יָאֶה.

Modest in kingship, properly redeeming, His righteous say to Him:

To You and to You, to You just to You, to You even to You, to You, LORD, is the kingdom.

For to Him it is fitting, for to Him it is suitable.

עָנָיו בִּמְלוּכָה, פּוֹדֶה כַּהֲלָכָה, צַדִּיקָיו יֹאמְרוּ לוֹ:

לְךָ וּלְךָ, לְךָ כִּי לְךָ, לְךָ אַף לְךָ, לְךָ יי הַמַּמְלָכָה,

כִּי לוֹ נָאֶה, כִּי לוֹ יָאֶה.

Holy in kingship, properly compassionate, His hosts say to Him:
To You and to You, to You just to You, to You even to You, to You, Lord, is the kingdom.
For to Him it is fitting, for to Him it is suitable.

Mighty in kingship, properly supportive, His perfect ones say to Him:
To You and to You, to You just to You, to You even to You, to You, Lord, is the kingdom.
For to Him it is fitting, for to Him it is suitable.

He is powerful! May He build His house soon, speedily, speedily, in our times, soon.
God, build, God, build, build Your house soon!

He is chosen; He is great; He is outstanding; May He build His house soon, speedily, speedily, in our times, soon.
God, build, God, build, build Your house soon!

He is glorious; He is faithful; He is pure; May He build His house soon, speedily, speedily, in our times, soon.
God, build, God, build, build Your house soon!

He is pious; He is pure; He is unique; May He build His house soon, speedily, speedily, in our times, soon.
God, build, God, build, build Your house soon!

קָדוֹשׁ בִּמְלוּכָה, רַחוּם כַּהֲלָכָה, שִׁנְאַנָּיו יֹאמְרוּ לוֹ:
לְךָ וּלְךָ, לְךָ כִּי לְךָ, לְךָ אַף לְךָ, לְךָ יְיָ הַמַּמְלָכָה,
כִּי לוֹ נָאֶה, כִּי לוֹ יָאֶה.

תַּקִּיף בִּמְלוּכָה, תּוֹמֵךְ כַּהֲלָכָה, תְּמִימָיו יֹאמְרוּ לוֹ:
לְךָ וּלְךָ, לְךָ כִּי לְךָ, לְךָ אַף לְךָ, לְךָ יְיָ הַמַּמְלָכָה,
כִּי לוֹ נָאֶה, כִּי לוֹ יָאֶה.

אַדִּיר הוּא יִבְנֶה בֵּיתוֹ בְּקָרוֹב.
בִּמְהֵרָה, בִּמְהֵרָה, בְּיָמֵינוּ בְּקָרוֹב.
אֵל בְּנֵה, אֵל בְּנֵה, בְּנֵה בֵיתְךָ בְּקָרוֹב.

בָּחוּר הוּא, גָּדוֹל הוּא, דָּגוּל הוּא יִבְנֶה בֵּיתוֹ בְּקָרוֹב.
בִּמְהֵרָה, בִּמְהֵרָה, בְּיָמֵינוּ בְּקָרוֹב.
אֵל בְּנֵה, אֵל בְּנֵה, בְּנֵה בֵיתְךָ בְּקָרוֹב.

הָדוּר הוּא, וָתִיק הוּא, זַכַּאי הוּא יִבְנֶה בֵּיתוֹ בְּקָרוֹב.
בִּמְהֵרָה, בִּמְהֵרָה, בְּיָמֵינוּ בְּקָרוֹב.
אֵל בְּנֵה, אֵל בְּנֵה, בְּנֵה בֵיתְךָ בְּקָרוֹב.

חָסִיד הוּא, טָהוֹר הוּא, יָחִיד הוּא יִבְנֶה בֵּיתוֹ בְּקָרוֹב.
בִּמְהֵרָה, בִּמְהֵרָה, בְּיָמֵינוּ בְּקָרוֹב.
אֵל בְּנֵה, אֵל בְּנֵה, בְּנֵה בֵיתְךָ בְּקָרוֹב.

A PASSOVER HAGGADAH: GO FORTH AND LEARN

He is mighty; He is wise; He is king; He is awesome; He is exalted; He is strong; He is the redeemer; He is righteous; He is holy; He is compassionate; He is Almighty; He is powerful; May He build His house soon, speedily, speedily, in our times, soon. God, build, God, build, build Your house soon!

כַּבִּיר הוּא, לָמוּד הוּא, מֶלֶךְ הוּא, נוֹרָא הוּא, סַגִּיב הוּא, עִזּוּז הוּא, פּוֹדֶה הוּא, צַדִּיק הוּא, קָדוֹשׁ הוּא, רַחוּם הוּא, שַׁדַּי הוּא, תַּקִּיף הוּא יִבְנֶה בֵּיתוֹ בְּקָרוֹב. בִּמְהֵרָה, בִּמְהֵרָה, בְּיָמֵינוּ בְּקָרוֹב. אֵל בְּנֵה, אֵל בְּנֵה, בְּנֵה בֵיתְךָ בְּקָרוֹב.

⁵³Who knows one?

I know one.
One is our God in heaven and on earth.

Who knows two?
I know **two**. Two tablets of the covenant; One is our God in heaven and on earth.

Who knows three?
I know **three**. Three fathers; two tablets of the covenant; One is our God in heaven and on earth.

⁵³ אֶחָד מִי יוֹדֵעַ?

אֶחָד אֲנִי יוֹדֵעַ:
אֶחָד אֱלֹהֵינוּ שֶׁבַּשָּׁמַיִם וּבָאָרֶץ.

שְׁנַיִם מִי יוֹדֵעַ?
שְׁנַיִם אֲנִי יוֹדֵעַ: שְׁנֵי לֻחוֹת הַבְּרִית.
אֶחָד אֱלֹהֵינוּ שֶׁבַּשָּׁמַיִם וּבָאָרֶץ.

שְׁלֹשָׁה מִי יוֹדֵעַ?
שְׁלֹשָׁה אֲנִי יוֹדֵעַ: שְׁלֹשָׁה אָבוֹת, שְׁנֵי לֻחוֹת הַבְּרִית,
אֶחָד אֱלֹהֵינוּ שֶׁבַּשָּׁמַיִם וּבָאָרֶץ.

---

53 Who knows one? I know one. This song (and *Had Gadya* that follows), like the previous two, was not composed for the seder. It too is of a universal character, reflecting the significance to Judaism of the numbers one through thirteen. Nonetheless, as with the previous songs, the inclusion of "Who Knows One" in the seder liturgy is not accidental. The song's question and answer format matches various Haggadah passages and reflects the evening's emphasis on education and pedagogy. More significantly, the song highlights a theme central to both the Haggadah and the book of Exodus: knowing God and bringing knowledge of God to the world.

Exodus begins with the rise of a new Egyptian king "who knew not Joseph" (Exod. 1:8) and later declares that he does not "know God" (5:2). God ensures that Pharaoh and his people learn to recognize God via the Ten Plagues, which were designed to let them know of God's existence and presence in the world (7:17, 8:18, 9:14). Following the Exodus, Jethro comes to meet Moses and the People of Israel in the desert, declaring that he now knows God is the greatest (18:11). The manna rains from the heavens so that the Israelites might know the God who redeemed them from Egypt (16:6,12), and the *Mishkan* is built for the purpose of allowing the people to know the ways of

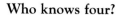

Who knows four?

I know **four**. Four mothers; three fathers; two tablets of the covenant;
One is our God in heaven and on earth.

אַרְבַּע מִי יוֹדֵעַ?

אַרְבַּע אֲנִי יוֹדֵעַ: אַרְבַּע אִמָּהוֹת, שְׁלֹשָׁה אָבוֹת, שְׁנֵי לֻחוֹת הַבְּרִית,
אֶחָד אֱלֹהֵינוּ שֶׁבַּשָּׁמַיִם וּבָאָרֶץ.

Who knows five?

I know **five**. Five books of the Torah; four mothers; three fathers; two tablets of the covenant;
One is our God in heaven and on earth.

חֲמִשָּׁה מִי יוֹדֵעַ?

חֲמִשָּׁה אֲנִי יוֹדֵעַ: חֲמִשָּׁה חוּמְשֵׁי תוֹרָה, אַרְבַּע אִמָּהוֹת, שְׁלֹשָׁה אָבוֹת, שְׁנֵי לֻחוֹת הַבְּרִית,
אֶחָד אֱלֹהֵינוּ שֶׁבַּשָּׁמַיִם וּבָאָרֶץ.

Who knows six?

I know **six**. Six orders of the Mishnah; five books of the Torah; four mothers; three fathers; two tablets of the covenant;
One is our God in heaven and on earth.

שִׁשָּׁה מִי יוֹדֵעַ?

שִׁשָּׁה אֲנִי יוֹדֵעַ: שִׁשָּׁה סִדְרֵי מִשְׁנָה, חֲמִשָּׁה חוּמְשֵׁי תוֹרָה, אַרְבַּע אִמָּהוֹת, שְׁלֹשָׁה אָבוֹת, שְׁנֵי לֻחוֹת הַבְּרִית,
אֶחָד אֱלֹהֵינוּ שֶׁבַּשָּׁמַיִם וּבָאָרֶץ.

Who knows seven?

I know **seven**. Seven days of the week; six orders of the Mishnah; five books of the Torah; four mothers; three fathers; two tablets of the covenant;
One is our God in heaven and on earth.

שִׁבְעָה מִי יוֹדֵעַ?

שִׁבְעָה אֲנִי יוֹדֵעַ: שִׁבְעָה יְמֵי שַׁבְּתָא, שִׁשָּׁה סִדְרֵי מִשְׁנָה, חֲמִשָּׁה חוּמְשֵׁי תוֹרָה, אַרְבַּע אִמָּהוֹת, שְׁלֹשָׁה אָבוֹת, שְׁנֵי לֻחוֹת הַבְּרִית,
אֶחָד אֱלֹהֵינוּ שֶׁבַּשָּׁמַיִם וּבָאָרֶץ.

Who knows eight?

I know **eight**. Eight days until circumcision; seven days of the week; six orders of the Mishnah; five books of the Torah; four mothers; three fathers; two tablets of the covenant;
One is our God in heaven and on earth.

שְׁמוֹנָה מִי יוֹדֵעַ?

שְׁמוֹנָה אֲנִי יוֹדֵעַ: שְׁמוֹנָה יְמֵי מִילָה, שִׁבְעָה יְמֵי שַׁבְּתָא, שִׁשָּׁה סִדְרֵי מִשְׁנָה, חֲמִשָּׁה חוּמְשֵׁי תוֹרָה, אַרְבַּע אִמָּהוֹת, שְׁלֹשָׁה אָבוֹת, שְׁנֵי לֻחוֹת הַבְּרִית,
אֶחָד אֱלֹהֵינוּ שֶׁבַּשָּׁמַיִם וּבָאָרֶץ.

God (29:43–46). Following the sin of the Golden Calf and the destruction of the first Tablets, Moses pleads to know God more intimately (33:12–16), and God reveals a list of attributes that are known in Rabbinic parlance as the *yud-gimmel middot* (thirteen attributes) of God (34:6–7). Thirteen is not usually considered a number of particular significance in the Bible or in Rabbinic thought, but strikingly, the song "Who Knows One" ends with the number thirteen, referring to these *middot* and thereby underscoring a core theme of Passover and the Exodus.

A PASSOVER HAGGADAH: GO FORTH AND LEARN

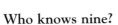

Who knows nine?

I know **nine**. Nine months of pregnancy; eight days until circumcision; seven days of the week; six orders of the Mishnah; five books of the Torah; four mothers; three fathers; two tablets of the covenant;
One is our God in heaven and on earth.

Who knows ten?

I know **ten**. Ten commandments; nine months of pregnancy; eight days until circumcision; seven days of the week; six orders of the Mishnah; five books of the Torah; four mothers; three fathers; two tablets of the covenant;
One is our God in heaven and on earth.

Who knows eleven?

I know **eleven**. Eleven stars; ten commandments; nine months of pregnancy; eight days until circumcision; seven days of the week; six orders of the Mishnah; five books of the Torah; four mothers; three fathers; two tablets of the covenant;
One is our God in heaven and on earth.

Who knows twelve?

I know **twelve**. Twelve tribes; eleven stars; ten commandments; nine months of pregnancy; eight days until circumcision; seven days of the week; six orders of the Mishnah; five books of the Torah; four mothers; three fathers; two tablets of the covenant;
One is our God in heaven and on earth.

תִּשְׁעָה מִי יוֹדֵעַ?

תִּשְׁעָה אֲנִי יוֹדֵעַ: תִּשְׁעָה יַרְחֵי לֵדָה, שְׁמוֹנָה יְמֵי מִילָה, שִׁבְעָה יְמֵי שַׁבַּתָּא, שִׁשָּׁה סִדְרֵי מִשְׁנָה, חֲמִשָּׁה חוּמְשֵׁי תוֹרָה, אַרְבַּע אִמָּהוֹת, שְׁלֹשָׁה אָבוֹת, שְׁנֵי לֻחוֹת הַבְּרִית,
אֶחָד אֱלֹהֵינוּ שֶׁבַּשָּׁמַיִם וּבָאָרֶץ.

עֲשָׂרָה מִי יוֹדֵעַ?

עֲשָׂרָה אֲנִי יוֹדֵעַ: עֲשָׂרָה דִבְּרַיָּא, תִּשְׁעָה יַרְחֵי לֵדָה, שְׁמוֹנָה יְמֵי מִילָה, שִׁבְעָה יְמֵי שַׁבַּתָּא, שִׁשָּׁה סִדְרֵי מִשְׁנָה, חֲמִשָּׁה חוּמְשֵׁי תוֹרָה, אַרְבַּע אִמָּהוֹת, שְׁלֹשָׁה אָבוֹת, שְׁנֵי לֻחוֹת הַבְּרִית,
אֶחָד אֱלֹהֵינוּ שֶׁבַּשָּׁמַיִם וּבָאָרֶץ.

אַחַד עָשָׂר מִי יוֹדֵעַ?

אַחַד עָשָׂר אֲנִי יוֹדֵעַ: אַחַד עָשָׂר כּוֹכְבַיָּא, עֲשָׂרָה דִבְּרַיָּא, תִּשְׁעָה יַרְחֵי לֵדָה, שְׁמוֹנָה יְמֵי מִילָה, שִׁבְעָה יְמֵי שַׁבַּתָּא, שִׁשָּׁה סִדְרֵי מִשְׁנָה, חֲמִשָּׁה חוּמְשֵׁי תוֹרָה, אַרְבַּע אִמָּהוֹת, שְׁלֹשָׁה אָבוֹת, שְׁנֵי לֻחוֹת הַבְּרִית,
אֶחָד אֱלֹהֵינוּ שֶׁבַּשָּׁמַיִם וּבָאָרֶץ.

שְׁנֵים עָשָׂר מִי יוֹדֵעַ?

שְׁנֵים עָשָׂר אֲנִי יוֹדֵעַ: שְׁנֵים עָשָׂר שִׁבְטַיָּא, אַחַד עָשָׂר כּוֹכְבַיָּא, עֲשָׂרָה דִבְּרַיָּא, תִּשְׁעָה יַרְחֵי לֵדָה, שְׁמוֹנָה יְמֵי מִילָה, שִׁבְעָה יְמֵי שַׁבַּתָּא, שִׁשָּׁה סִדְרֵי מִשְׁנָה, חֲמִשָּׁה חוּמְשֵׁי תוֹרָה, אַרְבַּע אִמָּהוֹת, שְׁלֹשָׁה אָבוֹת, שְׁנֵי לֻחוֹת הַבְּרִית,
אֶחָד אֱלֹהֵינוּ שֶׁבַּשָּׁמַיִם וּבָאָרֶץ.

Who knows thirteen?

I know **thirteen**. Thirteen attributes; twelve tribes; eleven stars; ten commandments; nine months of pregnancy; eight days until circumcision; seven days of the week; six orders of the Mishnah; five books of the Torah; four mothers; three fathers; two tablets of the covenant;

One is our God in heaven and on earth.

שְׁלֹשָׁה עָשָׂר מִי יוֹדֵעַ?

שְׁלֹשָׁה עָשָׂר אֲנִי יוֹדֵעַ: שְׁלֹשָׁה עָשָׂר מִדַּיָּא. שְׁנֵים עָשָׂר שִׁבְטַיָּא, אַחַד עָשָׂר כּוֹכְבַיָּא, עֲשָׂרָה דִבְּרַיָּא, תִּשְׁעָה יַרְחֵי לֵדָה, שְׁמוֹנָה יְמֵי מִילָה, שִׁבְעָה יְמֵי שַׁבְּתָא, שִׁשָּׁה סִדְרֵי מִשְׁנָה, חֲמִשָּׁה חוּמְשֵׁי תוֹרָה, אַרְבַּע אִמָּהוֹת, שְׁלֹשָׁה אָבוֹת, שְׁנֵי לֻחוֹת הַבְּרִית, אֶחָד אֱלֹהֵינוּ שֶׁבַּשָּׁמַיִם וּבָאָרֶץ.

54 One kid, one kid,

that father bought for two *zuz*,
one kid, one kid.

And then came the cat, who ate the kid, that father bought for two *zuz*, one kid, one kid.

And then came the dog, who bit the cat, who ate the kid, that father bought for two *zuz*, one kid, one kid.

And then came the stick, which hit the dog, who bit the cat, who ate the kid, that father bought for two *zuz*, one kid, one kid.

54 חַד גַּדְיָא, חַד גַּדְיָא

דְּזַבִּין אַבָּא בִּתְרֵי זוּזֵי,
חַד גַּדְיָא, חַד גַּדְיָא.

וְאָתָא שׁוּנְרָא וְאָכְלָה לְגַדְיָא, דְּזַבִּין אַבָּא בִּתְרֵי זוּזֵי, חַד גַּדְיָא, חַד גַּדְיָא.

וְאָתָא כַלְבָּא וְנָשַׁךְ לְשׁוּנְרָא, דְּאָכְלָה לְגַדְיָא, דְּזַבִּין אַבָּא בִּתְרֵי זוּזֵי, חַד גַּדְיָא, חַד גַּדְיָא.

וְאָתָא חוּטְרָא וְהִכָּה לְכַלְבָּא, דְּנָשַׁךְ לְשׁוּנְרָא, דְּאָכְלָה לְגַדְיָא, דְּזַבִּין אַבָּא בִּתְרֵי זוּזֵי, חַד גַּדְיָא, חַד גַּדְיָא.

---

54 One kid. The medieval Ashkenazic custom to conclude the seder with *Had Gadya* has become nearly universal. But *Had Gadya*, a folksong with parallels in other languages and cultures, does not touch upon obvious Passover themes, and its inclusion in the Haggadah is puzzling. Nonetheless, *Had Gadya* does poignantly convey one of the fundamental messages of the seder. The song begins with a father who purchases a kid that then is devoured, setting off a chain of violent events that concludes with God destroying the very Angel of Death. Once eaten by the cat, the kid cannot be recovered; nonetheless, that seemingly coincidental event is connected by an unbroken chain to God's ultimate display of power at the symbolic End of Days. Throughout the seder, we have attempted to recapture and relive history. As the night's ritual draws to a close, we concede that we can never fully reconstitute the past. But the past can be a point of departure with direct implications for all that the future holds in store.

A PASSOVER HAGGADAH: GO FORTH AND LEARN

And then came **the fire**, which burned the stick, which hit the dog, who bit the cat, who ate the kid, that father bought for two *zuz*, one kid, one kid.

And then came **the water**, which extinguished the fire, which burned the stick, which hit the dog, who bit the cat, who ate the kid, that father bought for two *zuz*, one kid, one kid.

And then came **the ox**, who drank the water, which extinguished the fire, which burned the stick, which hit the dog, who bit the cat, who ate the kid, that father bought for two *zuz*, one kid, one kid.

And then came **the slaughterer**, who slaughtered the ox, who drank the water, which extinguished the fire, which burned the stick, which hit the dog, who bit the cat, who ate the kid, that father bought for two *zuz*, one kid, one kid.

And then came **the Angel of Death**, who slaughtered the slaughterer, who slaughtered the ox, who drank the water, which extinguished the fire, which burned the stick, which hit the dog, who bit the cat, who ate the kid, that father bought for two *zuz*, one kid, one kid.

And then came **the Blessed Holy One** and slaughtered the Angel of Death, who slaughtered the slaughterer, who slaughtered the ox, who drank the water, which extinguished the fire, which burned the stick, which hit the dog, who bit the cat, who ate the kid, that father bought for two *zuz*, one kid, one kid.

וְאָתָא **נוּרָא** וְשָׂרַף לְחוּטְרָא, דְּהִכָּה לְכַלְבָּא, דְּנָשַׁךְ לְשׁוּנְרָא, דְּאָכְלָה לְגַדְיָא, דְּזַבִּין אַבָּא בִּתְרֵי זוּזֵי, חַד גַּדְיָא, חַד גַּדְיָא.

וְאָתָא **מַיָּא** וְכָבָה לְנוּרָא, דְּשָׂרַף לְחוּטְרָא, דְּהִכָּה לְכַלְבָּא, דְּנָשַׁךְ לְשׁוּנְרָא, דְּאָכְלָה לְגַדְיָא, דְּזַבִּין אַבָּא בִּתְרֵי זוּזֵי, חַד גַּדְיָא, חַד גַּדְיָא.

וְאָתָא **תוֹרָא** וְשָׁתָה לְמַיָּא, דְּכָבָה לְנוּרָא, דְּשָׂרַף לְחוּטְרָא, דְּהִכָּה לְכַלְבָּא, דְּנָשַׁךְ לְשׁוּנְרָא, דְּאָכְלָה לְגַדְיָא, דְּזַבִּין אַבָּא בִּתְרֵי זוּזֵי, חַד גַּדְיָא, חַד גַּדְיָא.

וְאָתָא **הַשּׁוֹחֵט** וְשָׁחַט לְתוֹרָא, דְּשָׁתָה לְמַיָּא, דְּכָבָה לְנוּרָא, דְּשָׂרַף לְחוּטְרָא, דְּהִכָּה לְכַלְבָּא, דְּנָשַׁךְ לְשׁוּנְרָא, דְּאָכְלָה לְגַדְיָא, דְּזַבִּין אַבָּא בִּתְרֵי זוּזֵי, חַד גַּדְיָא, חַד גַּדְיָא.

וְאָתָא **מַלְאַךְ הַמָּוֶת** וְשָׁחַט לְשׁוֹחֵט, דְּשָׁחַט לְתוֹרָא, דְּשָׁתָה לְמַיָּא, דְּכָבָה לְנוּרָא, דְּשָׂרַף לְחוּטְרָא, דְּהִכָּה לְכַלְבָּא, דְּנָשַׁךְ לְשׁוּנְרָא, דְּאָכְלָה לְגַדְיָא, דְּזַבִּין אַבָּא בִּתְרֵי זוּזֵי, חַד גַּדְיָא, חַד גַּדְיָא.

וְאָתָא **הַקָּדוֹשׁ בָּרוּךְ הוּא** וְשָׁחַט לְמַלְאַךְ הַמָּוֶת, דְּשָׁחַט לְשׁוֹחֵט, דְּשָׁחַט לְתוֹרָא, דְּשָׁתָה לְמַיָּא, דְּכָבָה לְנוּרָא, דְּשָׂרַף לְחוּטְרָא, דְּהִכָּה לְכַלְבָּא, דְּנָשַׁךְ לְשׁוּנְרָא, דְּאָכְלָה לְגַדְיָא, דְּזַבִּין אַבָּא בִּתְרֵי זוּזֵי, חַד גַּדְיָא, חַד גַּדְיָא.

THE *Seder*

The Seder Plate
הַקְּעָרָה

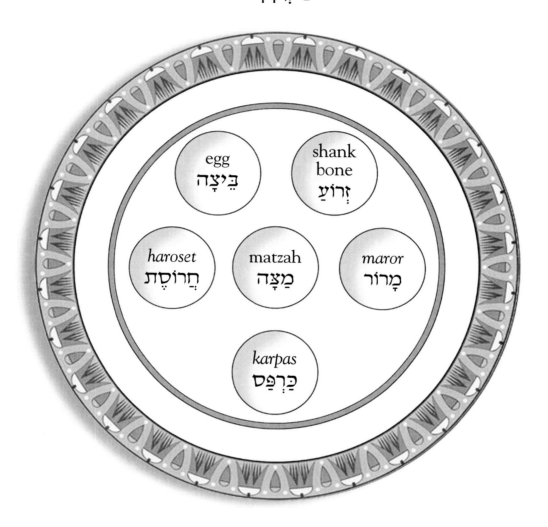

The symbolic foods are arranged on the seder plate according to custom.
This diagram reflects one common tradition.